From The Listening Place
Languages of Intuition

OTHER BOOKS BY MARGARET BLANCHARD

The Rest of the Deer
Restoring the Orchard (with S.B. Sowbel)
Duet

from the
LISTENING PLACE
Languages of Intuition

Edited by
Margaret Blanchard

"Life is a house made of sound and the people are made from that sound. . . .
It is, therefore, simply through listening, and using that listening and paying attention,
that one finds the guidance of the Great Mystery along the path of life."
—*Joseph Rael, Beautiful Painted Arrow,*
Being and Vibration

"Mind pictures brought feelings and feelings dragged out dramas
from the hollows of her heart."
—*Zora Neale Hurston,*
Their Eyes Were Watching God

ASTARTE SHELL PRESS   PORTLAND, MAINE

Astarte Shell Press
P.O. Box 3648
Portland ME 04104-3648

The following pieces, previously published, are reproduced here by permission of author and/or publisher:

Margaret Blanchard and S.B. Sowbel, "Intuition and Problem-Solving," *Restoring the Orchard: A Guide to Learning Intuition* (Ft. Ann, N.Y.: Tara Press, 1994).

Clarinda Harriss, "The Red House Dream," "Sub-Atomic," and "Speculation: A Dream of Perfect Clarity," *The Night Parrot*, Galway, Ireland: Salmon Publishing, 1988.

Angela de Hoyos, "Some People Sing," *Pax International Journal of Art, Science & Philosophy*, Vol. III, 1985-1986, Nos. 1 & 2, Winter; "This Deathless Birth of a Poem," *Tonantzin*, Guadalupe Cultural Arts Center, Vol. 6, No. 3, October 1990. Reprinted by permission of the author.

Ines Martinez, "The Singing Antelope," first published in *Daughters of the Fifth Sun: Contemporary U.S. Latina Writing*, Edited by Bryce Milligan, Mary Guerrero, Angela de Hoyos (New York: Putnam/Riverhead, 1995).

Alice Sadongei, "What Frank, Martha and I Know About the Desert," *A Gathering of Spirit: Writing and Art by North American Indian Women*, Edited by Beth Brant (Rockland, Maine: Sinister Wisdom Books, 1984).

Library of Congress Cataloging-in-Publication Data
From the listening place: languages of intuition/edited by Margaret Blanchard.
    p. cm.
  Includes bibliographical references.
  ISBN 1-885349-05-X (alk. paper)
  1. Intuition (Psychology) 2. Women—Psychology.   I. Blanchard, Margaret, 1938—.
  BF315.5.F76 1997
  153.4'4—dc21
                                   96-39490
                                   CIP

Cover: Gail Wheeler
Design: Sylvia Sims
Printed in Canada by Webcom, Toronto, Ontario

10 9 8 7 6 5 4 3 2 1

Dedicated to
Barbara Singer,
artist, healer, scholar, community activist.
1938-1995

Table of Contents

INTRODUCTION:
FROM THE INSIDE OUT
Margaret Blanchard

We've heard many stories about how people's native languages have been lost or stifled: the Irish forced by the English to give up their mother tongue; Native American children trucked off to government schools to be punished whenever they spoke the language of home; the Chicana language suddenly labeled foreign when the border shifted; and the many immigrants to this country whose voices were silenced by the deaf ear of Standard English—so different from the inner ear of the Statue of Liberty which, I imagine, welcomes to our common language, and puts to use, a multiplicity of idioms.

On another shared level we've been cut off from a native tongue by the dominance of discursive language which deems as superior statements of so-called fact, the generalizing, categorizing and statistical tongue of bureaucrats, politicians, social scientists, and academicians. This is the language which objectifies, distances and judges, which Ursula LeGuin calls the Father Tongue. It dismisses our stories as anecdotal while insisting on hard data. While this empiricism can liberate us from superstition and prejudice, it also tends to uproot some of our most profound ways of knowing.

Although most of us know this discursive idiom and some of us can even speak it well, there is another language which is native to all of us and, actually, spoken by more of us than the abstract dominant dialect. This is the language described by Zora Neale Hurston:

Mind pictures brought feelings and feelings dragged out dramas from the hollows of her heart. (*Their Eyes Were Watching God*)

Each of us has the capacity to speak this language. It is the language of intuition with its vocabulary of feelings, grammar of mind pictures and syntax of symbol and story. Because we are intuitive, we are, at least,

1

bilingual.

Intuition is a realization of wholeness which is simultaneously internal and external, an insight which gives us everything at once, if only momentarily. This realization is what Mozart described when he spoke of hearing a whole piece of music as a single sound. The wholeness we realize is not abstract generalization but the energy, animating spirit, soul or dynamism of an experience. This insight usually finds form in images or symbols and often plays out its dynamic dimensions through story. It tells truth from the inside out.

When, as with contributions to this book, those images are authentic and vital and those stories are deeply felt, the result is, as one contributor, Laura Filipp, describes it, "more than an idea or direction I'm moving toward—it seems like a solid thing. Instead of just a jumble of fleeting images and symbols and scenes, it's something real, something I can pick up and hold in my hands and carry around with me."

This language has been dismissed as insignificant compared to abstracting discursive language because it is considered merely subjective. In order to make our voices heard in public, in order to validate our observations, in order to generalize about humankind, the argument goes, we need to give up this childish, womanish speech and do Big Talk. But even Jesus, when he taught in the temple at the age of twelve, spoke the intuitive language of parables. For many cultures, like the Western Apache, who solve personal and tribal problems by evoking ancestral pictures in their minds, intuitive language is a mature and communal mode for the exploration of reality.

Intuitive language, in truth, provides a bridge between the subjective and the objective because it emerges from an intuitive realization of wholeness which is simultaneously internal and external. And just because any one intuitive insight is naturally personal does not mean it is not also socially relevant. We know that while each subjectivity is unique, it also participates in a more communal dimension which has layers of the collective consciousness as well as of the collective unconscious. So when one person's intuitive insight is expressed in symbol or story, it often can be recognized by or provide insight to another person's. From this expanding resonance, a different kind of generalization occurs.

The fact that intuition, like statistical information ("50% of Americans" referring only to white Americans) or philosophic truth ("All *men* are created equal"), can set forth false universals speaks to its potential for generalization. While inadequate archetypes or myths are more accurately described as "partial," "limited," "distorted" or "exclusive" rather than true or false, their capacity to describe a fuller human condition than the merely subjective or idiosyncratic cannot be disputed.

Take, for example, the false universal of the Sun God. When we explore the source of this image, the radiant human face of one's primal caretaker, the Sun God becomes more commonly female. As art educator Rhoda Kellog discovers the circle face in children's art from a wide variety of cultures, psychologist Daniel Stern describes the total absorption of an infant in the mother's face, and anthropologist Patricia Monaghan reclaims the sun as goddess in many ancient cultures, we can put the pieces together for a portrait of a more inclusive archetype of solar divinity.

Through a sharing of stories, collective insights are constructed and new social visions are born. From the story-telling process of consciousness-raising which characterized the civil rights movement of the 1960's and the women's movement of the 1970's, social transformations have occurred. From the more recent convergence of the stories of Americans from diverse cultures, a multi-cultural awareness has grown, challenging the stereotypes and oversimplifications of the categories of abstract generalization. When expanded to include a whole culture, this story-telling process produces archetypes and myth, symbols and stories of peoples which reach back into their histories and embrace them as a whole. While the abstract thinkers are busy constructing, deconstructing and reconstructing their categories and generalizations, the story-tellers are weaving authentic wholes just by speaking naturally.

I'm thinking, for instance, of the story by Anna Lee Walters, "The Devil and Sister Lena," in which a Navajo woman goes from church to church on Sunday, infuriating the missionary by her refusal to choose one form of worship over another. How can she practice her tribal ritual as well as attend a Catholic Mass and a Baptist revival? he demands to know. But she refuses to fit into his categorization. All religions, she recognizes, hold a strand of truth, and she is just as capable as anyone else of weaving them all together.

This is not to say that knowing discursive language is not important, just as knowing English has been crucial for most of us Americans. In fact we need the empirical data of science, the abstract truths of philosophy *and* the symbols and stories of intuition to see the many facets of any real whole. This balance of powers is crucial to democratic discourse. But for us to reap the full benefits of being bilingual, or multi-lingual, we need to bring the dominant language down from its throne and see how useful it can be when integrated with the dialect of intuition.

At the same time, we need to invite Intuition to renounce her shrine so she can serve us better. Like a woman on a pedestal, Intuition is now so mystified, so idealized in some circles, that she bears the aura of all our psychic and spiritual longings. For her to perform the everyday magic which is her reason for being, she needs to be liberated from those ex- alted expectations and allowed to move freely among us. Like the Victo- rian "Angel in the House," she must be wrestled with so she can discover her full and gritty potential in our lives.

The stories and myths which are the products of intuitive language are currently being uncovered, rediscovered and explicated by ethnogra- phers, mythologists, and Jungian analysts as well as by artists and writ- ers. What this book emphasizes is the creativity by which we produce such products and the languages by which they can be expressed. For only if we value this language for its process, not just for the treasures it has created, will our bi- or multi-lingualism become a vital part of our collective conversation.

This language we share begins and ends with intuition yet usually requires some discrimination and analysis in the middle. The creative process itself often starts with an intuitive flash, proceeds through ex- perimentation and selection, often chaotic, and finally pulls together an artistic whole. In varying ways the works in this collection embody both sides of our whole language. Some employ a kind of code-switching, integrating both the intuitive and the analytical. Others begin with the intuitive, the image or story, and end with some more discursive reflec- tion on their process. Others begin with the more rational standard and then fly off into the creative. Because each one is unique, they show how varied the languages of intuition can be. Rather than being set against each other in the argumentative polarization characteristic of much pro- fessional discourse, these pieces resonate to make a unified but multi- faceted whole.

The idea for this book on intuitive languages came to me while I was writing *The Rest of the Deer: An Intuitive Study of Intuition*. Images of the work of some of the most creative people I know flashed to me while I was struggling to explain intuitive process. I kept wanting to refer to their work as examples of what I was describing, as sources of spontane- ous insight into the workings of intuition. But much of their work had not yet been published; some of it had not even been documented yet.

When called upon, however, to share the fruits of their gardening, many were willing to do the work of harvesting that produced this cornucopia of intuitive languages.

At a working group meeting of contributors in August of 1994, we brainstormed on names for this book (the title was chosen by a vote of contributors) and agreed on an order of contents which models intuitive process, moving from dreams to symbols to stories to wider applications for healing, teaching and social action.

In varying ways, these individual pieces demonstrate one or more of the stages of intuitive process:starting with an open mind; dropping into unique personal experience, sometimes through empathy or identification with another person or another reality; centering in that experience; viewing it from all sides; getting in touch with the unifying energy of that experience; finding an image to express that dynamism; telling the story which grows out of that image; and allowing that story to expand in meaning and in the context of other stories, including the larger, cultural contexts of symbols, archetypes and myths.

Although this book is not officially connected with Vermont College of Norwich University, it is no accident that many of the contributors are associated with either the Graduate Program or the Adult Degree Program of Vermont College: two core faculty, four field faculty, one consultant, and ten graduates from the Graduate Program; two core faculty from the Adult Degree Program. This book was also supported in part by a research and publication grant from Norwich University. Five of the contributors are also graduates of the Union Institute, four of whom had as their core faculty, Dr. Elizabeth Minnich.

Special thanks should go to Nora Nellis and Sherry Kaufield, who did painstaking line editing of the first draft of this book and to S.B. Sowbel and Paddy Reid, who made consistently valuable contributions to the collective process which has so enriched this book.

Because of the variety of its contents, this book could be used as a reader in any number of courses across the curriculum: composition, psychology, creative arts, women's studies, education, ethics, as well as interdisciplinary courses on themes related to creativity, multiple intelligences, the environment and multiculturalism. It is also useful for anyone researching the creative process and how it converges with personal growth, healing, teaching and social action. [For further educational applications of this process, please see *The Rest of the Deer* (Astarte, 1993) and *Restoring the Orchard* (Tara, 1995).]

As this gathering of speakers demonstrates, our intuitive languages validate a common but misunderstood way of knowing, intuition; describe a process which offers insight, creativity, and healing to many dimensions of our lives; and use modes of articulation which are not only powerful and effective but also counter the false generalization and excessive categorizing which plague our ordinary discursive language.

These languages are particularly relevant to women's studies and multicultural studies. With them silenced populations find voices true to their own experiences, while the movement from symbol to archetype to story-telling and myth allows for diversity without hierarchy within the larger community.

The range of experiences within this book models the kind of diversity within unity which intuition can generate. Ages of contributors vary from twelve to eighty-one. Roots include Native American, Native Irish, Native Italian, Native Chinese, French-Caribbean, Chicana, Russian Jewish, several varieties of hyphenated American (African, Chinese, Italian, Irish, Lebanese, French Canadian, Russian, Filipino) as well as many of mixed blood and varying economic beginnings. Contributors live in all parts of this country and beyond, from Texas to Illinois, from Vermont to California, from North Carolina to Maine, from Baltimore to Dublin, Ireland, on a ranch outside of San Antonio to a loft in Soho to a shack in the woods to an inner-city apartment. These differences have not led us either to violence or debate but to the shared ground of intuition within whose sphere we can hear and appreciate our unique variety of intuitive languages.

❀

I. DREAMS: *Elusive Messengers*

This first section, "Elusive Messengers," describes how these writers have netted the elusive messages which came to them in dreams and visions, with almost magical results: the delightful and insightful poems by Clarinda Harriss; the evocative pilgrimage described by Amanda Joyce; the poetic self-portrait of a psychic by Terry Iacuzzo; Shirley Geok-lin Lim's meaningful exploration of the clash and convergence of different languages; the haunting dream-story of death by Inés Martinez, with her account of its inception; Verbena Pastor's powerful dream poems; Freida Chapman's naming of images before words and names before names; and Barbara Singer's evocation of the maternal muse of creativity and healing.

Clarinda Harriss is chair of the English Department at Towson State University and editor of the New Poets Series. Her most recent books of poetry are *The Night Parrot* and *License Renewal for the Blind*, winner of the 1993 American Chapbook Award. Intuitively she knows she would like to spend an additional life as an aquatic mammal in a southern sea.

Amanda Joyce grew up in southern New Hampshire amidst mills, tanneries and peculiar factory smells. She spent each summer at Seabrook Beach, where she was mainly underwater. When she's not dreaming, she supports herself in a variety of ways—painting, working on boats, cooking and accounting. She has a recording of selected writings, *Popping Out of Mother's Arms*, and a short novel, *Hook Bay Stories*.

Terry Iacuzzo is a professional psychic and videographer who lives in New York City.

Winner of the Commonwealth Poetry Prize in 1980, **Shirley Geok-lin Lim** has published four collections of poetry, a book of short stories, two critical studies, and a book of memoirs. Her co-edited anthology, *The Forbidden Stitch*, won the 1990 Before Columbus American Book Award. Feminist Press will soon publish her memoir, *Among the White Moon Faces*. She is Professor of English and Women's Studies at the University of California.

Born a female Mexican-American and raised Catholic in New Mexico, **Inés Martinez** has exercised and revelled in the freedom that 20th Century America could afford to even such as she. A professor of English, she is a 1987 winner of the New York Foundation for the Arts fellowship in fiction. Her first novel, *To Know the Moon*, was published in 1993.

Verbena Pastor has a waking life apart from her dreams; she is core faculty in the Graduate Program at Vermont College. She also lives a third life as a poet and fiction writer. She owes a special debt to her Muse, whom she also calls intuition.

Freida Chapman, a native Chicagoan, lived in Manhattan for 20 years, where she was an editor for hospital workers Local 420 AFSCME. Since moving to the Adirondacks in 1991, she's devoted time to writing poetry. Her poems have been published in *13th Moon*, *Catalyst* and *Black Bough*.

A native of New York City, **Barbara Singer** lived in Austin Texas, where she distinguished herself as an artist, an art therapist, and a community arts activist. In 1992 Barbara received a second master's degree, in psychotherapy and art therapy, from the Graduate Program of Vermont College. Barbara lost her two-year battle with cancer in the summer of 1995.

❂

Shirley Geok-Lin Lim

Terry Iacuzzo

Amanda Joyce

Inéz Martinez

Verbena Pastor

Barbara Singer

Freida Chapman

. Not pictured: Clarinda Harris

POEMS
Clarinda Harriss

The Red House Dream

On a white January night
Jennifer dreamed she asked me
"How can I get the red house
out of my head?"
and dreamed I said
"Oh Jennifer, just go live in it."

Next day Jennifer's friend Jennifer
told me she'd dreamed about Jennifer.
Jennifer was translucent
and exuded white light
that filled the red house.

All February I dreamed all
young women named Jennifer
were dreaming of women named Jennifer.
Their white light
emitted a clear, piercing hum.

By March my red house
was crowded with Jennifers.
Thousands of jostling Jennifers
all translucent and glowing.
Their white light
made me deaf and crazy.

On the first night of spring
my dreams asked my Jennifers
what to do about Jennifer dreams.

"Oh," they said, "just go live in them."
So I did.

Sub-Atomic

I think I could love the God of tiny physics
his brown Jewish eye clenched around a jeweler's glass
his thick fingers stuffing whole universes
into infinitesimal glass bottles.

Such patience, so abstract and grandfatherly!
I remember what my grandfather told me
through a clatter of plastic teeth
with his good eye locked on a bottle

he was filling with a clipper ship
and his bad eye (amber plastic) locked on me:
Things can be divided in half forever.
For instance one bomb can destroy half the world

and the remaining half with its bomb can destroy
half itself, and that half can bomb half itself
and that half can bomb half itself and so on, but always

one little piece will be left over and on that piece
God with his toothpicks and his weensy stones
will build little New Yorks, little Walls of China

and what have you. This is the comfort I sleep on,
and in my dreams—always large, always crude—
tiny grandfathers bloom in the sockets of my fallen teeth.

Speculation: A Dream of Perfect Clarity

What if the mind were something
round and heavy, something like some kind
of ball whose property it is
not to bounce but to roll heavily along grooved air
toward some wicket or other waiting space
(ball, as in croquet, bowling, billiard or bearing):

what if my mind were such a ball
and, propelled by a whack
from some cosmic mallet, cue or piston,
dropped this minute through this bed
taking with it my head and body,
the knotted sheets and the lover trussed therein
each dragging our respective dreams
each dream with its cast of thousands and in each
character a separate tiny mind heavy as mine
and my lover's and each other's:

would the gravity of the situation
pull each ball through the molten center
to arrive (scalded bald and pure)
at the appointed hole full of nothing
but Answer, Truth, Correctness, Perfect Fit, whatever,

or would that ecstasy of thud and jostle
thrust us scatheless through the cleansing flames
(our little crust of selfness thus
baked forever to our surfaces)
to burst at random through the other side
and wake as always, warm and dirty, wondering
only for an instant where we are?

❁

IT IS TRUE FOREVER
Amanda Joyce

When I woke up this morning, I knew that this would be a day for us to walk up the side of the mountain. The sky is always a hard, hurting blue, almost as hard and as harsh as the veins in the stones, when they send us up the side of the mountain. They do not know or care how far we climb, or which of the old paths we take, because when we return our bags are always filled with the stones.

Our stones are good, we know what they want us to find. We have the good eyes and the good hearts for finding stones. We have the strong legs and the sure feet. And we have the thick, wide chests to get enough of the piercing thin air and the heavy soft arms to balance ourselves.

We alone. The little boys envy us so. They long to be the ones to bring precious things home. But they are quick and light-footed and full of impatience. They cannot find the stones and they cannot hold them.

Like mountains ourselves, we alone find the true stones, the needed ones. The old people have a saying, "It is true forever" and they say it often as they look at what we have brought back.

The stones must be taken from the bags one by one, warmed by the hands, passed from one to another. They must be seen and accepted. The bluest of blue and the palest of blue are the most treasured.

They fuss over us before they send us up the mountain. They give us sweet things to eat and they touch us for good luck. When we return, they leave us to ourselves. We are so far away, they say, too strange from the thinness of the air. We have our own warm spot, and we rest while the young ones sleep and the Old Ones whisper over our stones. "It is true forever!" we sometimes overhear.

We each have our own stone. We wear it secretly, as close to the heart as we can get it. We would never wear stones we had not first offered the Old Ones. It is a hurting thing to hold back. These are stones the Old Ones Rolled Away From the Fire. They do this when they look and hold and whisper and get nothing back.

When a stone is Rolled Away, it can be walked upon or played with.

The little boys throw them at the sky. We laugh when we see them do this. We know that the stones are the sky.

The stones we wear are True Forever. The Old Ones were not heartless or blind, but the truth of our stones was so hidden that no one could see. We knew our heart stones would be Rolled Away. We waited and listened and we found them.

Now, we are high on the side of the mountain again. She stands a distance away from me, looking around in all directions and bending over to find stones. She is red like blood and black like rock. Her long plaited hair shines hard in the sun. She never turns around to look for me because she always knows where I am.

She is my sister, and I am hers. We know this, but the Old Ones have never said so. It is seven days of walking for her to be here. The Old Ones send for her when it is time to gather more stones. They send her back once the stones are gathered.

Sometimes I share her journey in my dreams. Other times she wakes me and I am surprised. There is a story about why we live in different places among different Old Ones, but we have not been given the story. We know that something must have happened to our mother's heart, and we were Rolled Away.

I look over at my sister often. I gather stones more slowly and have a smaller bagful because of all my watching. She is someone that I know. I want the knowing to be down inside me like the blue in the stones, and True Forever.

●

TO DRINK THE DREAM
By Terry Iacuzzo

We sit together at my table. It's the first time she's come to see me. "There's a man lying in a bed. Starched white sheets secured tightly beneath the mattress; he cannot move. His motionless face stares into emptiness." I swallow and grip my chair. "Three women surround his bed. They feel helpless. They know that nothing they can do will work anymore. I'm upside down. 'Oh my God, don't drop me! Please don't drop me!' Across the room two women hold a young boy by his ankles upside down outside an open window. The world below an eternal mouth eager to devour him if they should weaken and let go. 'Breathe! Come on breathe!'" I look to the man in bed. I shiver in terror and sadness.

The woman at my table is crying. "Oh my God, it all makes sense. That episode he told us so often. When he was a child he suffered from asthma. His sisters would flip him upside down and hold him by his ankles out the window to get him breathing again, and he must feel like that right now. He's just had a very bad stroke and he cannot move at all."

"Your father's always felt his life was in their hands. Now he wants them to let him go. His entire life was defined by those events in his childhood. And he now finds himself waiting for his sisters to say it's all right, you don't have to breathe anymore."

I sit with a man at my table. He is curious about me, skeptical but open. "What would my life have been like if I had made another choice?"

"A woman stands in front of a row of houses. Each one looks the same. Each one painted white with a neatly trimmed lawn and automatic sprinkler. I see you walking toward the house and two small children are running to greet you. You are telling her about your job at the canning factory. 'Kathy, I'm bored and unhappy and we need a new car.'

"My God, I'm seeing that life, the life you didn't choose! There's a big canning factory in this town. Everyone works there. These houses were built by the company. It seems all right, but everyone does the same thing day after day."

"I was engaged to a girl named Kathy and Westfield is a one company town. I broke off the engagement to take a job in the Middle East. I often wondered. . ."

A woman sits at my table. My heart knots with pain and longing. I feel a hand push me back with the force of lightning. "There was a brief but intense bond here, a passionate abandoned encounter without a name. Your grief is holding you back and you must let go. Was this only yesterday? It hurts my soul. This man is married. I know his conflict, but he is not joining you. Stop going by his house. Stop suffering. It has been six years, hasn't it?"

All my life I have been in search of the ancient lost city inside myself. I knew the world of the spirits. I prayed to the martyrs and saints and believed I was chosen. I crossed my fingers and hoped to die as I stared up to the sky, waiting for a descending ladder. My dreams were my awakening state and I was sleepwalking during the day. I could conjure up a snowstorm when I wanted to stay home from school. I could step into a movie screen and live in another story. We spent every Sunday at the great Niagara Falls, and I would float myself behind her majestic veil and walk where the daughters of ancient tribes live in safety. I could fly with the angels, speak in tongues and breathe underwater. I longed to know love and love lost. I waited for a miracle. I prayed to be holy. I was magic, I was thirteen, I was the last of my tribe. That's when my brother taught me to read the Tarot cards, and I found the language needed to tell myself it was all true.

With all of that gypsy mystery, clairvoyant understanding, I have been completely baffled how I spent the last twenty years in three small rooms in an apartment in New York City, having done several thousand psychic readings. All kinds of people climbed six flights of stairs to ask me all sorts of questions. Each person a walking library of stories they have lived and stories they want to live and what does it all mean? Each person having their own system of metaphors, their own internal language, wishes and fears. I was asked to decipher all of it and I did, and I stayed and I surrendered to it. I had other psychics read me and at sixteen was told that several thousand people were waiting for me to tell them what to do. I thought maybe it meant I would grow up to be a cruise director or a traffic cop. "Are you lost, lady?" "What time is shuffleboard?"

And here I am doing all those psychic readings at my table next to the bathtub in the kitchen. Up and down the stairs.

Intuition is knowing something without knowing why. It is a signal to me from my mind body that my life force is thirsty. If I can't articulate this thirst, I feel blocked and filled with anxiety, a kind of psychic constipation. Doing readings seems to relieve the anxiety. Without the readings I am a radio dial without a channel. Doing too many readings leaves me confused and unable to make logical decisions like when to stop pouring boiling water into a cup or what to do in a grocery story.

I come from a family of psychics. Doing readings was our family business. As children we were encouraged to live in our imagination. My mother took our dreams seriously and always viewed them as prophetic. She believed that everything had a reality somewhere. She told us that fairies, angels and ghosts were surrounding us at all times and that Dracula, werewolves and gypsy curses were to be taken seriously. I was terrified and taught how to be strong. I learned respect and fear and acquired incredible power. If a wish could come true, then I better know what I was wishing for. If a thought could kill, then I better be ready. We were an unusual family who knew of things most people feared. I took delight in our uniqueness, but I secretly longed to be part of a normal family— like I saw on television—you know, *Ozzie and Harriet, Father Knows Best. . .*

Living for so many years in the intuitive realm has been a natural unnatural wonderland. Being psychic makes sense to me in the controlled environment of a personal reading. Someone sits in front of me. I begin talking to them easily as though I have known them forever. I review their life and tell them what I see ahead. It sometimes appears to me like a drive-in movie screen. I watch and retell the plot. Sometimes I just say things I suddenly have always known. Once in a while I actually hear a voice whisper in my ear. I have also been able to enter a time of possibility to give details about a life that might have been if the person had chosen differently.

What I find most interesting are the uncalled psychic experiences. I was once in the middle of dinner when a feeling of sadness overwhelmed me. I found myself in an airport in Texas. A young woman was giving her baby to a couple. She was grief-stricken. I looked at the baby and felt its entire life shift before me. I looked at the woman and felt her coming years of sorrow and regret. What was I doing there? This scene has haunted me for years. I never have been able to explain it.

Another time, on the subway in New York City, I looked up into the face of a man. He was handsome in his three-piece suit. Our eyes met and I found myself standing in a hotel room. A woman was lying on the floor. She was dead and I knew he had killed her. My staring made him very nervous and he left the car. The next day I read in the newspaper that a woman had been discovered dead in a hotel room. They assumed she had had a casual love tryst. No clues were found. I have never spoken of this until now.

Through my readings I have traveled vicariously all over the world and through the spectrum of emotions. I often wonder what purpose this has. I grab the air for an answer and beg my sleep for a dream.

What is the reason for the recurring dream? The subconscious mind screaming and pushing. "Listen to me! Pay attention!" Over and over again. It shows us two sides of a mirror. One is the reflection of my own life, the other the prophetic inspiration of what is to come. Both are intimidating and mysterious. I beckon to those dark waters as I fear their undertow. The more it frightens me, the more I understand it. I can't wait to enter my evening dream theaters.

To interpret the dream which reveals my own life, I spend much time analyzing the symbolism and synchronicities in my daily life. Everything means something to me. To interpret prophetic dreams, I remove my reasonable thinking and absorb the process emotionally. The accuracy of the language in the prophetic is as hidden as an autistic child's mind. Only by observing with an empathic heart will the events be revealed. The only way I will get to know that language is to get out of the way and feel. I can be fooled by the literal, by the expectation that history repeats itself or by the magnetism of the catastrophic imagery. Between the two dreams, the personal and the prophetic, lies my world and sometimes I cannot tell the difference between the three.

I have had several recurring dreams throughout my life. One that I feel is a mirror of my life and my work as a psychic I call the Torso Dream. There are many variations. In one, I am alone in a bed. I am a torso. No arms, no legs, my head, my trunk. I am completely depressed. I cannot go anywhere. I have only my mind. I can speak but I cannot walk or hold anything or anyone. A friend stands next to my bed and is thrilled for me in my condition. Now I can write, I can write my story, the things I know. I am perplexed and angered by her enthusiasm. I do not say anything. I am an animal trapped. END.

In another torso dream I am in Buffalo, New York, where I spent my childhood. Standing near my elementary school on a very rainy evening, I witness a young boy hit by a car. He is repeatedly hit by several passing cars driving at high speeds. His arms and legs are severed. I watch what remains of him, a torso desperately trying to stand up and save himself. I do not respond. I am shocked by the horror. I stand there hoping he'll live, hoping he'll die. In the distance I see a rabbi going for help. END.

In a third torso dream I am in an open market place in a country like Morocco. A stranger approaches me and places a bundle in my arms. I take it with apprehension. He tells me to take the bundle to the scales to be weighed. I place it in the bucket of the scale. Another man adjusts the weights and measures and then unwraps the bundle for me to see. There, staring into my eyes, the torso of Jesus. His eyes are bleeding and his head is crowned with thorns. I am shocked and terrified. His eyes do not leave me. END.

Another recurring dream is about the sun and the moon. I started having these dreams around age twelve just before I learned to read the Tarot. It has slight variations, but basically is as follows: I am usually standing in a field, the same field every time. A warm sun glows in a turquoise sky. The field is quiet and a slight breeze gently moves the tall grass. Sometimes I'm alone, sometimes I'm with someone I know. We talk about how perfect this day is. Then in the distance we notice the sun becoming brighter and next to it appears an enormous full moon. The sun and the moon slowly move closer and closer together. They merge and there is a great explosion. The sun and the moon break up into millions of particles of light and rapidly start coming toward us. These particles pierce our bodies with tiny holes. I look down at my hands and legs and watch the light flow through me. The entire landscape is also filled with holes. I am ecstasy. At the same time I know this is the end. I have had this dream hundreds of times.

For years I have also dreamt of wild horses. These haunted animals appearing in my dreams always seem lost and out of place in the surroundings. Sometimes they just stand silently by my bed as I watch myself asleep. Their huge bodies moving gracefully around me. Their long, open noses filling the air with warm, moist breath. I'm sometimes standing in an empty house when the front door bursts open and the horses run up the staircase to the roof and out into the sky, leaving a gaping hole to the stars. I've seen families of homeless people transform into horses. Horses swimming underwater. Horses running through city streets. Horses trampling people. Objects turning into horses. And horses just motionless, just watching me. I wait for these night mares and I long to run with them.

These three recurring dreams speak to me both personally and prophetically. They are very complex, often revealing new meanings over time. I know the torso dreams tell me of the impact on my soul from doing so many psychic readings. The intimate psychic relationships I have with people I never touch or see again leave me feeling dismembered in some unusual way. They also speak to me of the power and the illusion of power our limbs afford us as human beings. Arms, legs, hands have allowed us to change the world. Without them we are humbled and reminded of our true animal nature. We also take our bodies for granted until some part is injured or removed. A torso cannot survive alone.

The sun and the moon coming together could mean the end of the world, or it could symbolize the transformation of the dark and the light—the oppositions of nature within myself and the world around me. The sun and the moon suggest how people mark time, counting the days we have left and recording our histories. If the sun and moon no longer had cycles, imagine how different our lives would be.

The wild horses reveal to me my own frustration of being trapped in a physical human body. I long to fly, to be wild in my animal nature. The horses show me the violence in the world and the helplessness I sometimes feel over things I cannot change. They show me that nature has its own continuing evolution regardless of humans.

I have great respect and gratitude for the psyche that has given me the vision of these dreams. They are filled with mysterious clues to my unknown self. I wait for night.

I stand here all alone in this room. The walls are so white, so bright. There's nothing here but a white painted table in the middle of this room, and the bright sun hurts my eyes. It is quiet. I wonder what I'm waiting for. On the table is a tall glass half filled with red liquid. "Over here. Here, over here." A voice, I think, is calling me. "Here, over here." I don't see anyone. I look around, but there's no one here. "Please, here, over here." My God, the voice is coming out of the glass. "Please don't let me dry up inside this glass. Drink me. Give my life meaning. Please drink me."

I don't hesitate. I pick up the glass, put it to my lips and drink it right down. I can stare into the red ocean inside me. I am the drink. I taste myself. This liquid is me. I am no longer the same person. I am no longer anyone. I am no longer a mind. I am red, passion, blood. I am no longer waiting. I know in this white room I had no choice. I had to drink the dream.

❀

POEMS
Shirley Geok-lin Lim

Learning English

A change of heart.
An English phrase, a Western idea.
I couldn't understand
its meaning. A child,
I knew hearts did not change—
grew older unfaithful
forgetful, but were the same
father, mother.
Unfaithful
forgetful, but still father mother.

It wasn't like changing
shoes, one pair of shoes
for leather heels
tap-dancing semaphores
of excessive meaning.
Or like simple translation:
ditditdit dahdahdah ditditdit.
It was like learning
to let go and to hold on:

a slow braking, shifting
gears, an engine
of desire on a downhill
slope, momentum of vocabularies
carrying the child
to foreign countries,
to families of strangers,
an orphanage of mind,
and technologies of empire.

It was more like cry,
a beloved country, and
see, traveler, on a hill,
by the wall, exchanging
what must be changed
forever, good-bye, farewell
the different words working
to say what is
unchangeable. Say, father,
mother.

The Fortune Teller

When the old man and his crow
picked the long folded parchment
to tell my fortune at five,
they never told about leaving,
the burning tarmac and giant
  wheels.
Or arriving—why immigrants
fear the malice of citizens
and dull shutterings of those
who hate you whatever you do.
My mother did not grip
my hand more possessively.
Did I cry and was it corn
ice-cream she fed me because
the bird foretold a husband?
Wedded to unhappiness,
she knew I would make it,
meaning money, a Mercedes
and men. She saw them shining
in the tropical mildew
that greened the corner alley
where the blind man and his
moulting crow squatted

promising my five-year-old hand
this future. Of large faith
she thrust a practical note
into the bamboo container,
a shiny brown cycliner
I wanted for myself, for
a cage for field crickets.
With this fortune my mother
  bought,
only the husband is present,
white as a peeled root, furry
with good intentions, his big
  nose
smelling a scam. Sometimes,
living with him, like that
black silent crow I shake
the cylinder of memory
and tell my fortune all over again.
My mother returns carrying
the bamboo that we will fill
with green singing crickets.

The Gift

At eight I become an animal.
Hunger sniffs, growls
at every corner, the dragon
stomps and dances on my poor head.

Every tree's a meal—
butterfruit pulped in
fuzzy jacket, stone guava
with gravelled core, even

tropical cherry-berries
which squish like bird-shit.

I hide in every corner
place where you can never
find me—dark under
hibiscus edge

cool by a back drain.
Crawl into my skin,
keep under cover,
listening to the quiet,

to the noisy dragon
spitting and shaking. She
and I were born together,
but I am wild.

I want to eat grass,
frangipani white
as sugar crusts,
just as the sun eats me,
melting in drops,
and licking like a lolly.

My Father from Malaysia

My father from Malaysia
stands under a tree in China
fifteen years ago. A lichee tree
in Canton's People's Park. Mr.
  Wer
who is also at the Clinic
takes the picture with slightly
shaking hands. It is a frugal
  picture,
black and white, two inches by
two inches, sent across two
  oceans,
creased by crazy white lines like
a cracked egg, although for fifteen years
I have preserved it in plastic
between student visas, in a suc-
  cession
of wallets, between checkbook
and dollar notes. He is gaunt,
he who loves oyster omelets,
long noodles, pure white of pork
  fat
between skin and lean.Now he
  counts
his white blood cells, reciting
numbers in letters home as he
recited mahjongg scores a year

ago.
He will not let the Malaysian
doctor cut his throat. He writes,
Chinese medicine can also
calibrate blood-cells. I am un-
  housed
in yet another country.
I do not know how to write
to him. I do not have his mother-
  land
address. I do not pick up
the black coffin telephone.
No one tells me he's dead
till he's been buried.

Today I would call Canton
person-to-person. I'd say,
I've booked a ticket for you
to Sloan-Kettering. See, I have
  bank
accounts and dollar notes to save
your life here in another country.

Instead I write this poem.

Listening to the Punjabi Singer

Her Urdu voice rises in the performance room.
I could have been married for twenty years
to the man she's singing for—the beloved
who does not return her love and vanishes
forever. Always suffering Asia!

I yearn to be her this evening.
Suffused, securely my own woman,
I play at nostalgia, imagine—
eyes closed—Malaysia now, as if
twenty years have passed and nothing's died.

Not the dream of marriage, of one brown
family and nation. From back-of-the-room
middle age spins fantasy and regret.
Singles the concrete bungalow
in Petaling Jaya, one of thousands

of a race: Malay, Chinese, Indian,
and Eurasian hardened in the same
shelter, if not skin. In front of the white
stone an iron gate, bars, curlicues,
three-inch chain and lock. By the gate
hibiscus, oleander, jacarandas
with dirty plum blossom. Leafage I prune
with words threaten to overtake the evening
just as the singer has overtaken
me—back, in a language I do not know,

to the place of colored doors, the riotous
vegetation, choices, and wild consequences.

❁

The Singing Antelope
Inés Martinez

During daylight, I can dream I see what I see—my house stands still between rows of rooted poplars. At night, if I open my eyes, I feel the earth move, and shortly, my house and I float between treetops. It's my watching the moon—slipping from cloud to cloud. And the stars. But it takes much longer to see stars.

I know he never saw them, although—and I have forgiven him everything because of it—he pretended. He never cared about what was real as I did—only whether things were going as he wished. Lying came easily to him.

He's suffering now, there on that narrow hospital bed—perhaps most because there's no way to maneuver. When we come into life, one tube is all we need. When we die—he looks like a bug caught in a web. This is not how I've known him, how any of us have. My younger sister pleads when she visits, scolds him as if he's in a mad, fatal sulk. As eldest daughter, childless, I watch around the clock. He doesn't know how my presence buffers him, how I give him permission to be mortal. I doubt he'd want that from me, but it hardly matters. For years now, we've had to slip each other what we have to give.

When I was seventeen, his silhouette loomed in my doorway. The brightness of the light behind him darkened his face, his body, and rested in his own sense of himself as a figure not quite divine, but certainly not simply human. As a consequence he trusted himself to me and allowed me my own head. I believe I loved him more than anyone ever had, and so, inevitably, we dashed one another's hearts.

I hated him for lying to me—and, then, it was another woman, too. Mother had been right about that—the only victory life gave her, I'm afraid. I first saw the antelope during my customary escape from their mutual dismemberments. I lay on the garage roof watching for falling stars, dreaming of a young woman. Nights in the valley towns were rather quiet, then. We had automobiles and planes, of course, but not so many of them that darkness ceased belonging to itself. And our house was on the edge of the mesa stretching miles toward the mountains. I had more sky than I could see.

The creature simply appeared although it was so distant and dim I assumed it wasn't where I saw it. I'd always thought we made the constellations up, grouped the stars in familiar shapes so we could recognize them, like faces. And this creature was not quite an antelope, either. For one thing, it had five legs, two coming out of its left haunch. And its tail had the sweep of a comet.

The cry of my parents' rage broke through the house, swelled into the night. I thought perhaps they might murder each other, and I felt the oddest peace. The urge to throw myself between them or to besiege God with prayers simply was gone. I was willing for even death to happen—I mean, even though it was they rending each other, I took what they were doing on myself. I can't explain. Only, for once, I both cared and didn't care with all my heart. And then I was free. Death felt perfectly inevitable; I, inexplicable; the world, absolutely open.

Getting ready for my journey was innocent. I took some water and a jacket. There was no moon and no way to know where I was going except that flickering body of stars that apparently had descended to the desert.

I picked my way through the sagebrush and cactus talking with myself.

Why are you alive now?

I don't know.

Why here?

I don't know.

With these people?

I don't know.

As you are?

I don't know.

Joy seeped into me with the starlight, filling me like my own blood. I could have been anywhere or never, and Lena's face filled my heart.

Why not?

Oh God—his chest is heaving. If only I could breathe for him. No, no, that won't do—not even for a moment. His face is so empty now, except for pain. My lending him my breath would be a violence against all he has been.

He wouldn't forgive me Lena. I was the only child he never hit. My sister tells me he beat her the night he found out. I hadn't spoken to him, myself, in years. We didn't talk, really, until after I was forty and had betrayed Lena. I left her for a younger woman, much as he had Mother.

At first, I asked him whether he'd be pleased if I moved back to town. "It's too late for that," he said. The next time I saw him, about four years later, we talked like old lovers who no longer needed anything of one another. Finally, he asked me about Lena. And I told him in pieces as we walked the mesa. It was twilight when I told him of the antelope, of walking across the mesa under the stars, feeling the ecstasy of my mortality, drawing ever closer to the constellation that had somehow fallen to the earth. I walked all night, and indeed the stars grew larger, softer as I continued. The night was still an hour from dawn when I heard. I'd already seen it fully for some time.

It was taller than any building I had ever seen—tall enough to suck the earth it stood on toward the sky. Mostly, it was darkness. I could see it only by the stars that marked it randomly. Stars outlined its face, its long neck, much longer than any earthly antelope's. There was a star at the tip of one ear, and an arch of stars along a tail that shot from its three hind legs straight toward the heavens. Its hindquarters were lifted, and its body seemed to pour toward its shoulders, a vessel of night. The closer I came, the more it resembled my own soul during the moment before I move. It was drawn into a breath of poise and gazed down into the arroyos far below.

And then I heard it sing. My body folded, and I wept. Its song was eight notes, and they rose like a scale, but the closest scale I had ever heard to the intervals of the antelope's song was a psalm a visiting Greek priest had once sung in our church. And yet this song was as far beyond his as the universe is beyond the sun. The antelope repeated it again and again, this rising call weaving the earth to heaven in strands of longing and love. I then not only knew that I would one moment die, but I knew the moment did not matter, that the meaning of a life is instantaneous, its completion impossible. And I knew, then, that I would choose for love.

He listened to me gravely. "I, too, had a young love, once," he said. She had been beautiful and in love with him, and he had been over-whelmed and grateful. He worshipped her. Parents, fate, time intervened. He did not see her again until they each had raised children. She was still beautiful, and still in love. "I told her I did not want to sleep with her," he said. "I told her what we had was still perfect and that nowhere else did I still have that."

I have learned that loving is an art to be studied and served, so I don't know if I understood him or not. Perhaps he had his own visions. Perhaps, in some way, he even understands mine.

Last night, I held his hand as he fell asleep. Before he drifted off, he told me he'd been dreaming of his father, of trying to swim the river by his childhood home. He smiled. "You're the one who remembers dreams," he said to me. I hold his hand again and help him dream his death.

The Genesis of "The Singing Antelope"

A phone call and I was left imagining my father on a surgery table, the machine measuring his heartbeats flashing like an odds board.

That night I dreamed that my father was my navel to the earth. During the following days that image hovered at the back of whatever I was doing, now closer to awareness, now further away. Certain moments were numinous with it—a passage by Philip Glass on the radio—a sculpture by my friend. Such moments and the image worked in me until one night as I lay with my eyes closed, the fallen constellation of the antelope in the desert sang for me.

The story begins with a waking dream, a memory of a childhood night, and it ends with dreams, a sleeping memory of the story's father and the wishful dream of its daughter.

The center of the story is yet another dream—a vision on the night mesa—fallen stars assuming shape and voice to sing across dimensions of being.

And through the substantiality of the dreams, facts are woven, facts fragmentary apart from the dreams—facts of fear and anger, love and betrayal, illness and death.

So in the story imagination rubs pieces of inner and outer worlds against one another. "The Singing Antelope"—for me, a falling into a constellation of the feelings of having and losing one's navel to the earth.

THE LINEN DOOR:
DREAMS, INTUITION AND CREATIVITY
Verbena Pastor

It's a conundrum. I think I know what intuition is, though conscious knowing, the intellectual exercise mediated by language, is the opposite of intuiting. Perhaps I only "feel" what intuition is. Yet intuition teaches and directs, in the way dreams instruct.

Instinctual apprehension, awareness, being at one with one's self: seldom our waking minds attain the certainty we hold in the paradoxically ephemeral world of our dreams. An interesting reversal takes place in sleep: "we" sleep, and the "dormant" issues in our lives come awake.

Old fears, unresolved conflicts, anxieties, expectations and secret hopes, unconfessed desires, childish grudges, spiritual hankerings: these are the faces, the places of dreams. The deceptively harmless, linen-clad portal of sleep ushers us into a world where temporal and geographic restrictions are non-existent. The dead speak to us. Gods and humans and animals mingle in a colorful harmony that would satisfy our ancestors' trust in the Peaceable Kingdom.

Our waking knowledge assists us in discerning the shadowy images, but only to a point. When logic fails—and how can it not, if automobiles fly and flowers talk?—intuition becomes the function. We make instinctual sense of hidden relationships, emotional connections, and gracefully move through rooms that often resemble Saint Teresa's mystical "interior castle."

But what's the use of dreams to the creative mind? Is there a transpersonal dimension to what we can acquire through them? Can dreams assist our creativity?

Artists like Goya, Kafka, Haendel thought so. Goya's nightmarish visions of personal and communal anguish; the Kafkaesque Gregor Samsa, who awoke from his dream transformed into a cockroach; Haendel's own admission that "The Messiah's" music was revealed to him into a dream-like state—all point to a tenuous yet resilient connection among dream, intuition and creativity.

Freud and Jung, founders of modern psychology, made dreams the cornerstone of their therapy. They believed dreams to reveal the hidden and explain the inexplicable: and if Freud's dream therapy often indicted the client's past, Jung's more positive approach admitted that the future can be foreshadowed in dreams.

More than this, in Jung's own words, the dream of a multi-storied house assisted him in developing his highly original system of analysis.

Once the Spanish poet Federico Garcia Lorca said that three spirits assist our creative minds: the angel, the Muse and the "duende." He warned that they must not be confused with one another, because their gifts are different and to different aims.The angel guides and protects. The muse directs. The "duende," a divine yet earthy spirit, possesses and inspires. For Lorca, inspiration is closely bound to intuition, and its locus is unconscious, unbidden, trance- and dream-like. May not then our night dreams, too, be a source for creative inspiration?

The following excerpts from personal dreams, some of them disturbing, all of them significant to me, are accompanied by poems which ventured forth from the same inner place of fear and love. The linen door of the dream world was ajar long enough for me to slip in and out, bearing gifts.

Dream, February 11, 1993

"I'm in the dark, narrow hallway of an old hotel. On the floor are scattered coins I know to be two thousand years old. I also know there are two hundred thousand ways of contacting the invisible world."

Message: The unconscious mind precedes our birth in a long line of experiences.

The Soul Market

The caravans gather at dusk
on windy crossroads in the desert
where purple hills skirt the distance
and set limits. At night
the caravans begin to move,

lumbering, wheeling, taking the round
orbits of the stars along their trails,
and the boys walk wide-awake behind the carts,
pulling small dogs by bits of string,
seeking the fairy hems of female spirits
in the purple black hills.
Old men discern the path in the equal sand
and have no expectations; they know the stars,
the muted shapes along the slipping surface
of the desert, the magic flimsiness of impressions;
they are not deceived nor hopeful nor
do they look back; all that's behind
for them is windswept barrows in the sand
where the dead are buried, the midden pits
of old camps, overturned water jugs and
reclining trees across the water holes.

But the boys tremble with the night
and feel the sting of stars prick them through the pores,
hear the shift of the sand roll over dunes
in gritty swells; their ears
are keen: their eyes capture the lonely arc
of meteors and the darkling hems
of the purple hill women, dancing, dancing
at the horizon, linking all directions.
And they forget their mothers' ankles and their sisters'
thin arms, but the trail
speaks to them and the night behind
speaks to them from the barrows and midden pits and the boughs on
    the water holes,
and the old men's forgotten childhood care.

Tomorrow
they will get to the city.
The caravans will be red and green
and women will wear sandals to pass the gate.
Old men will loiter outside the walls
in halfhearted barter, knowing that it is

just one more town with stalls and markets
and latrines, and another gate that leads out.
The boys will wonder at the gate,
face the hinges, reach for the strength of the jamb,
and feel their heart rejoice as they go across.

Dream, August 3, 1993

". . .A young girl about twelve years old, pitifully skinny and ragged,
comes trembling and asks for food. I go inside to get her something to
eat, and when I return, she's so desperately famished that she's scratch-
ing the dirt and devouring it. . ."

Message: The inner self needs nourishment and shelter.

Filia Mystica

My soul-daughter has taken the road
where dust collects, and the long rows
of carved columns lie. The wind has done
its work. It has danced and worn out,
taken, deposited, lifted up. The air
has not seen it, but infinitesimal
friction smoothed the joints before weakening them,
rounded, flattened, made snub. The face
of each stone was changed. Rain
fell in the clefts, and the pitted surface
became marble cups. The eaves molded
and dried up, insects smaller than a gnat
found homes and burrows from the wind. Shelter
was and shelter is, to different species.
The dust collects in the pauses of the wind,
away from March and the other hard-breathing months;
traces of past travellers
stamp the dust with the ghosts of hesitancy
or intention, a toe print deeper than the other,
widened by stopping to deliberate,

or marred by an attempt to turn upon the round
hinge of the heel.
My soul-daughter gathers her skirts and
picks her steps, leaving the full imprint
of her child foot in the dust.

Dream, March 20, 1995

"I am one of several prisoners in the garden of my parents' house. We are being punished and the guards shoot at us. We all race across the wall and escape."

Message: The insecurities and restrictions of childhood must be integrated and left behind.

Going Out, Out

I have said yes enough times. Locked the door,
swept the threshold, put away the jars,
stacked the dishes. I have replaced books
on the shelves and let the fly out
not to kill her, made sure that the shade fell
on the side of the room where the plants
thrive in the coolness. Cobwebs have
been wiped from the corners, the ceiling is
inviting the darted glare of marigolds
from the yard. I am putting my hat on.
I walk outside, cross the green,
and drop the key
into the well.

Dream, July 3, 1994

"I am in an underground tunnel. My long-dead mother attacks me and I must defend myself, pinning her to the floor and bearing my weight down on her until I subdue her."

Message: Spiritual independence requires a struggle.

Getting Free

I had to kill my mother in order for
my sisters to live, out of love for them,
because their sisterhood was more important
than my bonds to her. The blanched bones
I stacked by the road, in a place sheltered
from the wind, where the vines formed a bower and
red berries will grow swollen in autumn.
I'd like to call it a May shrine, but
the chalk Madonna has since had enough
of rosaries: beads won't do it this time.
Gaudy necklaces and ribbons of grosgrain
lie in boxes on the shelf, with
the collection of mismatched buttons from
incestuous uncles and dull cousins.
There are no offerings to this murder shrine.
The act itself is celebration, a mass
of the dead, this symmetric heaping
of calcified material. The bone of my small
finger has long been lit before it
like a pencil-thin candle, white
against the green.

Dream, May 19, 1993

"In a restricted, cabin-like space. I sit in front of a middle-aged woman, waiting for a beatific vision. When the vision doesn't come, I am disappointed. Then I realize that a divine sweetness radiates from the face of the woman."

Message: Spiritual initiation begins in unlikely places, when we least expect it.

Asleep in the Garden

It's taken years in the bark of the tree,
feeling my roots and dirt and sappy lymph,
caught in the case of scabrous wood.
The garden
was closed at both ends;
it was night. No one knew. The stars
were distant and unaware. Branches creaked
on branches. The two faces of each
leaf had too much intimacy to speak
their different colors.
And
I don't recall dawn
coming—it might have been the sailing rise
of the moon for all I know—but the dark
opened like an eye. The flimsiest stars withdrew
and sank into an infinite backwards.
Then
the irritant,
the bump, the passage of an insect on prickly
legs, the gem on the bark, poking,
poking, birthing a green shoot.

The bark has torn asunder.

Dream, December 9, 1993

> "A priest asks me questions, and I answer.
> 'Do you know me?'
> 'No, not really.'
> 'Why?'
> 'Because I only met you a short time ago.'
> 'But don't you feel we met before?'
> 'Yes, but that would imply metempsychosis.'
> He smiles. 'Sometimes I think that's possible. . .'"

Message: We are the part of a continuum broken by individual lifetimes.

Ephemera

Saguaro flowers bloom one day,
unfolding overnight from tightly bound
testicle-like, scaly buds. Only the ants
first presumed of tightness and of closure,
prophesizing the sweet, darting across
the bulbous heads while the sun went down.
After, the circle of each bloom cups out
in the dark.
Bats flutter by
on gauze thin wings to suck the sap, then bees and wasps
at dawn drone in and out
of the deep yellow core;
next are the mourning doves, in the blaze of midday; last,
as the flowers shrink into flimsy fists
on soon to be detached stems
against the purpling sky,
the ants.

The Gardens of Adonis last but one day.

Homenaje a Federico

To Federico Garcia Lorca, who feared lizards and believed in dreams.

Señor Lagarto hides under a rock
in his green coat.

Señorita Fly alights on the leaf,
dashing in her shiny body suit and wings,
heedless, modern, à la mode, debonaire,
cariñosa. She knows what's what. She's
daring. The transparency of her wings
contains at least twenty cathedrals,
three movie houses and an arena.
She's flown to Cuba and walked the dung piles
in Nueva York—plus her appearance in Buenos
Aires, by popular request.
Male flies have dashed themselves
against windshields
because not one of her ten thousand eyes
looked their way.
Saint Michael has plucked one feather
from his right wing
to offer her a drink of sweaty blood
from the calamus tip.
Women have stilled their fans
and men
curled their whiskers
(there is talk in Granada
that nuns deserted matins
to see her). Revolution in the Basque country.

Señor Lagarto darts
from under his rock
and eats the fly.

❂

POEMS
Freida Chapman

How We're Called

Slavery names. Resonant
proud—

Solomon Cotton, great
Solomon Cotton, grand
Solomon Cotton, father
never disavowed,
but died
in childless sons.

Daughters,
generations removed
from American
genesis, gave birth

to Lumumbas, Abdullahs
Jamahls and Kenyattas,
names bespeaking Africa
last
and first.

Last Will

I see a gathering of friends
on bluffs above the timeless river
a place for words. Something said about the best
remembered things. About the mingling of ashes,
leaves and stones

where scattered kin
congregate, amazed at the moving
stream, speak of wildflowers on the shore;
taking some comfort in beauty.

Not unlike
where you and I love to stand
watching the heron, in the same silence
that was in the beginning, before
we found our words.

❋

THE MATERNAL MUSE
Barbara Sturgill Singer

Transitional space is round and infinite, sometimes hexagonal. You stand in the middle. It folds and unfolds. Its colors are pinks to purples to dark blues. It's deeply textural, rich and warm. When you are in it, time ceases to be.

This summarizes what artists have responded when I asked them what transitional space would look like if they could paint it. "Transitional, or potential, space" is what pediatrician and psychoanalyst Donald Winnicott called a special area of creative consciousness in the development of the human psyche.

Winnicott saw the potential for creative ability being formed from the earliest relationship between mother and infant, "the nursing couple", as he called them. The role of the good-enough mother is to create an environment which holds the infant in a close supportive way yet allows her/him at times to be alone, to simply be. If the holding is too much, the infant feels overwhelmed and anxious, as if s/he must fill the mother's needs. If the holding is not enough, the feeling of loneliness, the need for connection becomes a haunting refrain. But if the holding is enough, the baby learns trust.

With trust, s/he creates a new kind of connection whenever the mother must appropriately withdraw. In an act of tremendous creativity, s/he transforms a transitional object such as a teddy bear or the corner of a blanket into a reassuring symbol of union with mother. This object transports the baby to an environment which exists somewhere between reality and fantasy. This third internal world develops as the mother and child agree that the transitional object is under the control of the baby's creativity, intimately connected to her/his imaginative ability throughout life. Here, in this intermediary space, creativity and play merge.

I think of my own Polish peasant of a mother, her warmth and softness, her entire personality which helped me become the person I am. After dwelling in her love for me, I learned to share her love of humanity. Growing up in New York, I fell in love with art, the museums and galleries but also the city itself, its aura spilling over with light, shape, form, design, movement and human drama. Creating my own art, I felt a delicious oneness with the universe I am just beginning to understand.

Art itself is transitional space, not only in its complex relation of negative to positive space, but also its mediating space between the work and the viewer. When I was a young girl in New York City, my mother used to take me to the Museum of Modern Art. I remember my favorite painting, called "Hide and Seek," of a wonderful tree filled with children hiding in the leaves and branches. Now, many years later, I can still feel the pleasure of finding those children.

When art interacts with therapy, clients can enter their own transitional space, to be restored to their capacity for symbol-making, the courage of creativity, the spontaneity of play and self-discovery through images. As multiple connections are brought back into consciousness, their inner lives are enriched with meaning. The transitional space of the drawing paper, for instance, bounded by its own edges, contains and is contained by the therapeutic alliance. The client is given control over the size, shape and contents of this container. Within this space the conflict between fear of isolation and fear of engulfment can be enacted visually.

The therapist provides the safety which holds the space secure while restructuring takes place, sitting quietly while the client works, making no demands so the client is free to experiment with the art itself, to wait for the truth to emerge. As one client describes the process, the art making "starts out fun. Then it gets kind of painful. Then something takes over—I don't know what it is, but I have to keep going until I'm done. My own work sometimes shocks and surprises me, but I have to keep doing it."

Allowing creativity to emerge as the act of an authentic self restores our capacity to return to transitional space, which trauma and its consequences have destroyed. During and after trauma, that transitional space crumbles, separating us from our resources for internal security, spontaneity, discovery and growth. The world is not to be trusted when the structures deep within can no longer hold, collapsing in on themselves. As our ability to create meaningful symbols freezes, our interactions with the outside world generate more and more anxiety.

Such was the case with Nancy, a 19-year-old woman traumatized physically and emotionally by a bus accident while traveling in Mexico.

She had gone there in defiance of her parents—an angry and controlling father, a passive, depressed mother—carrying her own baggage of unexamined pain, grief and anger. After a year of self-discovery and connections with other young seekers, she was ready to come home when the accident occurred, leaving her paralyzed and isolated. Another part of her—tough, resilient—emerged out of the numb twilight of her shock.

Finally her father found her, in constant pain, close to death, in and out of consciousness, and rescued her, to deliver her to the impersonal drama of modern medicine. As Nancy disappeared beneath the onslaught of tubes, incisions and injections, her body became the property of the hospital, while the new identity within her, detached but fighting for survival, took over as slowly she began to heal.

Scarred and confused, she finally emerged from the hospital, not sure who she was. Blamed for the accident by her stunned family, she ran away again, this time to Oregon, where she slid through a series of relationships, jobs and classes, still in physical pain. Further operations, including a hysterectomy, led to further recriminations from her family. She felt she could never repay them for depriving them of grandchildren. Finally, she divorced herself from Nancy and renamed herself Eli. After five years, we met in a bookstore and immediately connected. She began therapy soon after.

To develop a common language and to build trust—a bridge in and out of a transitional, supportive, non-judgmental, healing space—we used art. Our work together was helped along by the commonalities of a similar ethnic background and a love for art. We created maps to express feelings and to describe events beyond words. The edges of the paper made a frame within which we could work, a holding device within the holding device of our alliance.

After Eli felt safe enough to play with the art supplies, she then led the way by devising her own language of shapes, lines and colors. This in turn opened up for her the transitional space which had collapsed with the trauma of her accident. Each art piece expanded this space to establish new comfort zones. This process of reclamation was deepened by a series of poems Eli wrote to go with each major piece of art. As she reclaimed her creativity, her image of herself as helpless diminished.

Returning to the accident was the hardest bridge to cross, blocked by the natural protective devices of denial and shock. We learned the feel of resistance, its form and color. It took on a language of its own as we gave

it space and respect. The pain, isolation and violation of lying naked in the hospital, cut open, no one bothering to pull up a sheet, was too awful at first even to draw, or, once drawn, to look at.

But the accuracy of Eli's art work increased as she trusted the therapeutic holding enough to express her pain. Sometimes the art was ahead of comprehension. Sometimes we waited patiently for the nausea and dizziness to subside. Sometimes we could say nothing, awed by the art's ability to mirror a pain that was beyond words.

Beyond the accident was childhood and a reconnection with Nancy and the heartfelt feelings within her which were ripped out by the accident, "leaving a dark, empty, neutralized existence." When Nancy drew, her pictures showed a deep rage covering a nearly broken heart, the grief of betrayal, the loss of youth and innocence, the loss of her parents. Beneath this were issues of growing up second generation American in a conservative Jewish family, the gender contradictions between her and her male siblings, the sacred obligation in her tradition to bear children, the patterns of abuse and blame, shame and anger.

As Eli progressed, so did her artistic ability. She began to incorporate into her sense of self the identity and feel of an artist. As she made career plans, it became evident that her creativity was not isolated to fine art but would be part of all her future choices.The fact that her work was in some sense her offspring, worthy of nurture and respect, helped too. The dichotomy between Eli and Nancy grew smaller as each felt recognized, mirrored and accepted. After two and a half years of art psychotherapy, Eli at last came to appreciate a life which stretched out before her. A glimmer of authentic self had burst through the rigid walls of internal collapse where "each moment of life brought with it the fear of death." She realized that her true self had suffocated when trauma collapsed her transitional space; with healing she breathed air into that space and opened it up again.

It's a myth that creativity originates from a mysterious, otherworldly place. True, the impulse to create is notoriously fickle, as capricious as a breath of wind, an intimate smile or a sudden splash in a quiet pond, as breathtaking as an ancient Goddess or wryly significant as a lucky coin or an old Smith-Corona. Some wait and others woo in an attempt to cajole that longed-for muse to stay a little longer.

But as Winnicott reminds us in his poem, "Sleep," all we need do is let our taproots down to the centers of our souls to "suck up the sap from the infinite source of [our] unconscious and be evergreen."

❀

II. SYMBOLS: STARS IN THE STREAM

The charged quality of symbols which are harvested from the dream or trance state is characteristic of this second section, "Stars in the Stream." Beginning with S.B. Sowbel's profound description of an inner journey through the dead of winter in "The Mole," we move to Jackie Brookner's powerful sculpture and her poem which describes it, shapes behind words of our connection to the earth. The eloquence of Angela de Hoyos' use of symbolic language is evident in the originality and playfulness of her poetry. In describing the interaction between her personal mandalas and Mayan huipiles, Gail Wheeler helps define a new theory of knowledge. The fresh and vital images in Lewanda Lim's poetry speak of translating symbols from one culture to another. John Berdy extends this exploration of archetypes into the transcendent dimensions of music. In describing her creative process as an artist, Francelise Dawkins gives words to many ineffable facets of intuitive expression. The clarity and depth of the images in Barbara Trumbull's poems reveal the experience and skill of a lifetime. Clara Cohan's essay describes how in the creative process the artist like a magician transmutes images from spiritual inspiration.

S.B. Sowbel's poetry and artwork have been published in a variety of publications and she has written *The Next Step: A Participatory Guide for HIV/AIDS Prevention Education* and co-authored with Margaret Blanchard, *Restoring the Orchard: A Guide to Learning Intuition* and *Duet: A Book of Poems and Paintings*. At present she works as a counselor and life credit evaluator for adults while living in a shack with mice, moles and bats across from "the" beaver pond in upstate New York.

Jackie Brookner is a sculptor who lives in New York City and deep in the Adirondack woods. She was Guest Editor of the *Art Journal* on "Art and Ecology" and teaches at Parsons School of Design and the University of Pennsylvania.

A native of Mexico, **Angela de Hoyos** moved to San Antonio with her family when she was two years old. She has published five books of poetry, including the internationally acclaimed *Woman, Woman*. Her work has been translated into a dozen languages. DeHoyos is the recipient of numerous awards, including one in 1992 from the Guadalupe Cultural Arts Center, in 1993 for Distinguished Recognition of Chicano Studies and in 1994 the First Annual San Antonio Poetry Festival Life Achievement Award from the Texas Commission on the Arts.

Gail Wheeler is associate professor of art and education in the Adult Degree Program at Vermont College of Norwich University, receiving her Ph.D. in Art from the Union Institute in 1992. She has lived and studied in Ecuador, Mexico and Bali. She has conducted a cross-cultural book exchange between children in Guatemala and Vermont and a cross-cultural art exchange between children in Vermont and Indonesia.

Originally from the Philippines, **Lewanda Lim** has lived in North America for nineteen years. A painter and printmaker, she has been writing poetry for eight years. She speaks two Filipino languages but is most comfortable writing in English. She lives in Queensbury, New York.

John Berdy is a psychotherapist who specializes in the use of sound and music. John is also a mediator, composer and performer of classical Indian music. His B.A. in music is from Union College and his M.A. in counseling psychology, from Vermont College. His recording of North Indian classical bamboo flute music is entitled "Journey to Qayyum."

Francelise Dawkins, a native of Paris, France, with Caribbean ancestry, has lived in the U.S. for 16 years. A translator, workshop leader of French-Caribbean folk dancing and a French teacher, she is a nationally exhibited textile artist whose work has received many awards. It is featured in the 1992 *Black Family Dinner Quilt Cookbook* and at the Museum of the American Quilters' Society. Bi-racial, bilingual and ambidexterous, Francelise feels that individuality is the authentic way to unity.

Barbara Cole Trumbull received her M. A. in creative writing and creativity in elders from the Graduate Program of Vermont College at the age of eighty-one. "As a result I can now say 'yes' to myself. This is a quest I have been on all my eighty years. I feel I have become a new being. Nothing can be more surprising than a new being born in us."

Clara Cohan has been a self-supporting artist since the late 1970's. Diversified in her use of media, she has worked with natural colors of sands making mandalas, has sandblasted images on stones and loves working with oil paints, painting people in their urban settings. She lives in Arizona in a house she designed and helped build.

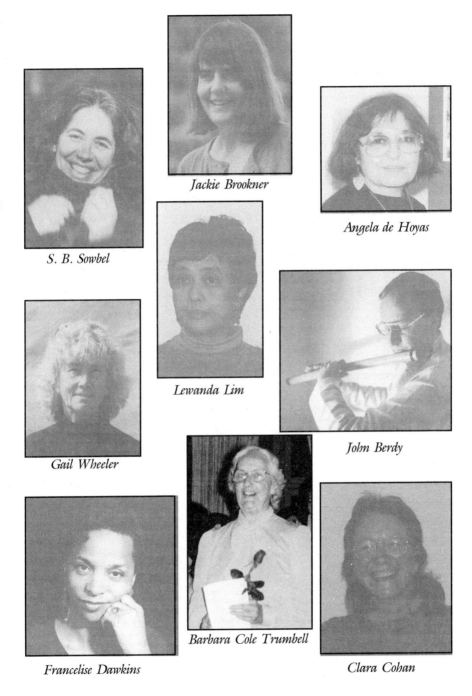

Jackie Brookner

Angela de Hoyas

S. B. Sowbel

Lewanda Lim

John Berdy

Gail Wheeler

Barbara Cole Trumbell

Francelise Dawkins

Clara Cohan

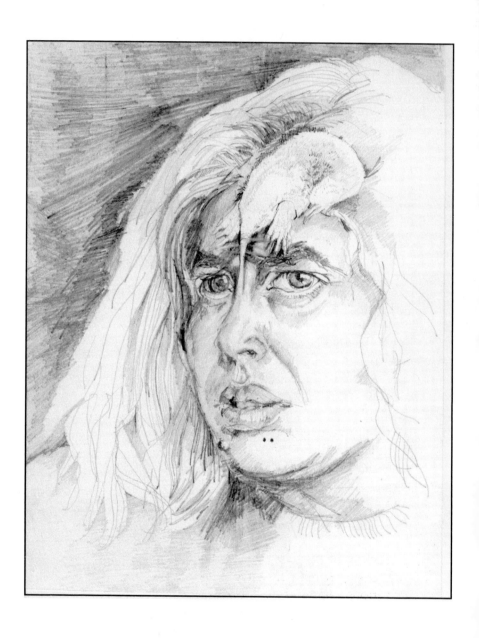

THE MOLE
S.B. Sowbel

When I was 20
I had a dermatologist
    excise a mole from my right cheek
        (there was a "growth"
        and in keeping with many world views
        growths must go.)
He offered to remove the mole on the left side
    of my chin as well
        (unsightly—benign—
        but cosmetically offensive.)
I refused
feeling no flesh of mine
    would be torn severed
    as I had been
    from my sister, my mother and my grandmother
unless death was in question.

Without that troublesome growth
I felt light and unbalanced
only the mole on my chin
would anchor my face now
and it tipped the advantage
    to the left

    Left to its own devices
my remaining mole sprouted soft hairs
of various lengths and colors
    a soft mossy mound
    of black, chestnut and silver.

I thought little of it, consciously
accepting it like a home-ly
bit of furniture, seasoning with age.

But then—I moved
to a cold and rustic shack
in a northern, wooded grove
    few neighbors
    little contact.

And who should join me?
    but a crowd
      of noisy, furry
        moles!
As if all the growths
    cut-off for fear or pride
lay safely dormant till their disposal
and then ran for cover
    tunneling through the earth
    to safety
      from knives and judgement.

I like to think we arrived at the same time.
But I spent several weeks
    ignoring our former bond
trying to sweep them from my shelter.

Finally,
fed up with my stitched-closed recall
and having fought four-foot snow drifts
    to reach me, leaving their own
    safe burrows beneath the earth
they thrust through the haze.

One brave and cheeky mole
in the early hours
—pre-dawn—
raced to my inert form

and bit me
    on my chin
    across from the left
    one.

The shock,
    less of recognition
    than trespass
shook buried memories
from their crusty place.

And all manner of clues, hints, keys
dropped from cupboards
    of disuse
and displayed themselves.

    I ran.
And for two days, refused to return.

Then, I accepted the call
and let them lead me
    fully and with abandon.
Entering deep tunnels
    furrowing through snow,
    tedium and sorrow.

Eventually
I learned to close my eyes and ears
    and allow
only the pulses of things
to speak to me.

The codes—
    like the dit-dash
    of early speechless speech—
flooded the burrows.
Some rapid, heavy and staccato
others, steady and serene.

We ate worms—and bugs
of infinite texture and variety.
We moved through rich, dank dirt.

I ambled with the best of them.
I shoveled my path.
I tenaciously held my place.
I shoveled my path.
I crushed any intruders' attempt
        to ignore my territories
        (regardless of relation.)
I shoveled my path.
I slept.
And I shoveled my path,
        powerful shoulders and limbs
        making cylinders of spaciousness and access
where none had been.

But it was clear
        only a half-time internship
in deep dark tunnels
        would allow me
        to retain the ability
                to wear socks
                ask questions
                stand upright.

So with regret and an anxious squeal
I went up
        into the old world
        of dermatologists
        and furniture
resuming the near-pulseless tongue
        whose structures
        tried to replicate
        the intricate grammar
        and connection
        of the canals below.

It was hard.
The worst was the light.
Severe.
Intrusive.
Forcing thousands of details—
        all different—into view.

It was blinding.

Odd, the changes. . .
I had revered the northern light
        for its clarity of color
        crispness of line.
I had hung years of opinion and design
on its contours.
Now it seemed vulgar, brash, confining.
I yearned for northern dusk, dark.

So I'd wait for the loathsome edges to soften.

        Then, sitting in the dark
            thinking. . .
            an unnecessary frippery
      my tasks minimal
            shoveling
            sleeping
            eating
            voiding
      I'd return to the sensing
      the pulse
            of dark, of box
            of window, of shoe,
            of bug, of rodent
            of heat, of paper,
            of need, of wet
            of rug, of air
            of sleep, of frost
            of ringing, of yellow

all rippling—towards and away
caressing impressions,
absorbing and releasing vitality.

And then back to the cacophony—oh the cacophony
machines, bodies and voices
languages banging, blurted, sung
like a damn army of jackhammers.

Deafening.

And I, who'd loved
the flurry of the marketplace
rushed to solitude and silence.

Only the pulse
of blue, of thick
of rough, of glass
of large, of plastic
of spit, of space
of nail, of sheet,
of crumb, of trickle
of glut, of metal
of acrid, of edge
of cringe, of lip
of fur, of clay
of fear, of mouth
of rock, of tender
could soothe me till my next foray up.

I began to exude a furtive air
all crimped eyes and clenched ears.
It took effort to embrace amenities
so removed from the pulses.
(I'd have preferred to curl up
like the headless worms
stored below
waiting to serve
another's needs).

But still I needed to "walk" both worlds.
And as I dragged my tunnel-craving self
through the turnstiles of civility. . .
    I noticed others

In that same odd pose
    heads tilting
as if to receive
an electric message
    of compression
    or advance
    or green.

I was stunned.

There were some
    above ground
who synchronized to the pulse,
    out of desperation or predilection.
The blind ones, the inarticulate ones, the searching ones.
They offered solace and science.

Together—in stolen moments
we'd check our hypotheses of pulse
examining the blue/yellow shift
    of sky and earth
listening for the thump, thump, thump
    of threat
paddling through watery metaphors
    of earth.

And the growth of speechless speech
    continued to seep into our lives
    (furry, round and fast)

And so. . .more or less alien
    to my sketchy past and others

I practice the faith
    required
    to carve
        through a wall
        of impacted earth
    or wander into a densely peopled room
and find a path.

❀

THE BACK OF NAMES

By Jackie Brookner

Before words, behind names.
Where? Who names
whose body?
My own our own earth's.
Standing,
an act of relation—
to time, to memory, to earth,
to each other.

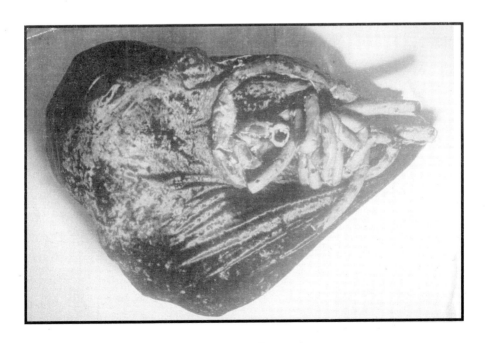

POEMS
Angela de Hoyos

Some People Sing

for Gwendolyn Díaz, who wants to know how my poems originate

but I drool my best jewels
when that cold shower
tickles my chin.

. . .stand on one foot
to soap my toes:
the magic of words
trickles down my nose.

—O Muse, would you
come again at will?
(I'm scrubbing my back.)
. . .Metaphor? Simile? Dactyl?

—You'd better hurry
to paper 'n' pen!
I'm afraid we won't
come by again. . .

—Then, patience! let me
dry my feet.
Let's not jeopardize
the image. . .complete!

—Quick! be quick!
I am your poem
conceived in water.
I will be born.

This Deathless Birth of a Poem

"And I may return
if dissatisfied
with what I learn
from having died."
                        - Robert Frost

we are sitting
at this table
  at this table
  we are sitting
eye to eye
like a pair of
mortal enemies
  alert, aware
  that our love
expressed or
unexpressed
is certain death

but we hiss
and spit in
joyous unison
    the creative fire
    the deadly venom

and bare our
fangs in mutual
bifurcated loversmiles
for one
deathless moment—
    long enough
    to breathe our
    last breath

❀

KALEIDOSCOPIC KNOWING:
THE ART OF INTERACTIVE PROCESS
Gail N. Wheeler

When we hear the term *old masters*, images come to mind of individuals, specific paintings, a particular group of artists, those who, over time, have achieved fame and prestige. We usually visualize men. If we were to use the feminine parallel, *old mistresses*, images of denigration, contempt, and abandonment come to mind. We have no language to respectfully describe or include women artists historically. The term *old masters* genderizes what society considers to be art.

As we know, women have always produced art, but our culture has not recognized it. Women have been left out of art history and their work considered craft and inferior, most likely because it was useful, completed at home, inside the house. It certainly was not considered to be fine art.

The art historian Griselda Pollock, while looking at how women were excluded from art history, focuses more specifically on examining the "rules of the game." Pollock raises the concern for ". . .how and why an art object or text was made, for whom it was made, [and] to do what kind of job. . ." (Pollock, 1988, p. 26). She insists that art history remove art as "aestheticized object" and that women's art be placed in its historical and sociological context. Women's production of art has been different from men's because of differences in our social/cultural experience throughout history. Patriarchy has determined artistic merit based solely on the experience of white males, neglecting to include the experience of women. I do not mean to imply by this that all men fit into the prescribed patriarchal construct. I'm simply stating that historically, women's social/cultural experience has not been taken seriously in relationship to their art. This exclusion is not limited to the art world. In general, traditional academic, medical and psychological settings have neglected women's experience. Patriarchy has elevated the analytic over the intuitive, the objective over the subjective, the separate over the connected. That which is outside of us, separate from feelings, separate from body, is what is valued in the patriarchal construct. Women's art and women's ways of creating meaning encompass feelings, the personal, *inner* thinking and knowing. *Outer* thinking and knowing is relegated to what has been the acceptable norm in patriarchal institutions. I'm not suggesting that all women use only intuitive, subjective, inner thinking, or that all men use only analytic, objective, outer thinking; clearly, we all use many types of thinking. What I am talking about are contrived constructs which have excluded women's experience.

Corresponding exclusions are seen when viewing traditional cultures as well. Lucy Lippard (1990) discusses the construct of inner and outer knowing from a cultural context: "The question of difference and separation is not only being played out on the level of personal subjectivity, but is also paramount in discussions of the relationship between "First" and "Third" World cultures. . ." (p.13). Jamake Highwater (1981) describes how the linguistic skills of the dominant culture set "primal" people apart (and *beneath*) those from industrialized nations. Patriarchical positions usually place verbal (outer) knowing, other than poetry, in a dominant position, and inner (visual) knowing in a subordinate position.

Whether we create meaning from outer, separate, analytic positions, from inner, intuitive, connected positions, or from both, and whether or not we assign gender/culture labels to varying positions, we are talking about different ways of viewing and understanding the world. Living in different surroundings influences the various ways in which we see and create meaning. Dualistic divisions negate the fact that two supposedly opposing conditions are connected; they are actually on a continuum; they are a whole. By speaking in dualistic terms, we avoid opportunities to see the continuum, the whole. We stand in one camp or the other.

My work, through creative visual process, psychological probe and intellectual pursuit, attempts to understand interactive process between such dualistic divisions and to bring them into relationship. It attempts to value both inner and outer knowing, to see how a visual inner landscape informs outer thinking and how outer linguistic and artistic application informs inner knowing. My work strives to illuminate, respect and celebrate difference and at the same time to illuminate, respect and celebrate sameness and commonality. It sees difference *and* commonality as vital to creation of artistic work, to education and to gender and cultural compatibility. Differences should not be divisive but instead enable us to see how diverse colors, shapes, and textures enrich a textile, painting, ethnic group or culture. Sameness, on the other hand, should not be isolating and exclusionary but instead something which enables us to see tone, value and hue as solidifiers.

Martin Buber's (1970) *I-Thou* relationship presents one model for looking at interactive process. He examines the nature of interaction between self and other, whether that other be a person, animal or inanimate object. Buber distinguishes an *I-it* interaction from an *I-Thou* relationship. An *I-it* interaction is an experience between *I* and the world, but the world does not participate. The world is object, separate from self. *I* dominates. An *I-Thou* relationship, on the other hand, establishes a relationship of mutuality. *I-Thou* involves the world and endows both objects and people with meaning through love. The difference is in the nature of the relationship.

An *I-Thou* relationship, says Buber, is *reciprocity*, it involves action from both sides. Other is not passive, but an active participant. In *I-Thou* reciprocity, there is distinction, but no division. *Thou* includes the divine, the divine in *I*, the divine in *You*, the divine in *other*.

My goal has been to work with image in a way that nourishes a reciprocal *I-Thou* relationship between inner knowing and outer knowing, between self and other, between the subjective and the objective. I began my exploration with mandalas (*mandala* is the Sanskrit word for circle). Mandalas have been used in almost every culture as a means of uniting opposites.

> The word *mandala* literally means "association," "society." The Tibetan word for mandala is *kylikhor*. *Kyil* means "center," *khor* means "fringe," "gestalt," "area around." It is a way of looking at situations in terms of relativity. . . .(Trungpa, 1991, p. 15)

I was using the mandala to better understand what's inside (the circle) and what's outside and how to invite interaction between them. It was through painting that circular image that I began to see the connection between my compulsive making of mandalas and my compulsive concern to understand the dualistic divisions between inner and outer thinking and knowing. For a long time I fell into a dualistic trap and kept the two separate. I was creating mandalas "in the closet" for personal understanding and well-being and studying dualities "out in the *real* world" for my doctorate. Finally, I came to a position where I could see the relationship between them.

From that point on, the circle (for me) became a kaleidoscope. I saw the kaleidoscope as my metaphor for reciprocal, interactive thought because a kaleidoscope takes outer images and through the use of inner mirrors reflects the varying parts. Color, shape and tone interact in multiple ways. Looking into a kaleidoscope, one can see colors change when juxtaposed next to different colors. In a similar way, our thinking and actions might change when juxtaposed next to different people or groups. We could say that outer activity, processed through inner thoughts and feelings, mirrors the varying aspects which create dialogue and form meaning, just as outer images, processed through inner mirrors in the kaleidoscope, create designs which reflect diverse configurations of color, shape and tone. Inner and outer inform each other in reciprocity. There is no hierarchy.

My use of the mandala, an image which traditionally has clear and distinct boundaries yet whose purpose is to create a unified whole, was to gain greater understanding of the kinds of boundaries which separate and those which connect. I examined the connections betweeen traditional mandalas and personal spontaneous mandalas. My personal mandalas explored issues concerning the separation and individualism which I, a woman raised in a multi-cultural society, experienced. For comparison, I examined the huipiles (overblouses woven and worn for centuries by Mayan women in Guatemala) as mandalas from a unified traditional culture. I chose the Mayan communities of Guatemala because of my affinity with this group of women and because they seem to have transcended the arbitrary boundaries which separate inner and outer knowing. They have retained interactive process through family, community and spiritual connection. Their art is integrally related to their lives.

My attempt to draw parallels between my personal spontaneous mandalas and the Mayan women making their traditional huipiles is that I might glean a better understanding of the interactive process between internal and external knowing. The following excerpts from my journal express my artistic, personal and intellectual explorations with focused attention on the outer compositional features of the mandala as they reflect my inner personal feelings. I began making mandalas long before I had an awareness of their uses, as a matter of fact, long before I knew the word *mandala*.

I use them to get into my self and to get out of my self. I begin to have a relationship with them. I am compelled by them. As time goes by, I begin to see how they are connected to many parts of my life. And yet, I am never satisfied with them. They have their grasp on me, a dualistic hold, and I need to understand why. My process is an attempt to allow my inner awareness to speak first, and then to develop a relationship with the drawn images, bringing outer thought to inner awareness.

James Hillman(1972), Mary Watkins(1986) and Shaun McNiff(1992) describe a similar process for dialoguing with images. They speak of personifying the image, having a conversation with it. However, the images they use are what I might refer to as representational or pictorial images: images from dreams or drawn/painted identifiable images. I avoid the use of predetermined images and try to allow images from my unconscious to flow without conscious intervention. I focus on compositional features of my work rather than analysis of representational images. Henry Schaeffer-Simmern (1961) used a similar technique when working with children in a mental hospital. He focused specifically on each child's composition rather than on his/her psyche and found that their behavior and reflections of self grew out of compositional reflection on the paintings. My work attempts to combine features from both camps—dialogue with image and examination of composition.

In order to close out conscious thought, I always begin my drawings by sitting quietly for a few moments. With pen or brush in hand, I go immediately to the center of the prescribed or imagined circle, and allow the lines, forms or dots which emerge to be put down. I follow my hand. As a rule, I don't think ahead of time about what I am going to do. As I become more involved in the process, I sometimes experiment with conscious application.

Most likely, because I have the images go directly to the paper and bypass the step of having images first emerge in my head and subsequently put them down on paper, they are often abstract and geometrical rather than representational. Attempts to draw visualized images become conscious endeavor to make a reasonable facsimile of what I have visualized, and for me that is a very different process. I get too caught up with my ego and conscious process when I work that way.

There are times when an image haunts me; something is going on in my life which is all-encompassing; a particular image keeps appear-

ing in my head. In that case, I find that as I am drawing or painting, that recurring image might appear on the paper, in which case I elaborate on the image. As I experience this dynamic, I observe the visual/verbal, inner and outer distinctions and look to see where and how the boundaries between them play with and against each other.

Composition of art work tells us as much, if not more, about our inner selves than analysis of an expressed symbol. It is the ongoing relationship with multiple images which give meaning rather than analysis of one or two symbols or images. It is through the unfolding from one drawing to the next, over time, that we may begin to piece together relevant and diverse elements which have deeper meaning. Ongoing process suggests relationship, a continuous relationship which over time changes, grows and deepens.

Drawing mandalas may bring me to a point of balance and harmony; however, the drawn mandala does not have the dynamics of a work of art for me. There is no action within the balance; it does not contain inequalities and contrary forces in my life. It is symmetrical, balanced, perfect. Am I doing this for artistic design or for a healing, knowing

process? I am actually striving for both. They should not have to be separate. The enclosed mandala seems to satisfy my knowing process but does little for my aesthetic sensitivity.

It seems to float in the air, not connected to anything. Outside the circle, there is void; inside, there is only harmony. The energy is immobilized within the center.

What does it mean that I want to break out of the mandala, the symmetry, the boundaries? Does it mean that because I have ordered my confusion, I can now put it aside? Does it mean that I have not yet integrated chaos into all aspects of my life? Or might it mean that a quest inward will eventually return to an outward quest?

What I seem to be describing here is my being outside of a contained mandala, controlling and manipulating it, or being within a free mandala, experiencing all of the internal/external relationships. Inner distinct from outer—and I'm trying to soften those boundaries. The circle holds paradox for me—both connection and isolation, inner and outer knowing, balance and tension. I am polarizing contrast against harmony yet they both are needed for deeper significance in the visual process.

I need to withdraw from the world for quiet, reflection and renewal (in the mandala), but at the same time I want to be in the world for motivation, interaction, relationship. Can I, can the image, illustrate both simultaneously?

Jung saw creating mandalas as an integrating force, yet for me, the boundary of the mandala keeps the forces separate. Can I maintain the calm me while in the chaos, or invite chaos while in calm space? My quest becomes how to have boundaries without creating a dualistic in here or out there approach. I want relationship with the multiple, strong, clear others without losing "I" in the process.

I don't want a blending of the contrasting elements, their distinctions blurred. I want to sharpen the meaning of both and yet keep them in relationship. Do I choose the mandala because its lack of stability reflects my own lack of stability? Or do I choose the mandala because it creates stability for me?

Dondis (1973) says that there is no stability to the circle and that we supply it with stability visually by imposing a vertical axis or adding a horizontal base. So once again we find a paradoxical situation where the symmetrical mandala traditionally is considered to be a symbol which will help reconcile instability, yet visually is a stressful image because of its having no stability. The need for harmony and resolution becomes clear *within* the context of the contrast.

Is my relationship with the mandala similar to its traditional use in other cultures? Is it similar to the Mayan woman's relationship to her huipil? Her culture has the stability of using symbols in its huipiles which have been handed down through generations. The huipil has both a vertical and horizontal base. When the Mayan woman puts her huipil over her head, she is in the center of her universe, for she has created the universe in her huipil. She weaves the stability of hundreds of years of cultural history into her work.

My struggle with the power of forces outside the circle are twofold: how to give credence to others' ideas, thoughts, perspectives, wishes, without abandoning my own personal ideas, thoughts and perspectives. Outside the mandala, I am controlled; inside, I control. Thus, the intense need to understand *self* in relation to *other*—control or being controlled. Must it be one or the other? In a different yet similar context, I ponder the invasion into the lives of the Mayan women by outside forces. How can they maintain their *centers* while *others* outside their boundaries are influencing and invading their very way of life? Mayan women honor their huipiles in spite of the fact that wearing them announces their status as "Indian," and can possibly mean death, rape or torture. Honoring my mandalas certainly does not carry the same kind of weight as the huipil to the Mayan woman, but it carries an internal weight with which I struggle. Political, economic and religious changes influence the way the huipil is worn and woven, yet the Mayan women continue to weave. Somehow, they have managed to make gradual, subtle changes while still maintaining their centers, their identity and their culture, and this they have done for literally hundreds of years. However, current forces are driving rapid change with no opportunity for gradual acculturation.

Arnheim (1988) has developed a complex theory of the center and its relationship to boundaries in visual composition which helps me begin to see an "action of forces" which I might use. He describes the "action of forces" as centricity and eccentricity: centricity is the tendency to understand things moving toward or away from self, *self-centered*; eccentricity is awareness that my center is only one among many and that other centers cannot be ignored. There is reciprocal interaction between them all, a fundamental task of life, according to Arnheim.

He also sees the power of gravity at the center of the earth as one which is used in composition, because ". . .it dramatizes the pervasive human conflict between powers trying to pull us down and our own striving to overcome them" (p. 7). The pure circle, floating in space, does not illustrate the gravitational pull.

For the Maya, the gravitational pull seems to be strong and evident; they have that force working for them. Their connection to the mysteries of the earth, their relationship physically, emotionally and spiritually to terrestrial wonders keeps them in direct contact with the gravitational pull. They have a relationship with their traditional communities to keep them grounded as well. The huipil contains both centric and eccentric vectors and aligns itself with the gravitational pull. It includes the personal and the communal.

> *Jung's perspective, when he says: "I felt the gulf between the external world and the interior world of images. . . . I could not yet see that interaction of both worlds. . . . I saw only an irreconcilable contradiction between "inner" and "outer" (p. 194), reflects what is going on for me.*

I sometimes feel the need to withdraw from the world for spiritual atunement. And I simultaneously feel a tension pulling me back into the world with all its conflicting tensions. Contained mandalas bring me to a place of security, comfort and stillness, almost the stillpoint. I can feel the center. When I think about a large, free mandala, it feels like a dance, expansion, movement, everything flying around, a whirlwind, open, risk. The question becomes, is there a place in between? How do I integrate each? How do I bring the spiritual and the mundane together? Would in-between be bland?

I begin to see how working with symmetrical, enclosed mandalas might be an evasion of the tensions between eccentric outer powers and centric inner powers and avoidance of the gravitational pull. The symmetrical mandala keeps me within the dynamics of centric powers alone. By squaring the circle, breaking the symmetry, playing with multiple centers, experimenting with various kinds of boundaries, I might allow eccentric forces to enter the dynamic and to invite more complex relationships.

When I view pluralism as diversity within unity (a unified whole?), I am stuck inside the mandala. There is diversity, but the diversity is confined within the circle. By transforming the rigid boundaries between various tensional opposites and observing many centers, I am now able to view diversity differently. I am able to integrate unity into diversity, rather than the reverse. For me, unity has to do with an interaction taking place at any given moment in time, at a given place. It is not an ongoing, continuous feeling. I might have unity with a person or an object when I am intensely involved in reciprocal relationship. When I disengage, I am not experiencing unity; connection is still there, but not unity. Diversity comes into play because there are many people, objects, ideas, cultures, groups with whom I interact at varying points in time. Unity exists in time. When I am painting a mandala, I am in unity with it; nothing else exists. Once that union is broken, when I have finished the painting, the relational unity is no longer there; a unified painting is. A connection may still be present, but with distance and time, the relationship changes.

Rigid circles keep the interactions within; opening the boundaries allows the center or centers to interact and correspond to the elements existing outside, inviting and accepting a diversity of ideas, views and opinions.

I begin to see how the many communities to which I belong, just as the many selves within me, interact with the differing communities to which others belong. I have left the realm of dualism and joined the realm of pluralism. I am not part of just one community, one culture like the Maya. I am many of them and belong to many of them. I am a North American who has lived in Central and South America with a deep sense of my own and other cultural differences and can speak only from those relationships. I am a strong, independent woman who has made her way alone and also a shy, dependent woman who relies upon others. I am simultaneously fearless and afraid. I am many.

What I have been describing is creating meaning through interaction and dialogue with images. Meaning comes through a continuous inter-action. The mandala and huipil have been my metaphor. Connections are rooted in problem-solving situations, making meaning of life and in attempting to understand self in relation to community and to the world. This journey of mine with the mandala continues but in a slightly differ-ent form. The mandala has helped me understand and *see* in different ways. I don't reject the enclosed, symmetrical mandala, for I see it as necessary at certain times, a possible beginning for yet another inner journey. It has its value in ordering and creating form when life seems scattered and out of control. Using the compositional features of an im-age through an ongoing dynamic relationship empowers understanding. We are not fixed, static creatures, and the movement and growth which I continually experience is more clearly illustrated through an ongoing relationship with my changing images. Image has the power to change me; the image may change as well.

The huipil of the Maya has been, and is continually, facing change. No longer is the Mayan woman able to complete her huipil in synchro-nization with her own time and cultural traditions; political oppression, the need to make money and changing values force a different relation-ship. How long will the Mayan women continue to wear and make huipiles of meaning for themselves? For many right now, this is an impossibility. My hope is that the direction of change will not eliminate their commit-ment to culture, to tradition, to relationship, but that they may continue to retain their centers in the face of change and movement and growth, in just the same way I hope I may retain my relationship to my centers in the face of change and movement and growth.

I have discussed my struggles with the concepts of unity and diversity, wanting the unity and community which I saw in the Mayan culture and living the individualism and diversity of being North American; I wanted the unity of the mandala while valuing the diversity of other painted forms. I wanted to be able to experience unity and diversity simultaneously.

I was finished. Or so I thought. I felt that I understood something about myself and about dualities; I believed that I had a better understanding of unity and diversity. I had closed the door on mandalas for the time being. I was ready to open new doors but was not sure which ones to open or where they might take me. For a while I was stopped. Stuck. I had nowhere to go. I was in chaos and confusion. I tried using a different medium. Until this point, I had been painting in gouache, a medium in which it is difficult to blend lines. Painting in oil might give me a chance to work with softening or blending those hard lines. It was unsettling to be learning a new medium, to have no focus, and my work reflected my chaos. I wanted to complete paintings which softened the boundaries, and I didn't want to paint mandalas, objects, landscapes or bodies—so what was left?

I struggled with technique. I layered paint. Might I consider painting landscapes, people, objects? I experimented with them all. I tried new techniques. I painted a shell. I wiped the excess paint away with a cloth— and began to feel as though I was taking off layers of myself—exposure. A shell. Yes! The shell gave me an opportunity to paint an object with a defined shape. I could clarify the boundary, but still see other things within the defined shape. Then I saw the shell as boundary. After struggling with inside or outside of the boundary, why not paint the boundary itself?

Trungpa, in his book *Orderly Chaos: The Mandala Principle*, discusses the conflicts which arise when dichotomizing inner and outer thinking and suggests that the ". . .only thing left to relate with is the boundary. . ." (Trungpa, 1991, p. 5). He believes that the realm of dualism creates a situation based on territory or boundary. By working with the boundary as space, we have an opportunity to give up the ". . .whole trip of boundary and space and provide the basic ground" (p. 7). Attempts to paint the shell as basic ground have given me an opportunity to explore its meaning, color and form from a different perspective.

As I explore color, I begin to see that what feels right is to use opposite colors for the figure and the ground, including hints of each within the other. I place some of the ground color in the shell and some of the shell color in the ground. Opposites interact to make composition more interesting. They have reciprocal relationship—the orange gets blended with the blue—a dab of blue is placed in the orange; one is bland without the other. I begin to see that if I can absorb a part of you inside of me, I understand you better, and if you absorb some of my color, we have an opportunity for reciprocal relationship. I maintain my integrity, and you maintain yours; there is distinction but not division.

The shell, I begin to see, is very similar to the mandala. It is a mandala. The form is geometrical, and there are numerous variables in each geometrical form. As Bachelard (1994) says: ". . .*a shell* stands out from the usual disorder that characterizes most perceptible things. They are privileged forms that are more intelligible for the eye, even though more mysterious for the mind. . .it is the *formation*, not the form, that remains mysterious" (pp. 105,106). I begin to see that using the shell as basic ground opens new doors for exploration. Boundaries take on different meaning. The shell and the creature inside actually have many kinds of boundaries. The shell serves as boundary to protect the creature from outside elements. The shell itself has another boundary between its rough exterior and its smooth, slick interior. In addition, the inhabitant has its own completely different set of boundaries. It can choose to remain inside or peek and extend its body outside; however its ". . .part that comes out contradicts the part that remains inside. Everything about a creature that comes out of a shell is dialectical" (p.108). Some creatures abandon their shells. The hermit crab inhabits the shell of others. As Bachelard says, these examples furnish a ". . .phenomenology of the verb 'to emerge,' and they are all the more purely phenomenological in that they correspond to invented types of 'emergence'" (p. 109). My explorations with the mandala and the shell illustrate my own form of "emergence."

As I wipe away excess paint and blend the edges, I find myself becoming one with the object. Where my mandalas consisted of a dialogue between myself and the painted image, painting shells elicits a dialogue not only between myself and my painted image, but between myself and an enigmatic object outside of myself, as well as between the object (shell) and the painting—a more complex form of reciprocal interaction. I see boundaries as more intricate in their multifarious roles. I'm interacting with an object outside of myself, using the boundary as ground, and

begin to see that boundaries between inner and outer, personal boundaries and boundaries in a visual image are equally complex.

I'll probably stay with shells for a while, but already my thoughts are
focusing on other objects, other kinds of boundaries. Perhaps someday
soon I'll begin to paint people as boundaries—boundaries between what's
innermost and what's outside. The challenge for me would be to paint
people as basic ground, not as objects. Giselda Pollock was concerned
with the patriarchal view of art as "aestheticized object." Are my shells
"aestheticized objects?" They just might be. Is it possible for me to paint
them as boundaries, as basic ground? Will it be possible to paint people
as boundaries—as protectors and connectors—not as "aestheticized objects?" Will it be possible to see others who are different, as connectors
or protectors, not as objects?

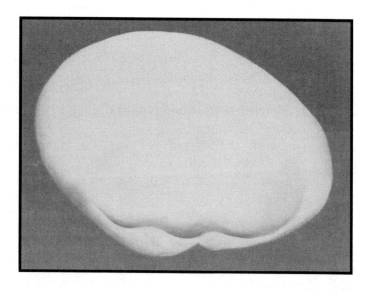

Suzi Gablik's (1991) book *The Reenchantment of Art* looks at postmodern
deconstruction of art and considers ". . .new forms emphasizing our
essential interconnectedness rather than our separateness, forms evoking
the feeling of belonging to a larger whole rather than expressing the
isolated, alienated self" (p. 6). My work with the mandala has expanded
from its original purpose of understanding and expressing my "isolated,
alienated self," toward one which includes multifaceted and broader im-

plications of connectedness. Gablik sees a new paradigm emerging, one which ". . .reflects a will to *participate* socially. . .thinking [which] involves a significant shift from *objects* to *relationships*" (p. 7). She comes to conclusions similar to Pollock, who sees the "aestheticized object" as obsolete, and determines an ". . .ecological perspective [which] connects art to its integrative role in the larger whole and the web of relationships in which art exists" (p. 8). My quest inward has given me a depth of understanding necessary for greater outer participation.

I live with multiple and clearer boundaries today, not hard edges, embrace the tension and contrast of appropriate design and celebrate my emergence toward more complete and richer relationships. And, like the kaleidoscope, with a simple turn of the wrist, new images emerge and new relationships are formed. I interact and dialogue with multiple wholes in reciprocity, knowing that with a turn of the cylinder I will be in dialogue with another whole—another unity within diversity.

WORKS CITED

Annis, S. *God and Production in a Guatemalan Village*. Austin: University of Texas Press, 1987.

Arnheim, R. *The Power of the Center: A Study of Composition in the Visual Arts*. Berkeley: University of California Press, 1988.

Bachelard, G. *The Poetics of Space: The Classic Look at How We Experience Intimate Places*. Boston: Beacon Press, 1994.

Buber, M. *I and Thou*. New York: Charles Scribners Sons, 1970.

Dondis, D.A. *A Primer of Visual Literacy*. Cambridge: The MIT Press, 1973.

Gablik, S. *The Reenchantment of Art*. New York: Thames and Hudson, 1991.

Hillman, J. *Re-Visioning Psychology*. New York: Harper and Row, 1975.

Hillman, J. *The Myth of Analysis*. New York: Harper and Row, 1972.

Highwater, J. *The Primal Mind: Vision and Reality in Indian America*. New York: Harper and Row, 1981.

Jung, C.G. *Memories, Dreams, Reflections*. New York: Vintage Books, 1989.

Jung, C.G., von Franz, M.L., Henderson, J.L., Jacobi, J. & A. Jaffee. *Man and His Symbols*. Garden City, NY: A Windfall Book, Doubleday and Co., 1964.

Lippard, L. *Mixed Blessings: New Art in a Multi-Cultural America*. New York:Pantheon Books, 1990.

McNiff, S. *Art as Medicine: Creating a Therapy of the Imagination*. Boston: Shambhala, 1992.

Pollock, G. *Vision and Diffrence: Femininity, Feminism, and the Histories of Art*. New York: Routledge, 1988.

Watkins, M. *Waking Dreams*. Dallas: Spring Publications, Inc., 1986.

❀

POEMS
Lewanda Lim

Second Generation

For my children
I cook rice every day
and salted baby shrimps
on open-window days.

I steeped their tongues
in a basket of native sounds.
On their young brown heads
I painted my childhood.
Tropical lushness, succulent papayas
pink guavas, orange mangoes
red bananas, torrential rains
choral frogs, ponderous carabaos
paradise farm, nature spirits
and malevolent witches.

But now sharp lights
are blurring my ethereal sketches.
Their tongues stumble through
half-remembered phrases.

So I cook rice and salted baby shrimps.
They will not taste forgetting.

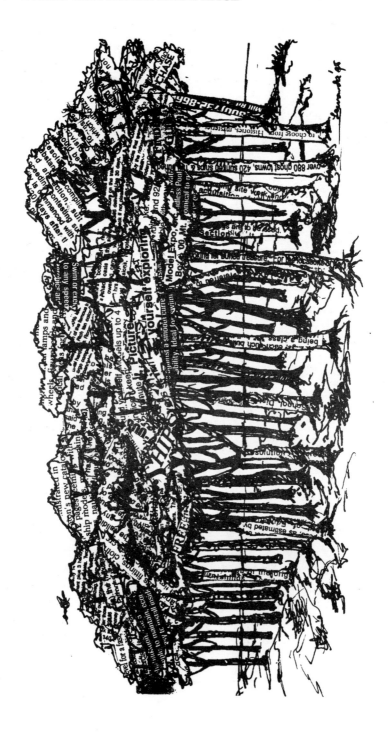

The Stranger

She is a stranger
self-consciously stalking the unguarded
forest of words
Aiming to catch bright creatures
of a borrowed language.

Crisscrossing her forked trail
To hunt words uncaptive,
she falls into trap-holes
in-between the lines.

Words are fireflies
flickering in the wings of night
They are grace
falling into her open jar.

❁

WHAT DOES AN ARCHETYPE SOUND LIKE?
John V. Berdy

Some Basic Sounds of Our World

Randall McClellan, a music therapist and educator who is learned in the music of western and non-western cultures, suggests that there is a genre of pan-cultural healing music which contains characteristics that extend beyond any culturally defined musical forms. He believes that this music, which may have its roots in the most ancient musical traditions of the world, possesses a potential for healing at deep levels because it appears to be connected more to the rhythms of nature than to human cultures. This type of music, which is comprised of elements found in all the musical cultures of the world, is described quite poetically by McClellan in the following passage:

> On every area of Earth it continually invites us to be still, to listen, to feel its resonance within, and to experience the stillness where spirit may speak to us in a language that is beyond words. It echoes the sounds of Earth which have been its inspiration. Its quality is tranquility; its emotion is joy of spirit."[1]

According to McClellan, the most fundamental elements of this type of music come from the most common sounds of the Earth. The continuous timbre of wind and flowing water are mirrored in music by the drone, which is a continuously sounding tone or set of tones found in every musical culture. Next, the Earth is filled with the repetitive sounds of insects, frogs and birds, whose rhythms are mirrored in music by the ostinato, which is a repeated melodic and/or rhythmic pattern also found in every musical culture of the world. Then McClellan tells us that the ocean, which is a universal symbol for the unconscious and the source of all life, contains both the drone sound in its continuous roar and the ostinato in its relentless rhythm pounding the shores. The elements of drone and ostinato are found in the spiritual chants of most religions. McClellan wonders whether this is due to the fact that on an unconscious level they symbolize water and air—the necessities of life.[2]

I tend to agree with McClellan, who also feels that drones and ostinatos are essential components of healing music, and I would add that these most basic sounds of nature and music have within them qualities of the archetypal realm.

> All the mythologized processes of nature, such as summer and winter, the phases of the moon, the rainy seasons, and so forth, are in no sense allegories of these objective occurrences; rather they are symbolic expressions of the inner, unconscious drama of the psyche which becomes accessible to man's consciousness by way of projection—that is, mirrored in the events of nature.[3]

I believe that the calls of some birds and animals are archetypal. The cry of the loon, for example, is a direct link to the archetypal quality of solitude (the tarot Hermit or Crone card) as reflected in its natural habitat—areas that are remote from the world of human activity. The primary characteristic of the loon is that it is forever seeking habitats in nature that are as far removed from human contact as possible. The archetypal quality of the loon's cry is also colored by a sense of longing; a feeling for something at a distance. I am speculating that the cry of the loon is indeed archetypal—that is, it is a sound that evokes an auditory memory from the depths of the collective unconscious of humanity—based upon the assumption that it will evoke these feelings no matter what culture or landscape people come from. Two contemporary haiku poets manage to distill into just a few words the archetypal quality of the loon's call:

> Loons cry—
> the deeper silence
> behind. (Lewis Sanders)[4]

> alone on the lake
> until the loon's cry
> . . . still alone   (Sandra Fuhringer)[5]

Within the haunting call of the wolf we may find something archetypal connected with the sacredness of family and immediate community (wolves mate for life) combined with a recognition of the importance of maintaining one's individuality. The lone wolf on the hilltop affirms its connection to the group by sending forth its cry. It is a sound that bridges heart to heart.

The song of the humpback whale is another sound that links members of a group, for it has been discovered that this sound can travel through vast expanses of ocean. The whale (according to some Native American traditions) is also said to hold ancient memories and records stretching back to the earliest days of life on this planet. Perhaps that is why the writers of one of the the feature length "Star Trek" movies chose the humpback whale as a creature whose consciousness was sought out by some colossal, interstellar space vehicle which entered our galaxy from some unknown starting point and departed just as mysteriously.

And the sound of the seashore would not be complete without the cry of the seagull, whose shriek evokes the sense of searching and longing for a stable home, as it forever alternates between feeding and resting on the ocean and nesting on land. However, my words hardly express the poignancy of a famous poem by the Chinese poet Tu Fu (Tang Dynasty) entitled "Night Thoughts While Travelling":

> A light breeze rustles the reeds
> Along the river banks. The
> Mast of my lonely boat soars
> Into the night. Stars blossom
> Over the vast desert of
> Waters. Moonlight flows on the
> Surging river. My poems have
> Made me famous but I grow
> Old, ill and tired, blown hither
> And yon; I am like a gull
> Lost between heaven and earth.[6] (transl. Kenneth Rexroth)

Interestingly, all of the nature and animal sounds I have described above are "best sellers" in the form of audio recordings, both alone and combined with music. I think these sounds nourish some of the deeper layers of our psyches, especially those of us who live somewhat removed from the natural world in cities and populated suburban areas. And I believe that the sounds of some of the more "primitive" instruments, such as the Australian didgeridoo, are also being utilized in the musical textures of many new age compositions because they too embody archetypes of sound that relate closely to the natural world. "Rain sticks," which sound amazingly like falling rain, are also popular today.

Musical Instrument as Archetype: Instrumental Timbre

The specific tone quality, or timbre, of an instrument is the first thing we notice when listening to a piece of music. If we don't respond positively, if we don't resonate to the timbre of a musical instrument or ensemble of instruments, the music is not likely to move us deeply. By the same token, there are certain musical instruments or families of instruments which seem to have universal appeal extending across cultural boundaries: the drum, the bell or gong, the flute, the harp, the lute, and the oboe. One might add to the list the group of bowed string instruments, although they are essentially lutes (with or without frets) that are played with a bow.

These instrumental groups certainly fit the definition of archetypal, since they appear in almost all cultures, and the tremendous variety of forms that each family of instruments takes essentially represents variations on a basic theme. For example, the "drum" is the archetype and the Irish bodhran, African djembe, Indian tabla and Middle Eastern dumbek are but a few manifestations of this instrumental archetype. Of course, the basic blue-print, "imprint" (as Jung sometimes calls it) or archetype of each instrumental form carries with it a primordial quality that the physical instrument reproduces or translates into audible vibration.

Archetypal does not necessarily mean appreciated or enjoyed alike by all cultures (with the exception of scholars or academics, I suppose). The manifestation, or concretization (to use another of Jung's terms), of an archetypal musical instrument will just as often be culturally bound. Indians tend to be much more receptive to the sound of the Western guitar than we are to the north Indian sitar. However, the large north Indian bamboo flute (which is an instrument I perform on) is regarded as having quite a pleasing sound to Westerners, whereas the Indians seem to be lukewarm or indifferent to the timbre of the Western classical silver flute.

To offer a brief taste of the possibilities inherent in the exploration of archetypes within the sounds of musical instruments themselves, I would like to quote some metaphoric gleanings on this subject by the Native American teacher Joseph Rael (Beautiful Painted Arrow):

> BELLS: "Bells originate from the idea of insight. Bell means in metaphor the 'strike of light' that slices the ice crystals that are filled with wisdom. . . . The bell sound carries with it the power to awaken and lift that which it awakens. . .. The bells bring into consciousness an element of vibration, or energy, that connects the mind to the heart and the heart to the mind. The bell also connects the heart to the periphery of the circle of consciousness."[7]
>
> DRUMS: "Drumming opens up three basic vibrations. Drumming awakens the self. Drumming heightens the ability of perception, and drumming enables the person to see into the deeper realms of the self. . . . Drumming creates in the psyche of those people who listen to the drum, a sense of abundance, a feeling that there is more than enough in life to sustain life. There is the feeling of strength, of being able to step forth with whatever one wants to change, because the power to sustain that change is in the drumming. The drumming sound helps persons listen to themselves as they really are."[8]
>
> FLUTE: "The original idea of the flute was that it was the way by which the cycle could be completed between the masculine and feminine energies. In traditional Native American practices, the young men would play the flute for the young women in order to keep alive that ancient tradition of the visible calling the invisible. . . . The flute is an instrument connecting the two worlds, the non-physical with the physical. The breath of the flutist is the breath of God coming through a hollow reed; the sound is that of the invisible lover courting the visible lover, the metaphor of the lover and the beloved."[9]

Rael's metaphors surrounding the flute are quite remarkable in that they could just as well be applied to the flute-playing god of the Hindus, Lord Krishna. And yet we may need to travel no farther than the American Southwest in order to find an archetypal relative of Krishna.

Krishna and Kokopelli: Flute-playing Archetypal Cousins?

The current popularity of the Native American flute is responsible for sparking my original insight about the archetypal nature of the sounds of certain musical instruments. The traditional Native American flute is a form of flageolet, or end-blown instrument, carved out of a single piece of cedar. It is very limited in its range and tonal capacity: most instruments encompass little more than an octave and are usually tuned so that only a few scales at best are possible on each flute. Consequently, most musicians have several flutes.

The music that these flutes are capable of producing is restricted to quite simple melodies. Yet, I watched as people would come into a local new age book shop, show an immediate reaction to the sound of the Native American flute when a "demo" recording was being played, and then rush to the cash register to buy a fistful of CDs or tapes of them. I thought I should buy a Native flute for myself, change my name to "Singing Deer" and become a millionaire. This got me thinking.

I realized that it was *the sound itself* of the flute that was grabbing people, and in particular, the simple, haunting refrains of the Native American melodies. Since these compositions from any sort of musical framework—not just a Western perspective—are hardly enthralling, people had to be captivated by the very sound of the instrument.

People are moved deeply by this music and for reasons that are probably unconscious part of the time. They are responding to something very old that they have forgotten for centuries and only now are awakening to. Whether they know it or not, they are being revitalized and inspired by an archetype of sound. In the case of the Native American flute, perhaps they are "remembering" the magic of Kokopelli, the legendary flute-player depicted on petroglyphs of our own Southwest; or, upon hearing the distant tones of the flute of India, the part of themselves that dwells in the collective unconscious may be experiencing nostalgia for the playful, loving aspect of the Divine named Krishna.

> Krishna is pictured in Hindu symbology with a crown of a peacock's feathers, playing the flute. Krishna is the idea of divine love, the god of love. The flute is the human heart, and a heart which is made hollow, which becomes a flute for the god of love to play.[10]

> The flute is an instrument connecting the two worlds, the non-physical with the physical. The breath of the flutist is the breath of God coming through a hollow reed; the sound is that of the invisible lover courting the visible lover, the metaphor of the lover and the beloved.[11]

Rael's words might just as well have been written with the Hindu god Krishna specifically in mind. As a divine incarnation, Krishna appears in many forms. In the form known as Govinda, Krishna "carries a flute, whose haunting melodies draw the love of his playmates as the Lord himself draws the human soul. . ."[12] The statues and paintings portraying Krishna holding his flute to his lips symbolize the sweet call of the Divine, and all the gopis, or cow-herdesses, who are romantically attracted to Krishna through the melodies of his flute, represent those of humanity who hear the Song of the Divine.

Krishna as a divine incarnation is quite a romantic figure. He is truly the "invisible lover courting the visible lover." Rael's metaphoric comments about the flute may point to one of the deepest archetypal levels of this instrument. And Inayat Khan's remarks about the heart needing to become a hollow reed for the god of love to play upon may give us some insight as to why the sound of the flute is so touching, so poignant to many people.

Whenever the flute appears in Native American traditions, its role is customarily as a courting instrument. A young man will try to attract a young woman by the beauty of his flute compositions. One of the most popular images today in decorative art from the Southwest is that of the legendary flute-player Kokopelli. Kokopelli's image appears on petroglyphs throughout the American Southwest where, despite the multitude of variations on the representation, the one absolutely consistent characteristic is that he is always playing a flute. Krishna and Kokopelli are indeed archetypal cousins.

Kokopelli is often interpreted as a hunting shaman and rain priest who calls the clouds with his flute, which he also plays in order to bring warmth to the earth in Spring and to melt the snow so the crops can be planted.[13] The stories say that first he melts all the snow and ice with his flute, then, with more wonderful melodies, the birds, insects and animals appear one by one and join him in his music. Soon Spring has fully blossomed and the land is ready for planting.

Interestingly, the greatest number of stories about Krishna are also set in the springtime, and important festivals for Krishna, such as Holi, take place in the spring. One of the most popular *ragas* (melody-forms) in North Indian music associated with spring, called Hindol, literally means "Swing" and it refers to Radha playing on a swing during the nicest time of spring while she waits for Krishna to visit her.

When an image really captures the attention of people on a large scale—as we can observe with the current popularity of the Kokopelli design—we cannot ignore the distinct possibility that something powerful is being brought to consciousness. There is more to the connection between Kokopelli and Krishna than merely the coincidence that they are both legendary flute-players. Rael's metaphors for the flute ring true on a profound level. Now that the Woodstock II Concert has come and gone, and the undergraduates are pulled more than ever toward degrees in business and other economically practical vocations, maybe a portion of the general populace is still hungering for the magical flute-player, and the funny, earthy picture of Kokopelli is filling that need for us today.

There are ways in which people can gain a sense of how different instruments impact them personally on an archetypal level. Ultimately, the personal response is probably more important that any broad pronouncements.

I have asked workshop participants, for example, to be willing to imagine themselves as a particular musical imstrument which expresses who they are at their present juncture in life. Someone may have lived a ten-year period of his or her life resonating to the soulful, poignant timbre of the oboe or English horn, and now the deep, rich sound of the cello, with its incredible several-octave range expresses this person's inner nature. This is quite an easy exercise to do because most people are familiar with enough musical instruments to make a choice—the voice being one of them, of course—and they usually have a current favorite instrument or ensemble sound. However, this metaphor of imagining oneself as a musical instrument through which the soul expresses itself helps people to become more introspective than just registering a sound preference that has an appeal for them.

Some Suggested Criteria for Identifying the Archetypal in Music

At this point I wish to venture some suggestions as to how we might know when we are in the presence of a musical archetype. We may have good reason to suspect that we have contacted an archetype of sound and music if one or more of the following subjective conditions can be verified.

An archetype of sound and music:
    •affects the emotions with great intensity due to its numinosity.
    •produces a powerful stream of images or thoughts, often of a symbolic nature.
    •activates synchronistic events or forms a nucleus around which synchronistic events seem to gravitate.

Whether one experiences primarily powerful imagery or an intensity of feeling or both depends upon how visually oriented someone is and how attuned one is to his or her emotions. Whether or not one experiences an increase in synchronistic events depends upon how much a person is already in the habit of noting synchronicities in one's day-to-day life. I think that the first item on my list is generally the most reliable and accessible, provided that there is an understanding of the depth of feeling involved. I am not speaking here of evocations of sentimentality or feelings associated with unexamined neurotic frustrations of life and relationship of the kind that comprise the subject matter of so many popular songs found on AM radio programming. I am referring, rather, to a depth which generates tears, laughter, wonderment and a host of bodily sensations. It may move us to reverence, gratitude, tranquility, forgiveness or one of the transpersonal emotions which seem to incorporate several feelings all at once.

Music of an archetypal nature opens us to a depth of feeling beyond that of the passing surface emotions of daily life, although they too may get drawn along in the wake of the great archetypal energy. I am speaking of music which moves us so deeply that we are somehow changed forever; we are not the same person after listening to it. And it is usually a mistake, after this happens, to go back again and again looking for the experience to recur. We may return to certain pieces of music with renewed appreciation and enjoyment and continue to enjoy them for years.

Transformative experiences also have a synchronistic quality to them and activate powerful images and thoughts. That is why, perhaps, Jung makes such a strong connection between emerging archetypes and synchronistic events. At certain moments in our lives, there are unexpected, non-linear, unplanned intersections of, say, physical location, emotional content and relationship with person or thing, which become charged with the numinous for reasons we cannot comprehend. These are events where the laws of the outer "world of appearances" do not apply.

Here, lightning bolts may just as easily travel from tree to tree and from earth to heaven as from cloud to mountaintop. In this universe snow falls upward in order to unveil the green and brown earth of springtime in full bloom. Life and Death, who journey together doing a strange back-to-back dance just out of sight of each other, suddenly meet one day on the seashore of eternity and engage in a dialogue, as in the opening scene of Bergman's film *The Seventh Seal*. In one moment I am reaching into the cupboard for a jar of cooking spices while preparing dinner, and all of a sudden, for no apparent reason, I am sobbing over the beautiful way in which a dying hospice patient searches for the meaning in life, while simultaneously understanding the significance of hundreds of hitherto unconnected events in my own life. It happens so quickly that language has no time to form. The mysterious doorway between the two worlds opens before us, and if we maintain full awareness at this instant, if we take care not to phase out, wondrous things abound. It is the doorway that Rumi speaks of:

> The breeze at dawn has secrets to tell you.
> Don't go back to sleep.
> You must ask for what you really want.
> Don't go back to sleep.
> People are going back and forth across the doorsill
> where the two worlds touch.
> The door is round and open.
> Don't go back to sleep.[14]

We cannot will these experiences to happen again. They come from some part of us that is larger than our personality (ego-complex, in Jungian terms). Therefore, we experience the archetypal in music as a matter of depth, not frequency. That is why there is such a strong correlation to the feeling function (in Jung's typology), which is also the "valuing function," a factor of intensity.

I can provide an example from my own personal experience. Right after undergraduate school I moved to Ireland with the intention of composing music in a serene, rural environment. Just before leaving for Ireland, I had discovered an old recording of Bach's "Partita No. 1 for Keyboard" performed by Dinu Lipatti. I was awestruck over the beauty of this recording by an extraordinary pianist who died tragically from leukemia sometime around his thirtieth year. [I have yet to hear a rendering of this work by anyone else that surpasses the grace and clarity of Lipatti's.] On my first trip to Dublin, I obtained a copy of the music for this partita so that I could practice it on my newly-acquired upright piano.

The Courante movement was my favorite. Although it took a considerable amount of practice before I could play it close to the proper tempo, when I was finally able to make it through the first section of the Courante relatively smoothly, something unusual started to happen to me. Whenever I got to a certain passage beginning around measure number 18, I seemed momentarily to enter an altered state of consciousness, during which I experienced myself stepping outside the flow of linear time and viewing the entire course of my life as a single, whole, multi-dimensional impression. The symbol that always came to mind was "The Road of Life" and I would see in my mind's eye an image of a road winding off into the infinite distance ,while simultaneously feeling a sense of the whole journey of my life from birth to death happening in an instant.

It is truly impossible to put an experience of a transcendental nature such as this into words. It was a feeling of having completed the entire journey of life infused with a quality of acceptance and the 'rightness' of every event. The emotions were some combination of gratitude, forgiveness toward myself and others, the wonder of the earth-plane experience, a sense of completion with a tinge of nostalgia to return—paradoxically interwoven with a feeling of nothing to do over—and finally, a knowledge that all was guided by a higher power or awareness which is supremely loving. All of this from a single page of music!

These transcendental experiences often translate so poorly into language that the result is likely to be either embarrassing or incomprehensible to others. This experience actually recurred several times, always happening at the same, precise place in the music and always with the same accompanying imagery and profound emotional content. For some reason, that passage of music was a doorway for me to a larger perspective, and my discovery of this particular work by Bach coincided with (to paraphrase myself) a synchronistic intersection of: physical location (Irish countryside), emotional content (a juncture in my life of transition and reevaluation) and relationship to person or thing (I was uncharacteristically solitary at the time and the catalyzing relationship was with an art object—Bach's "Partita No.1"). Then one day, this particular experience ceased as mysteriously and unexpectedly as it had started, leaving me, nonetheless, changed forever.

Notes and References

1. Randall McClellan, *The Healing Forces of Music: History, Theory and Practice* (Warwick, NY: Amity House, 1988), p.180.
2. Ibid., p.181.
3. C. G. Jung, *Basic Writings of C.G. Jung*, ed. Violet deLaszlo. trans. R.F.H. Hull (Princeton, NJ.: Princeton Univ. Press/Bollingen Series, 1990), p.302.
4. Bruce Ross, ed., *Haiku Moment* (Rutland, VT: Charles E. Tuttle, 1993), p.219.
5. Ibid, p.67.
6. Kenneth Rexroth, trans., *One Hundred Poems from the Chinese* (New York: New Directions, 1971), p.33.
7. Joseph Rael, *Being and Vibration* (Tulsa: Council Oaks Books, 1993), pp.161-162.
8. Ibid, pp.163-164.
9. Ibid, pp.167-168.
10. Hazrat Inayat Khan, *Sacred Readings: The Gathas: The Sufi Message of Hazrat Inayat Khan* (Geneva: Servire, 1982), p.122.
11. Op. cit., *Being*, p.168.
12. Eknath Easwaran, *Thousand Names of Vishnu*. (Petaluma, CA: Nilgiri Press, 1987), p.149.
13. Dennis Slifer and James Duffield, *Kokopelli: Flute Player Images in Rock Art*. (Santa Fe: Ancient City Press, 1994).
14. John Moyne and Coleman Barks, trans., *Open Secret: Versions of Rumi*. (Putney, VT.: Threshold Books, 1989, #91) np.

❀

"Remembering the future"
"Ethnikollage"

Francelise Dawkins

"Memory Pulse"
"Silkollage" 1993

Francelise Dawkins

"Sensing Streams"
"Silkolage"   Francelise Dawkins

CREATIVITY ON THE MOVE
Francelise Dawkins

Early in my Parisian childhood I felt the desire to create, as I observed artists in action around me, too absorbed in their art to allow me to join in the fun.

When hungry or sick, I had visions of beings appearing in bright lights, and, left unnoticed, I strived to create something with my hands. I remember the perseverance with which I used my fingers as knitting needles, determined to build a fabric out of a short piece of yarn, in vain. I remember the hours of aloneness spent "in the company of" fancy candies wrapped in shiny and colorful cellophane papers. To me, they resembled beautifully attired women in a ballroom, and I made them dance.

To be surrounded by undulating dancers in scintillating costume designs, cut and sewn by my mother on the unforgettable pedaled sewing-machine, filled my heartbeat permanently with the rhythmical powers of their music. The texture and flow of fine fabrics, dance and music illumined my inner stage.

Though the creative process had started within, from outside stimulation, it did not manifest itself right away. I was slowed down for being left-handed, an unforgivable bizarrerie in the old Europe of the fifties. Parents and educators accepted to show me how to sew but could not bear to look at me apply their skillful teaching in such a "gauche" fashion. I complied with their expectations and mostly observed or tried to explore on my own, secretly cutting fabric with the forbidden hand. My right hand had been "civilized" into writing, while my left hand had developed the gift of cutting. It, then, seemed natural to choose the medium of collages to bring my creativity beyond its cutting edge. Away from my inhibiting culture after I came to America, I found the courage to actualize my textile art.

At first, in Indiana, I worked as a commercial translator, a valuable bridging activity that made insertion easier into my newly adopted culture. Then I became a workshop leader in French-Caribbean folk dancing, to learn to explore and communicate my passion for movements. Textile art, therefore, came late on my creative path. In the America of Baby Boomers, I have accepted feeling like a late bloomer from afar: at first standing by, in awe, to admire the profusion of visual art in this country.

Having been confined to watch art in the making from childhood, I have taken the habit of using a long initial observation time. My creative process always begins unfolding slowly, a chrysalis, ready when ready.

I have come to cherish this "laziness" of mine, holding me still in the morning or late at night, before getting into the physical act of creating. Sublimated passivity or pure contemplation marks the first moments of my creativity. This apparent laziness represents, nevertheless, my busiest and most decisive time. Then comes the magic moment when, fully prepared mentally, I overcome "inertia" and leap into action with a passion!

At this point, my early conditioning calls for the energy of international music. It must reflect the mood of the moment and help me select among a vast collection of fabrics, while I dance and sing in the studio in joyful anticipation. The curiosity to actually see inner images brought into the outer plane fuels my desire to create. My heart is now beating fast. Adrenaline plays its part. My memory of what happens at that particular moment (which can last for hours) fades. I live the present as if I were a magnifying glass heightening up immediate reality, glorifying details, making abstraction of all else. Only one thing seems to count: what I am looking at, what my hands are giving birth to.

After years of meditation, more simply called "silent sitting," I have learned to trust the voice of an inner teacher. It started off as an inner dialogue between the censoring part of me that would infringe on my creative impulses and the other part, motherly, assured.

"The censor" and the "new nurturer" have now merged into one voice which feels sacred and leads me effortlessly through the creative "ritual." Still, there are undefinable manifestations to my creative process. As an example, while I create, interrupting me, even by calling my name softly, startles me and forces me to make a tremendous effort to respond. When resuming work I am surprised at what I have created, as if I were seeing it for the first time.

Thinking back on the quality of my creativity in motion, I can seize impressions, interpret symbols, visualize how designs are being born between the legs of the scissors. I am the midwife or the "wise woman," as we say in French. I create free shapes from my subconscious mind, evoking the noble elongation of a Mangbetu baby's head, a dancing spirit or a dolphin. When I get ready to sew designs by machine, I swing in the polyphonic rhythms of the flying needle, stitching miles of collage contours requiring patience and concentration. The slow beat of the labor-intensive work is played on the fast beat of the technological tool, an exhilarating combination, bringing inconspicuous harmony of contrasts, as heard in music of African origin.

Creating, as I have come to realize, is a very private meeting between the high forces of my imagination and myself, the channeled facilitator. Before "doing" it, I try to clear anxiety, to stay focused on the "vision," to decode it. I also have to dissipate any feeling of loneliness, to uncover the safe and comforting path to healthy solitude, where ego vanishes and where the insignificant is naturally eliminated. As spiritual and artistic skills sharpen, the discipline of clearing mind clutter purifies design and speeds up the creative process.

My creative adventures contain the key to my psychological and emotional well being. Every time I create, I assert myself authentically, with consideration for my individuality, as I live the paradox of inaction followed by deep absorption in action. This pattern assures my growth. Honoring my own creative style is how I keep the process "working." Any time I move away from this center of personal truth, my creativity goes hiding, like a neglected child pretending to disappear by staying out of sight for a while. Because it permeates my entire life, I miss its play and I feel empty. The creative act is positively addictive. It is the best journey I can pursue. It takes me to higher places and shows me where humanity connects delicately within the realm of beauty. By beauty I mean anything which gives love unconditionally. Creating is like taking another helping and another helping of the gift of love universally offered in a place of never ending creative abundance. It is handed to me as I reach out and serve it back, visually translated, to those who walk along less enchanting paths to get to it. Art is my service, my best way to express solidarity to others, since they are part of me.

A creative process is "language of the heart" in action. It perceives secret beats within common idioms, it hears ancient voices which the artist gathers into a new echo for the world. Because creating requires the discipline to act freely and the strength to stay focused on one's commitment for "vision" to be actualized, I see this process as my ultimate spiritual tool to self-realization.

Entering my third "art life" with writing (after dancing and textile art), I marvel at another welcome contrast: the power of my creativity to produce its own translucent merging of art languages with new ones. My writing seems ready to blossom on the fertile grounds of past revelations. Dancing energy has traveled from my body to my silk collages and now into my words. It leaps back into the "body-temple" of my soul to complete the cycle. I am on the continuous journey of renewed vision, serving life in all, feeling joy, assisting my dancing voice in its quest to move to the beat of the One.

✿

POEMS
Barbara Trumbull

A Gift

The blueberry bushes were a gift from my mother.
Over the years the bushes grew to resemble her,
beautiful, vigorous, fertile with blueness as she
with offspring. In the fall as other plants grow
grey, dull with the first touch of early frost, the
blueberry bushes take on color of fire and blood.

Dawn from my Hospital Bed

For Sharon Elizabeth Trumbull on her birthday

> Darkness almost complete
> With only the lights of the city
>   Across the river
>   To speak of human hands.

> The darkness becomes a dull mist
> Made beautiful only by its reflection
> In the snow on the roof
> And again as it makes visible
> The row of trees along the bank
>   Of the unseen river.

Grayness becomes smoke, rising
        From a distant smokestack
Speaking of another dirty day
        For countless, faceless people.

Then the star comes into view;
        Faithful, resolute Venus
        Taking center stage
            Bringing the dark
            The dullness, the pain
To their knees in adoration.

❀

INTUITION AND MY CREATIVE PROCESS
Clara Cohan

In my studio I have set up small altars. Various objects adorn the space. Mostly there are beautiful stones, little statues of Buddha, Ganesh, Kwan Yin, photos of spiritual teachers, and pictures or objects which represent beauty. On one altar is a small vase in which I place fresh wild flowers before I start working. I ask for guidance.

I sometimes light incense at the altars. The sweetness of the swirling, wispy, rising smoke sends my prayers in a symbolic, tangible way.

And then I work. I crank up the music—Led Zeppelin, Sweet Honey, or the Indigo Girls—and I keep the energy moving. Most of my clearest ideas come through when I am working, not from quiet meditation.

Intuition is not the idea which comes through; intuition is my "ear," the way I decode messages from their source into a comprehensible, audible, visual language. Sometimes I hear the message clearly; sometimes it get muddled up with interference from criticism, technical language, knowledge, ambition, parental and peer voices.

"Women Fishing" 8" x 10" Oil on Panel   Clara Cohan

I keep my mind receptive. If I find myself controlling the process, then I experiment, break the set pattern. If that doesn't work, I distract my controlling self by scrubbing the toilet, grocery shopping, working in the garden. Then new information comes through.

The guidance is subtle. . .a steady flow of impressions, directions to follow. I know what colors to mix, how to put them on the surface of the painting, how to interlock the shapes within the composition. The essence of the person I'm painting comes through.

Intuition connects me to a place of wholeness, a web of connections which is the source of daily decisions, creative form, my sense of truth. It's like a fiber-optic tube or a spinal column of nerve fibers which originate at the center of an immense 3-D mandala. The other end connects through the top of my head to every cell in my body.

I know I have followed my intuition when the image has a certain look and a particular feeling. The work engages me both as something familiar and comforting as well as something bigger than myself, something deep, timeless and true.

❀

III. STORIES: KINDLING THE FIRES

In this third section, "Kindling the Fires," we see how writers kindle the fires of intuition so they can sit around them and tell the stories which emerge from those sparks. Beginning with domestic settings which provide contexts for many of our stories, we move from Jan Wilkotz's delightful medley of animal and human voices in a light key to Alice Sadongei's poem about desert storytelling, then across the Atlantic to the Ireland of Paddy Reid's childhood where tales of loss were plentiful. Pat Monaghan's poems then tell the story of lifetimes of dealing with the effects of war.

Both Laura Filipp and Joyce Kavanaugh do a remarkable job of recreating experiences from childhood with the honesty and freshness of a child's point of view, open to the contradictions and ironies intuition provides. Laura Whiting tells a story of friendship when a girl's mother disappears.

Moving into the realm of fantasy, Kate Lipper describes a girl's discovery of two faces of magic, while Janet Calico explores what happens to a woman born with wings. Both tales show how stories emerge from deeply felt archetypes—Kate transforms the Demeter/Persephone pattern while Janet expands a contemporary symbol of women's empowerment. Finally, Nora Nellis tells the story in poetry and essay of how she explored her Native American roots.

Jan Wilkotz was born in Bakersfield, California in 1942 and educated at great length at the University of California at Berkeley; since 1973 she has taught English and women's studies at Maryland's Towson State University. Josie, born in upstate New York around the beginning of 1992, has certificates from Pet Depot of Timonium, Maryland. Faustina, adopted as a kitten from the Baltimore SPCA in 1983, and Lucy Primrose, found abandoned in local woods in 1990, decline further comment.

Alice Sadongei has been writing since she was fourteen. She writes about what is familiar about being Indian (Kiowa/Papago). She lives in Arizona.

Paddy Reid came to story writing by accident while working on a masters in bereavement counseling. The stories kept coming. During 1994 thirty magazines published his work. He lived in the U.S. Midwest for eleven years before returning to Dublin. "I write about an inner-city community as it dies before my eyes. My fiction draws primarily on those women and children I grew up with in this old red-light district. It saddens me that at the age of forty-four I have outlived many of my peers. Various problems, most recently heroin and AIDS, have utterly decimated this place. I'm compelled to tell these stories as a record of a forgotten place, now numbed deeper into silence."

Patricia Monaghan has written two books of poetry, *Winterburning* and *Seasons of the Witch*; three books of nonfiction, *The Book of Goddesses and Heroines*, *Working Wisdom* and *O Mother Sun: A New View of the Cosmic Feminine*, and has edited three anthologies, *Hunger and Dreams: The Alaskan Women's Anthology*, *Unlacing: Ten Irish-American Poets*, and *The Next Parish Over: Irish-American Writing Today*.

Laura Filipp is a college administrator who writes fiction every chance she gets. This story is taken from a novel-in-progress. She lives in Baltimore.

Joyce Kavanaugh lives and works in Brooklyn, New York, where she was born and raised. After obtaining her bachelor's and master's degrees, she now teaches literature in a night high school. She enjoys people, likes to learn, read, travel, talk and write. She is the author of two novels and is currently at work on her third.

Laura Whiting is thirteen years old and lives in Baltimore, Maryland. She is an artist as well as a writer. She was a member of the Heart Gang, described in *The Rest of the Deer*.

Kate Lipper is a thirteen-year-old eighth grader. She lives in Richmond, Virginia. She enjoys reading fantasy and suspense novels, as well as playing basketball, writing, spending time with animals and bike riding. Several of her ideas for an occupation are teaching either in the U.S. or in a third world country, writing or practicing law. She has a baby hamster whom she is training. "Wandering Heart" is Kate's first published short story.

Janet Calico is an artist and writer whose short fiction and artwork have been published in feminist magazines. She has taught creative workshops for writers and is currently revising her novel *Gifts*. Janet earns her living as a graphic designer and also makes dream catchers, goddess figures and other spiritual artifacts. She lives in Baltimore with a dog and calico cat and is active in the Inspiration spiritual community.

Nora Nellis, who lives in Lake George, N.Y., leads writing workshops she calls "Root Therapy." She received her B.A. in English from Skidmore College in 1990 and her M.A. in women's studies and creative writing from Vermont College in 1993 (with a scholarship from the Golub Foundation). Her poetry has appeared in various anthologies and literary reviews. She is currently working on a manuscript based on 1840 family letters.

❀

Jan Wikotz

Joyce Kavanaugh

Laura Whiting

Laura Fillip

Kate Lipper

Janet Calico

Nora Nellis

Not Pictured: Alice Sadongei, Paddy Reid, Patricia Monaghan

JOSIE'S STORY
Jan Wilkotz

June 20, 1993

Dear Margaret—

I'm glad to know the drive back north went easily and delighted that all of the puppies have found good homes. Thanks again for delivering mommy-dog Josie, whose coat grows glossier every day but whose appetite remains immense; it must have been a hard winter indeed for a homeless, teen-aged single mother of six. Despite a lukewarm and indeed very skeptical welcome from two eccentric, middle-aged cats, Josie appears to be settling in.

Josie's Tea Party

Jan returns home. What progress in dog behavior: the garbage has not been scattered all over the kitchen floor (the better to nose out the edible bits)! Josie appears from the general direction of the bedroom (beds *are* supposed to be off limits), looking quite pleased with herself. And in the little hall leading to the bathroom, there are two blue willow mugs and a glass catfood dish. All right side up. Indeed, aligned in a row. Josie sees Jan looking at these and her belly immediately hits the floor, tale thumping in a muted but regular rhythm that seems to communicate something like, "I was sure I heard you specifically mention that you wanted that pillow unstuffed/garbage unwrapped/cat food in little bowls on table cleaned up. I never would have done it if I hadn't thought I was helping out!"

"No, don't fret, it's OK this time," says Jan, bemused. "If only you could tell me, not even *how*, but *why*." But she hasn't, not yet.

Josie Gains Weight

That Eukanuba dog food is some stuff! Not only can Jan no longer count Josie' s ribs; it might take the untutored a moment or two to find them. Her summer coat is very silky but perhaps a little warm for a Baltimore afternoon at 98 Fahrenheit. "Josie," Jan says, "no more cleaning up the kitties' food." (Faustina gives a smug little grunt; Lucy sneezes with approval from the other room.) "It's Adult Maintenance Eukanuba for you." Lucy makes a foray into the spare bedroom, where I'm still keeping Josie's dish. Josie is torn: shall she put down her precious rawhide bone to go chase Lucy? If she does, won't Faustina finally display her true nature and steal the bone? Oh, as you pointed out to her, the myriad petty decisions confronting the plump and propertied classes are a great drain on the energy.

Josie and the Information Age

We set up the computer yesterday. I not only love it; I have fallen in love with it. Josie, ever quick to spot a rival (ask Lucy), is not altogether pleased, but right now she's napping comfortably at my feet, looking up occasionally with devoted eyes and ears set at the highest "adorable and affectionate" setting. And indeed she is a dear beast. Perhaps she can learn a bit about word-processing herself; kitties appear to be scouting the room with a view toward making their own plans. I actually feel a little uneasy about what these might be. Will report soon.

How could anyone prefer flashing lights and funny hums to someone warm and furry—with such devoted brown eyes, too. And helpful! I had to jump up on the kitchen table to clean up that cat food yesterday. Luv, JOSIE

July 17, 1993

Dear Margaret—

How very pleasant to get your note on an afternoon when my bathroom is being torn apart—and partly reassembled. We can only trust that the other part will follow tomorrow, and that water service will be restored by—well, in *time*. What to do, especially when the workman's daughter, an exceptionally beautiful African-American teenager, is on the sunny outdoor steps hugging her knees as if chilled, reduced to the last degree of misery—she probably wasn't really delighted to be chosen helper of the day anyway, but this is *too much*—by the large, obviously girl-eating dog, and, the very last straw, the Saturday afternoon Metropolitan Opera broadcast of *Madama Butterfly*. Best perhaps if I take advantage of recent large investments in technology and carry lovely new music machine into computer room, where aforesaid beast is by now used to stretching out on the floor under the printer and hoping for better times (Josie's opinion of *Madama Butterfly* is, perhaps luckily, not at present known).

THE FURTHER ADVENTURES OF JOSIE

Josie Gets Discovered

Act I: One day as Jan is being given her usual brisk afternoon outing at the highschool track, a tidy man with a small dog emerges from the underbrush. He takes one look at Josie and says in a distinctly Scots accent, "Gordon Setter!" before disappearing towards the tennis courts. A clue!

Act II: The Richards have come to dinner: Richard R., Jan's former student who has undertaken to introduce her to the computer age, and his partner, Richard S., whom we are meeting for the first time. Jan grabs Josie's collar as they enter, painfully aware ever since Josie lunged at a friendly and indeed dog-loving guest last week—teeth bared in truly embarrassingly clichéd fashion—that Josie does not enjoy meeting unfamiliar men. (It's Jan's theory that Josie's feelings are so different about women she doesn't know because one of them might turn out to be another Margaret.) But Richard S., it happens, once bred Gordon Setters and is quite pleased to spend a lot of time making friends. He says that not only does Josie look very like a GS, but that her mannerisms are equally familiar, from the demure feet-together pose to the thefts from the kitchen table (he has a Thanksgiving story about one of his mother's legendary chocolate cakes . . . luckily, in a family that at one time had 127 dogs— his mother specialized in Great Danes—much could be forgiven). Josie has a splendid time, even though the people eat all the dessert (cherry-apricot crumble with homemade vanilla ice cream).

Act III: Josie waits for the penny to drop: when will Jan realize that she is therefore a HUNTING DOG? And thus that when she freezes and points, any sensible owner would let her off the leash? How is she ever to earn her rations (not that this dry healthy stuff is worth a lot), not to mention keep in check the Bunny Menace that's obviously overrunning the county?

Josie's Cycles

If a hunting dog is not allowed to hunt, she develops eccentric longings: Josie's is to capture the large wheeled whizzing creatures that are always speeding down the narrow path from the pool or bearing screaming tykes around the track at a marvelous speed—and when she is forced to *walk*! Even on the 100-degree days when Jan unaccountably refuses to go over to the woods and track until it's almost too dark to see, the beasts speed by. Careless as ever of her own comfort when duty calls, Josie leaps at them in full cry no matter how short the leash; Jan, sad to say, often at this point screeches something impolite—about blistered hands? Josie is promised that they will next week sign up for the fall session of the most-recommended dog-training classes, the ones that were full this summer. Josie doubts that this will hold much in the way of her favorite moldy cheese or chocolate cake as a reward, but if Jan enjoys this sort of thing. . . .

Josie at the Opera

There's an interesting effect at the moment: the post-*Butterfly* feature is Puccini's greatest moments (most of them fatal, of course), while the teenager has taken Jan up on her offer of the little radio and is listening to rap. Josie finds the rap less hard on the ears. She likes danceable music best, actually, and can do a very nice three-quarters turn in midair, ears swinging. That's more fun than licking tears off Jan's face at the end of *Tosca*, but people, well, they're ODD, that's all there is to it. Nice in their own way, but the ones around here really do have a lot to learn before they'll be any good at hunting at all.

I could have been very helpful tearing up that floor in the bathroom, but whenever I try anything like that, I get scolded something terrible. And talk about noise—a nice useful bark is nothing to

a really determined tenor and soprano, especially, for some reason, when they're dying.
　luv to all, JOSIE

I can hardly believe it: first a troop wanders in this morning with an appalling array of power tools, and then, just when I've decided that anything that spooks Josie so much can't be all bad and that I might as well venture out for some breakfast after all, JAN GRABBED ME AND TRIED TO PUT ME IN THE CAT CARRIER. SUDDENLY I REMEMBERED THAT WHEN FAUSTINA CAME BACK LAST WEEK, SHE SMELLED LIKE VET OFFICE AND THAT NASTY DISINFECTANT THEY USE WITH THE— UGH—NEEDLES. *I am not having a good day. You probably need an extra cat up there, though. Just let me know when to arrive.*
LUCY PRIMROSE

SOUTHWEST AIRLINES IS OPENING AT BWI (I SUSPECT I'M THE ONLY ONE AROUND HERE WITH ENOUGH SENSE TO READ THE BUSINESS PAGE: I FIND IT A VERY SATISFACTORY PLATE); RATES ARE DOWN; I'M OFF FOR THE SUMMER TO PHOENIX. FAUSTINA

October 3, 1993

Dear Margaret—

Josie has been longing to write, but Jan has not been as cooperative as one might hope; not only does she spend long hours away from home these days (at "school," she mysteriously says), but she often seems testy and distracted—in a sort of, well, *floppy* way—when she returns. Here, however, and at last is an interim report on

JOSIE'S SCHOOL DAYS
I. Disgrace

"Josie," said Jan in that suspiciously bright tone, "*lucky* Josie! We're going to doggie school. It's the best doggie school; Tina is the trainer. You're just going to love it!" What Josie would have loved right about then would have been her dinner and a decent walk, but Jan had been told to bring her to class hungry (for the treats that would then be supplied for good behavior) and energetic.

So there they were, among the shepherds and Yorkies and Westies and a whole crowd of genial Golden Labs. They were there behind a little fence at the back of the pet store and all kinds of smells, all kinds of people, all kinds of food and medicine and dog messages . . . and here came this assertive person around in a circle offering little clucks of encouragement and an obviously spurious friendship to all the assembled creatures, who witlessly grinned or wagged tails or whatever it is that the unsuspicious see fit to do. Not Josie. She growled, a serious don't-even-think-about-calling-my-bluff growl, and when that didn't seem sufficiently discouraging, she barked as menacingly as she could manage, which was actually pretty menacing. Alone among the doggies at this exclusive training session, Josie did *not* like the much-respected instructor. Not at all. And she got shaken by her collar for it, and everyone watched. Jan really did not seem pleased, and the horrid lady with the strong voice didn't even go away: she seemed to teach most of the rest of the class from about two feet away. Josie spent most of the rest of the class on her back, hoping that Jan would pet her tummy reassuringly instead of watching with stupid approval as the other dogs vied with one another to show how *very* attentive to instruction they could be. And then it was time to go, thank heavens, but on the way out, Jan asked a distinguished-looking grey-haired woman whose little ball of fluff had been idiotically eager to obey, "Is that a King Charles spaniel?" And when the answer was "Yes, a Cavalier King Charles spaniel," she actually went on to say, "That's just what I'd wanted! But this dog needed a home . . ." and then, belatedly realizing how she'd given herself away, "but of course you're my favorite, Josie!" Ha! And the woman says she's in favor of democracy: her politics are disgraceful by seventeenth-century standards! Josie's tail drooped for quite a while.

II. Sleep-Away Camp

There she went again, using her "Aren't-we-a-good-little-doggy-with-no-brain-at-all" manner. "Josie, this is going to be *really* nice!" Lord deliver us. A long, long car ride, out to Street, Maryland, a place that seems to have hardly any streets at all, but lots of dogs, at Country Comfort Kennels. The main house is quite lovely, an old Victorian with a gazebo and little round stained glass windows; Josie was even quite taken by the numbers of interesting and interested dogs that greet her and busy enough tracing smells so that she barely heard the chit-chat about the Camp Special (nature walks! complimentary shampoo and dip!), but she caught on quickly when she realized *Jan was leaving*. Something about visiting a daughter. That small person who'd been introduced as the Beta dog was all very nice, but do you catch Josie having to rush off on any excuse to visit her *multiple* daughters? It seemed a very long time until Jan returned, at which point she heard that Josie had behaved well, had growled at no one, had *not* enjoyed her bath . . . Josie upon leaving deposited a very large evaluation on a trim little patch of lawn. Jan and Josie have both had colds this week, the direct result of all this unseemly rushing about the continent.

III. Star-Struck at Thornfield Hall

Classes of all sorts continue. Josie, supervised by the *assistant* trainer, has learned speedily to sit, lie down and then sit right back up again. More impressively, she has stopped barking at bicycles (she *hates* having her muzzle shaken). Jan has been teaching *Jane Eyre* for at least five weeks now and sees no sign of ever finishing. The William Wegman show has opened at the museum, showing thespian doggies acting out all manner of stories. Josie, putting various pieces together, has begun to see a compelling career move in her future. More to follow!

"There was no possibility of taking a walk that day." Jane Eyre, c'est moi! And this Brocklehurst person, I know him (or her as the case is) whenever I see him, and I tell everyone about it. I was meant to play this role—perhaps in a more popular form, though. Watch a theater near you!

Luv, JOSIE

She says there's a part for me, in a nice warm attic. I don't know; of course, she's highly unreliable and a little evasive about meal service. Don't you think a real director would understand that I'M a natural star?

Yr. LUCY PRIMROSE HEARTBURN

SHE'S NOT WHAT I'D CALL AN ACUTE LITERARY MIND. JANE EYRE, I REMEMBER CLEARLY, DESCRIBES HERSELF AS "POOR, OBSCURE, PLAIN AND—LITTLE." THIS GREAT HOUND? HARDLY. SHE TELLS ME I CAN PLAY MRS. FAIRFAX.

YR. OFFENDED FAUSTINA

January 19, 1994

Dear Margaret—

I'm sure that winter's fiercer in your parts, but that hardly consoles. This earthquake week I can't even whine my usual, "But I'm a second-generation Californian! I'm not genetically equipped to deal with ice!" I rather enjoyed the giant earthquakes of my childhood, but that was before I had a heavily mortgaged property of my own; I somehow doubt that I would have been tremendously composed if I'd been in L.A. Monday. Well, we hope that you all are making it through in good form and good spirits; here, from the frigid and uneventful wastes of Donegal Drive—is just a short report:

JOSIE ON ICE

I. THE WORST WINTER EVER

After twenty-one years in the East, Jan's beginning to catch on: it's not a good sign when the announcer on the classical music station starts laughing as he tries to read the weather forecast—and then spends the rest of the afternoon playing Beatles songs.

On the other hand, the local meteorological hotshot interviewed in the paper today refused to say that it was the worst winter ever—on the extremely shaky and indeed rather troubling grounds that winter is not yet over. He did admit that the average winter has one and a half ice storms, almost all followed by nearly immediate thaws, and that the current total of five storms, only one of which melted quickly, is a bit on the high side. He did not see fit to mention, though, that two more bouts of freezing rain are supposed to turn up in the next three days. Yet the supermarket wasn't very crowded when Jan got there this afternoon, even with two to five inches of snow predicted by tomorrow's so-called dawn, when the switch to freezing rain may begin. In other words, a lot of people hadn't yet been able to negotiate their streets; in addition to a *lot* of dog and cat food, Jan picked up another 40 pounds of kitty litter for her driveway, in hopes of being able to pull back into it when she got home. And so she did, and Josie was glad to see her look a little more cheerful now that she had acquired $82 worth of provisions. "It's enough to feed only a very small village," she explained to Josie, "and, considering that I may not get to the store again until, say, mid-April . . ."

Josie wagged her tail.

Really, Josie does try to be generally encouraging and even to understand why Jan is so reluctant to get the exercise they both so badly need. This two-footed locomotion does not seem to be at all practical for the humans, she notes; what did Jan mean this morning by saying that she couldn't walk down the driveway? It seems to be hard on their nerves, too. When, deprived of even a little trot up the street, Josie was showing a reluctance to dirty her own back yard both natural and commendable (and besides, there were so many fascinating small-mammal smells), Jan became quite impatient and, when they finally got back inside, actually started to whimper as she took her gloves off. She should have worn the lined gloves, Josie noted. This transplanted half-hardy semi-tropical routine of hers is a little old.

II. LUST IN A COLD CLIMATE

So Josie spends the days thinking about wildlife. She lies on the Indian-print bedspread, resting her chin on the window sill, and watches for the small creatures that eventually venture out to the tell-tale percussion of ice-coated twigs. Squirrels are quite an event, worthy of a circuit of the house, tail up, barking loudly, but RABBITS, now . . . she begins with a bark but quickly modulates into a truly uncanny serenade for which "whine" is far too pale a description. It makes one wonder . . . she is very fast . . . and was no doubt tremendously hungry last winter. . . .

On the other hand, she has become increasingly considerate of the kitties. Sort of. Should Faustina be attempting to settle on Jan's lap, she does put her paw up on Jan's leg in the famous submissive Gordon Setter pose in such a way as to bop the dear little cat on the head, but she doesn't try stalking the cats on their way to the litter box anymore—well, not while Jan's watching. If the door into the room with a view is closed, she'll take a nap with Faustina, on the sunny side of Jan's bed. And she was most concerned and dignified when Jan got the car stuck in the ice pulling back into the driveway after obedience class last Monday. But just let her see a rabbit. . . .

III. CAREER MOVES IN THE YEAR OF THE DOG

Once the car was freed from the ice—a mere matter of three or four hours' digging—Jan was pleased that they had made it to class. It had been graduation, after all. That last night, three doggies broke the Long Down while their owners were hiding from them in the aisles of the pet store: but not Josie. When everybody traded dogs for several minutes, one, too miserable with anyone else, had to be given back to her owner; but it wasn't Josie. When each owner stood by her dog in the middle of a circle while everyone else came up with a treat to pet the center dog, one dog was judged enough of a security risk that the instructor suggested simply offering the treat on outstretched fingertips and forgetting the petting; but Josie wagged her tail at everyone and hoped for more. So when two dogs were singled out, one as much improved but still in need of careful attention and a lot of work, the other, as simply most improved, you will correctly guess that Josie was the latter. Jan got her a pretty new collar as a present—Valentine scarlet webbing with leather trim that matches her own tan—and, more relevantly, promised her favorite kind of bone.

So now that Josie is educated, she wonders what line to take up next. Philosophy is always a possibility; she hopes Jan brings home Vicki Hearne's new book soon, after the review in the *Times* ran lines like, "Stanley Cavell, a great philosopher whose work is hindered because he owns cats, but no dogs. . . ." She wonders about political science: the mystery of the Chinese, for example, who officially still outlaw dogs as "bourgeois affectations," but who have now opened at least one park where dogs can be rented by the hour. She is of course still much drawn to stage and screen, but Jan is encouraging her to stop studying the Brontës and consider comedy. She has, Jan thinks, a certain Carole Lombard-ish air, including fine comic timing. There is for example the way she disappears— not so much as a jingle of tags—as Jan brushes her teeth, only to materialize as a dark shadow lying at the foot of the bed. She will not meet Jan's eyes, remembering when the bed was out of bounds, but even if the light's not on, you'd know she's there from the increasingly rapid beat of her tail as she hears Jan approach. A few weeks ago, she cracked up the whole obedience class: as they were all circling the ring, the enormous, sleepy Black Lab nicknamed Moose, a most friendly fellow, so far forgot himself as to hustle up and sniff Josie's behind. Josie turned and ran for Jan, sat up on her haunches and put both paws on Jan's arm with a most demure and worried air.

But whatever heights she reaches, she promises not to forget Jan, nor her friends in New York.

All right, obedience class had its moments. The night I let Tina scratch me behind the ears, everyone applauded. And it's true, I do like applause, although being scratched behind the ears is even nicer. But it's hard not to enjoy any outing at all in this odd season, with Jan so reluctant even to venture out the door. I would like it to go on record that I have not pulled her down on the ice, not once. If she'd get into the spirit of things and slide, like me, she'd have a lot more fun.

Luv, JOSIE

I tried one of my mad dashes through the door a week or so back and was astonished and dismayed that I had to turn right around and slink back in. Something very unpleasant seems to have happened out there. But this last week there have been birds about to watch through the glass. What with that, planning naps or deciding how to get up from a nap, I do keep busy.

Your unpleasantly chilled LUCY PRIMROSE

REALLY THIS WON'T DO. I AM NOT PLEASED, I TELL YOU. ENOR-MOUS CANINES INDOORS, SOME FORM OF FREEZE, I BELIEVE, OUTDOORS, LUCY NEARLY CATATONIC . . . I CAN NOT WAIT UNTIL I CAN GET MY LITTLE SATCHEL OUT THE DOOR. BUT I DO SEE THAT JAN GETS OUT TO THE STORE FOR LITTLE CANS OF CAT FOOD. THE VOICE OF HOUSEHOLD REASON, **FAUSTINA**

April 23, 1994

Dear Margaret—

Just an interim note: spring appears to be coming, and I'll report fully should this actually turn out to be the case. I myself have a hard time believing in May, much less June, but should rumor be accurate and summer be on the way, please do expect a visit from Josie and me. I didn't want to wait, though, to let you know about the important development in Josie's life.

She is no longer quite a country dog! She's been downright refusing to take walks in the rain. But she is spending many hours that the unobservant might call idle ("Josie, get out from between those sheets. Dogs do NOT nap with their heads on pillows! Josie, *you have gone too far!*") in deep meditation on a new cat-training program that may revolutionize life as Faustina and Lucy Primrose know it. But they too, of course, have their own plans. I'll let you know. . . .

Menus

Faustina: cream, chicken dinners, eau de tuna, cream, Alpo Dairy Cat (don't even try the Whiskas equivalent), cream, non-fat milk (**WHAT?**) SORRY! cream, left-over raspberry salmon with caramelized shallots (Faustina, there was no salmon left over. **WHAT? WELL THEN, LOTS MORE CREAM!**).

Lucy Primrose: Last seen licking the bottom of Jan's foot to wake her up from an entirely unnecessary nap. It could not be determined whether her purposes were culinary.

Josie: Don't go to any trouble, just show me how to open the refrigerator door.

❀

WHAT FRANK, MARTHA AND I KNOW ABOUT THE DESERT
Alice Sadongei

My mother
used to speak about Coyote.
She talked to Praying Mantis—
asked him
when rain was coming.
She taught me, Frank and Martha
to look for sap
on the greasy bark
of mesquite.
(the sap has crunchy, crystallized edges, a smooth
    wax-like center)
She told us
how to eat mesquite beans.
"gnaw on the ends, don't eat the seeds"
(the fiber inside the pod is sweet)
On zoo visits
we'd hear tales of Coyote.
"Coyote fell on desert sand
blinded by his vanity. Bluebird
laughed at him—now his coat is streaked and blotched."
Coyote knew
we were talking about him.

He'd let us look into his eyes.
My mother
would take me, Frank, and Martha
to the desert in spring.
"Stand
alone out here.
Don't speak.
Listen
to the desert."
My mother
showed us a purple desert flower
that looked like a rabbit.
(they grow near the highway)
There are patches of poppies
near my grandmother's village.

> Out there
> in the desert
> where there is nothing
> but heat and the wobbly
> shade of the mesquite
> tree, look around before
> you sit on a rock. There
> may be lizards or snakes
> sleeping under the cool
> stone.

❁

HOME
Paddy Reid

In all his nine years Liam Bollard had never been away from Dublin. He really missed the sounds of Portside Street. The cries of mothers calling while children ran the other way. The loud, cheerful voices of men leaving the Black Diamond pub at closing time. He even missed chasing after lorries to steal lumps of coal. Here it was so different. The sanatorium was too quiet. The other boys were mostly silent. Yes nurse, no nurse was about all they said. At night the distant clatter of trains made him homesick, even as it broke the silence. There were few other sounds. The squeak of a nurse's shoes, the banging of a door that didn't shut properly, the harsh coughs that sometimes jerked him awake.

Liam gazed into the bathroom mirror and didn't like what he saw. A skinny white face and close–shaven head. He ran a hand through black bristly hair and frowned. Ma wouldn't know him now. He returned to the ward and climbed back into bed. As he slipped into sleep he recalled the last time he saw her. . .

"I hafta go now, Liam." She ruffled his hair and kissed his forehead. "Don't cry–will yeh do tha' for me, love?"

Liam held her coat sleeve. "When kin I go home, Ma?"

He saw the pain that filled her eyes. She looked close to tears.

"I don't know, Liam. Only God knows." She managed a smile. "Don't forget to pray every night like I tol' yeh." She began twisting the end of her headscarf. "I'll see yeh nex' Sunday, love." She kissed him again and moved toward the exit door.

Liam ran to the east window and pressed his face to the cool glass as she passed by. Ma glanced up, waved, shook her head and moved quickly along the gravel path. She was almost running now, her head lowered. That's when he saw the Alsatian dog loping alongside her. Ma didn't seem to notice even when the dog howled at her.

Liam's bed was at the end of the ward. Other than for a crucifix over the door, the room looked bare. Nothing but row after row of gray-covered beds. A pot-bellied stove stood in the middle of the ward, but it still felt cold. Even after three weeks it felt strange to wake up in such a place. The moments between dreams and awakening were the worst. Sometimes he snapped awake at the sound of Ma calling him, but she was never there. Once he awoke to find the head nurse, Sr. Immaculata, standing over him, her face a shiny skull in a black cowl.

"Are we sleeping well, little man?" She spoke slowly, her words falling on him like sharp frost.

Liam quickly turned to face the wall. Ma always told him to think of something nice whenever he felt sad. As he slipped into sleep he brought an image to mind. Both of them walking along Dollymount Strand on a hot August day. He was five then, half a lifetime ago. Ma was laughing aloud, swirling around in circles in the seawashed sand, one hand gripping her shoes, the other holding up her long white skirt. She began splashing water in all directions as she moved closer to the sea. Liam stood on the white dry sand warily eyeing the blue-green waves that hissed and foamed around her ankles. It was his first ever visit to the seaside. He took one step towards her.

"Come on, Liam, it's only massive." She laughed like a child. "Last in is a cowardy custard an' gets no ice cream!" She beckoned him in, black shoes waving above her head. He ran towards her. Soon they ran along the strand, side by side, kicking up sprays of salty water. Their feet splattered noisily as they headed for the wooden pier.

"Whee! Isn't it only gorgeous, Liam?" She tossed her shoes into a sand dune. "Come on, let's play!" They began kicking water at each other. Liam laughed so much that tears mixed with salty spray. He had never seen her so happy. Finally they rested in the sand dune while Ma dried him down with a towel. In the distance he saw the silver bicycle cart of the ice-cream man, a shimmering blur in the setting sun. Ice-cream would taste so good. . .

Sunday came and Ma didn't visit. Liam saw nurses gathered in groups whispering, then glancing over at him. Even Sister Immaculata smiled at him. Were they sending him home? *That's* why Ma didn't come. He must be going home. The thought cheered him greatly. When he went to the toilet after lunch, he saw a newspaper lying scattered on the ground. He glanced at the date. Sunday, June 1, 1941. A familiar scene caught his attention. He knelt down and read the page, slowly mouthing the words.

North Strand. . . German Bombers. . .38 dead. . .many missing.

Liam looked at the photo, his heart racing now. It was his end of

Portside Street—or what little remained of it. Mostly heaped rubble with jagged beams thrusting out like long bayonets. He ran from the toilet. Two nurses chased and caught him as he rushed to the front door. One held him tight as he wept. Everything went blurry after that. When he awoke he felt as if he'd been sleeping forever. A deep, silent sleep with no dreams.

"Are we feeling better now?" Sister Immaculata managed a brief smile as she stood over him.

"The dog's barkin' outside again." Liam said absently.

"Silly boy," she said with a lipless grin. "There's no dogs around here."

The boy in the next bed came from Cork. Seanie was friendly and they talked about football and such things. Seanie's parents even brought presents for Liam the following Sunday. That same evening both boys stood by the front window, watching as Seanie's parents left to catch the train to Cork.

Liam stared at the railway tracks in the distance. "Which way is Dublin?" he asked.

"That way." Seanie pointed left. "Cork is down there." Liam peered into the distance to the right, but saw nothing, only fields and hedges.

"An' where are we?" Liam asked.

"Oh," Seanie laughed, "we're right in the middle of nowhere."

Liam frowned. It wasn't right. There should be streets with girls skipping and singing and boys playing football. Dogs barking and trams rattling by. "How far is Dublin?" he asked finally.

"Dunno. Far, I'd say." Seanie shrugged. "As far away as Cork is." Something in his voice made Liam look up. Tears welled in Seanie's eyes.

"Yeh wanna go home, Seanie?"

"Doesn't everyone?" Seanie returned to bed and climbed under the blankets.

It was the same every Sunday when the visitors left. All the boys were sad and tearful. Liam sat in bed and watched some go stand by the east window until Sister Immaculata ordered them back to bed. The ward was always so much quieter on such nights. Some kids cried softly while others lay staring up at the ceiling. Seanie buried himself under the bedclothes. Liam listened to low moans that finally settled into stillness.

"When kin I go home?" Liam began asking every nurse the same question. They just smiled. "Ask the doctor," one finally said. The doctor patted him on the head and said. "Not yet, son."

Finally he stopped asking.

"Seanie?" Liam called one night.

"Yeah?" A yawny answer.

"Will yeh be a farmer like yer daddy when yeh go home?"

"No." Seanie paused. "Too bloody hard."

"What are yeh goin' to do when yeh leave here?"

"Leave?" Seanie echoed. "I'll be with me Grandad and Grandma."

"Oh? Where do they live?"

Seanie laughed. "With Jesus."

"Wi' Jesus?" Liam was confused. "Why?"

Seanie rolled his eyes. "It's where we go after here–don't you know that?"

"No." Liam lay back, tucking the blanket under his chin. "Kin we not go somewhere else?"

"Such as?" Seanie asked.

"Home."

"No." Seanie sighed. "It's not up to us."

Nothing was said for a while.

"Is TB bad, Seanie?" Liam waited but got no answer.

Seanie lay sleeping, his mouth partly open, forming a small o.

Granny Bollard came to visit. He was glad to see her, even if all she did was bury her face in her blue-veined hands and cry. Her tears only made him feel worse, as if he were somehow responsible for her sorrow. That night he coughed so much that he felt his chest would explode from the effort. He must have fallen asleep for he awoke into silence and darkness. Somewhere in the distance he heard a train whistle. Was it going to Dublin or Cork? A dog barked. Rising silently from bed, Liam went to the east window. He watched the square yellow lights slowly drifting left. That's when he saw the Alsatian gliding easily over the moonlit field. The dog came toward Liam and stopped outside the window, pink tongue hanging. Sitting and waiting. Then it stood and wagged its tail rapidly. Come on! It called to him. Liam nodded and quickly moved back to his bed. Opening his bedside locker, he pulled out a woolly jersey.

"Liam?" Seanie whispered. "What–"

"Quiet!" Liam hissed, kneeling at Seanie's bed. "D'yeh wanta come wi' me?"

"Where?" Seanie asked quickly.

"Home." Liam whispered fiercely.

"I can't, Liam." Seanie's voice was shaky. "I hafta stay. . ."

"Why?"

Seanie sighed. "For Jesus an' Grandad–"

"Okay." Liam cut in. "I'll see yeh." He moved towards the side door.

"Liam?" Seanie called.

Liam returned quickly to Seanie's side.

"Take this for when you get hungry." He handed Liam a small blood orange.

"Thanks." Liam slipped out the side door as he'd seen the nurses do at night. He'd heard them complain that the door didn't shut properly. Outside, the dog came over and licked his hand once, then walked alongside him. Liam moved quickly down toward the tracks and found an old boreen road running alongside the railway line. He leaned against a telephone pole and peeled the blood orange. Sweat dripped from his body and began to cool on his skin. When the fruit was sucked dry he called to the dog.

"D'yeh know where I live?" Liam asked. The dog barked once.

"Please." Liam urged. "Take me home."

The dog whirled around and galloped silently along the path. Run! It barked, run! Liam nodded eagerly and began running. As he ran he started laughing. Just like he did when being chased by the fat lorry driver crying blue murder over his missing lumps of coal. It felt great to run in the dark. Whenever he slowed down the dog turned to him, tail wagging. Run! run! Liam ran, moving even faster than before. The dark-faced coalman would never catch him now. As the sky turned from black to gray, Liam realised he had never run as long, as fast, or as easily in his life. I'm goin' home, he told himself. At this rate he'd be all the way home to Portside Street before he knew it.

❀

POEMS
Patricia Monaghan

Hmong Pa-Ndau, Embroideries of the Laos Hills

A woman buys a dream maze in blue and red
on a patio in California while the sun
rages like a warrior, while the wind battles
with the sea for possession of the sand.
She does not know who cut and stitched
the runes of slavery in the cotton cloth,
what old mother bent beneath the mission tiles
to trace an alphabet of tribal names and reach
back over the Pacific to the peaks of home.

The woman takes the maze away, back across
the sea in the direction of the Laos hills
and hangs it on the wall above her bed.
She dreams: in a small neat hut, laughing,
away from any wars; in a trackless jungle, fleeing,
short of breath; explosions and escapes. She dreams:
solitudes and sorrows, forgotten families.
She dreams while an old woman who has sold
these dreams for bread sleeps fitfully, trying
to find the road back, trying to remember scenes
that shine like dragons' scales, weeping in her sleep
for the one time she forgot to trap the power
of dreams within a border of embroidered peaks.

The River, Constructed by Saddam Hussein and Named The Mother of Battles, Speaks

I was built in a rage of blame.
I was built in pride and anger.
I was built as a rippling flag.

But I am more than they expected.
I have planted small reeds
along my straight shores,
I have sung songs to waterbirds
who crowd into me, nesting.

I have deepened and settled.

In ten years date palms
will line my curving banks.
In a hundred years I will have
sloughed out lakes and passages.
In a thousand years more
islands will dot my surface.

And they will have blown away like sand.
They will fade like morning flowers.
They will disappear like light rain.

At Quartz Creek, at Fifteen

I climbed a knotty cottonwood and
carved my name; I have a short name;
it did not take long; but while I did
my brother, racing a boat around the lake,
fell in. While I was in the tree the boat
was lost, my brother saved, my father furious—

but there, surrounded by tree fleece and unaware
of any other threat of loss, I had slipped away

like the boat from my brother's control, had
felt myself slowly sinking under life,
had cried as I carved, wondering

would I remember my name blazoned
on a tree at Kenai Lake—sure I would
forget—crying for all I knew I had already
forgotten, all those times I knew

myself for just the time it takes to climb
a tree or uproot a wild onion or find the first
spring patches of asparagus, those moments
of myself, and certain I was I would forget
this one, certain I was this would be
the last, that I would soon forget
myself and die.

I fled into my tent and cried into my old brown
sleeping bag till dinner, when I sat pensive
and silent, trying to keep hold of that moment
while my father scolded and the babies screamed.

I have come to that lake for the first time since,
boats roar across its greenness and I do not even
search for that tree—in twenty years it will have
fallen—but the cottonwoods give me back that memory,
I send back to that girl some consolation—
my remembering her, my still remaining her—

my spirit touches hers, my own, and she
quiets, sitting at that redwood table,

she stares into the lake, she does not know
it is herself who comforts her, she will not
for many years know that.

❀

THE SMELL OF DIRT
Laura Filipp

With Grandpa Wojack dying, summer really speeded up. The next few days went by in a terrible flash, like a movie in fast motion; all herky-jerky, in bright, scary colors. Mama cried a lot. Daddy went around staring this mean stare. He wouldn't talk; Mama kept saying for him to get it off his chest, but all that did was make him leave the room.

I mostly tried to stay out of the way.

The first thing I did when I got a chance was go ask Denny what a heart attack was. He said your blood starts boiling and your pressure goes way up and your heart gets bigger and bigger until it explodes. "Like a big, old water balloon filled up with blood," he said.

I'm glad I wasn't there to see it.

Mama and Daddy spent two whole days at Kowalski's Funeral Home with Grandpa, talking to all our relatives who came to pay their respects. At Kowlaski's, we had our own little room. It was dark and hot and smelled like strong perfume and flowers and hot, sweaty people. Grandpa Wojack was lying on his back in a big, shiny box at one end— a coffin, or a casket— all dressed up in his best black suit. He was tucked in between white satin sheets, and his head rested on a tiny white satin pillow, with beautiful flowers in golden vases crowding all around him. There was white powder and rouge on his face and his cheeks looked all lumpy. They had his hands folded together over a black rosary. From across the room it looked like he just fell asleep saying his prayers, but if you knew my Grandpa, you knew that wouldn't be true; he never said a rosary or even went to church.

From up close, it didn't really look like him.

There was this little smile on his lips. I couldn't stop staring at that little stuck-on smile when Mama took me up to see him the first night. There was a hush in the room as we walked up; everybody was looking at me. I was so nervous about how I would act. Seeing Grandpa, dead, was such a surprise. But when I got up there, nothing looked real. It seemed fake, like they had made a big life-sized Grandpa Wojack doll or something, only they got the color wrong. There was a white velvet pillow on a small kneeler by his head; when we knelt down to say a prayer, my face was about two inches from his.

In the worst way, I wanted to touch his puffy white cheek.

"Mama," I whispered, "is he really Grandpa?"

She put her arm around me and took a breath. "No, honey, not anymore. What you see is just a shell, the body without the soul."

"Does he have his shoes on under the sheet?"

Acting like she didn't hear me, Mama crossed herself and stood up. Then she jerked me to my feet and pulled me through the crowd to the back of the room where a bunch of our relatives were talking. Our relatives were all these people who looked kind of familiar, but I didn't really know them. We hardly ever saw them. They kept giving Mama hugs and patting my head like I was a dog. Mama liked it. I didn't. I could tell Daddy didn't like it, either—he kept stepping outside for some air.

Supper was cold fried chicken and potato salad and glass after glass of cold iced tea, which I ate in the Ladies Lounge with Mama, Daddy's aunts and all the girl cousins. It was a tiny, peach-colored room leading to the bathroom, with a couch and comfortable chairs and a big picture of the Blessed Mother on the wall. After they ate, some of the old aunts rolled down their stockings, took off their girdles and stretched out. They talked about my grandmother, my Grandma Wojack, the one I never knew. Aunt Bertie, the fattest of Grandpa Wojack's sisters, fanned her face with the hem of her dress; I sat on a bench across from her watching the soft, creamy skin folds hanging down from her arms jiggle back and forth. "Not a day goes by I don't miss her," she said.

Then she turned to me. "Rose Marie, you take after your Grandma." They all stopped chewing and looked at me. "It's in your eyes," she said, "the way you hold your head."

They studied me—my eyes and the way I held my head. Then they nodded. I put down my iced tea. Mama gave me a proud little secret smile. Everyone loved Grandma Wojack. Such a fine woman, they said. But what a cross she had to bear.

Then a man knocked on the door, saying the Altar Sodality from Blessed Heart was here. Everyone jumped up and got dressed and combed their hair and rushed out to meet them.

The ladies from the Sodality had come to say the rosary for Grandpa's soul. They also came, Mama said, to remember Grandma, who used to be their President. There were about twenty women in the group, all dressed in black, filing into the two rows of folding chairs set up in front of Grandpa's body. Some of them were very old and bent over, with canes. Right away they all sat down, pulled out their rosaries and crossed themselves. "In the name of the Father and of the Son and of the Holy Ghost, Amen," they said, swinging their beads in wide arcs across their chests. Then they began the rosary, saying out loud one I Believe, an Our Father, three Hail Marys, and one Glory Be; then they started right in, without a pause, on the first string of ten Hail Marys. By then most of the women in the room had joined them, sinking down into folding chairs as fast as the men could set them up. They prayed in low, murmuring voices that rose gently, then fell, then rose again. After a few minutes, they got into a rhythm and started keeping perfect time with one another, making all the words run together like some long, sad line of a song sung over and over. "HAIL, MARY," they said, then rushed on, "fullofgracethelordiswiththeeblessedartthou amongwomenand blessed isthefruitofthywomb, JESUS," (at the name of Jesus they bowed their heads and took a breath, making a sound like a huge, soft sigh), "HOLY Mary," they went on, "MotherofGodprayforussinnersnowandatthehourofourdeath, a-MEN." Then another huge sigh of a breath and they began all over again, "Hail, Mary." On and on, and on. Through every one of the Mysteries—the Five Sorrowful Mysteries, the Five Joyful Mysteries, the Five Glorious Mysteries— fifteen Mysteries in all, with a whole rosary for each. At first, I tried to keep up with them, but it was like diving into a rushing stream; they rushed right over me. So I closed my eyes. After a while they sounded like bees buzzing or waves washing up on shore at the lake. I laid my head in Mama's lap. The praying voices carried me to a cool, quiet pond where I floated on my back, then fell asleep.

In a dream, Daddy carried me to the car and laid me down in the back seat; then he was carrying me again into the house. Mama undressed me and put me to bed.

I remember her tucking the sheet around my shoulders; the next thing I knew I was flat on my stomach, climbing the hill down at the construction site. I was alone. It was dark, the middle of the night. There was no moon. I could hear the bulldozer moving dirt on the other side of the hill as I climbed. At the top, I looked carefully over the edge, but all I could see was a giant black hole; it was so deep I couldn't see the bottom.

It looked like the deepest basement ever dug.

Suddenly the bulldozer appeared, slowly crawling out of the hole. The engine roared and strained as it lurched up the steep slope. It was so dark I couldn't make out the man driving, but when the bulldozer got to the top and the engine cut off, I saw him jump down. He stood there and looked across the hole in my direction. I pressed myself flat into the dirt; it was cold and damp, and it chilled me to the bone. I was shivering inside but didn't move. Suddenly he pointed right at me. "Hey!" he yelled. I jumped up and started to run, but all of sudden the ground gave way beneath me, and I was falling, falling headlong into the hole.

I landed in a pile of loose dirt. It was so dark I couldn't see; all I could smell was damp, dark dirt. I scrambled to my feet. Just then, the bulldozer started up with a roar high above me. Before I knew what was happening, I was knocked flat by a huge pile of dirt that hit me from above. I got up and tried to run, but my legs wouldn't move. I tried to scream at the man in the bulldozer to stop, but no sound came out. Then another load of dirt hit me; this time it almost covered me up. Then more dirt and more dirt and I was drowning in dirt and I couldn't see, it was in my eyes; I couldn't breathe, it was in my nose; I opened my mouth to scream and my mouth filled up with it.

"Help," I tried to yell, "help," and that's what woke me up, my yelling. Only then I wasn't yelling, just making little strangled whimpering noises in my bed, the pillow over my head. I threw off the pillow and sat up, sucking in air.

I hoped I didn't wake anybody up.

It was a few minutes before my heart stopped pounding, then it was quiet. The only sound I could hear was Daddy snoring. Relieved, I got up and went to the window. The moon in the sky looked far away and very white and cold.

After a while, I got back in bed. But I didn't go back to sleep that night; every time I closed my eyes I saw Grandpa's white face being covered with dirt.

Just like Daddy, I was afraid of Grandpa Wojack, and him being dead didn't really change anything. I hated going over his house; he was always giving me mean looks. He told Mama I talked too loud and made too much noise and she didn't know how to raise children but what could anyone expect, considering what kind of trash she came from. She would get real quiet when he said things like that. Later she would cry, but she didn't do it in front of him or Daddy.

She had her pride, she would tell me.

He didn't even like the way I ate ("Chews like a horse," he said). According to Grandpa, I couldn't do anything right. Last year, me and Mama were over there picking plums from his plum tree, the same one he was pruning when he had the heart attack. It was a warm, late-summer day. The long branches of the plum tree were hanging with the weight of bunches and bunches of fat, dark, purple plums, hundreds of plums. I loved plum-picking time, it meant all the fresh little sweet plums you could eat, plus plum tarts, plum dumplings, plum pies, and all winter, canned plums and plum jelly.

Grandpa Wojack was in the house, in his room, probably asleep in his chair. "Pick what you can. The ladder's out, the baskets are on the back porch; just leave me be," he said when he let us in. He saw us out to the back, then went into his room and shut the door.

We set right to work. Mama put up the ladder, picked up a basket and climbed to the top, unafraid. Leaning her hips into the ladder for balance, she picked off the plums with one hand, putting them into the basket she held with the other. To get the plums she couldn't reach, she'd give each limb a good shake, making them rain down on the soft grass underneath. That was my job, to catch what fell down to me. I'd gather the plums up, careful not to squeeze them too tight, careful not to step on any. I piled them into one big straw basket after another. The sweet, ripe plum smell made my mouth water, but I didn't eat even one. I wanted to fill up more baskets than ever before.

After a while, I had to pee. I held it as long as I could, but finally, I told Mama I had to go. "Well, go on ahead, then, Rose Marie—it's time for a break, anyway," she said.

I walked into the house quietly, careful not to bang the back door. When Grandpa Wojack was in his room with the door shut, it was best to leave him alone. The bathroom was down the hall from his room; I tip-toed past his door. I could hear him mumbling on the other side. He sounded mad. I wondered who he was talking to. In the bathroom, I peed quick as I could, flushed the toilet and jumped up and ran out. I was running down the hall when his door opened, and there he was, holding onto the door frame with one hand, waving his cane with the other. He had a mean look on his face. A sweet, spoiled smell came out of the room.

Right away, I started to back up. Grandpa Wojack, walking wobbly-like, came after me. I backed up to the end of the hall then just stood there, waiting; my heart pounding was all I could hear. He got within two feet of me and growled like a dog. "Little girl," he said slowly (sometimes he forgot my name), "little girl," he said again, lifting the cane above his head, "if you don't learn to walk so I can't hear you, I'm going to beat the living CRAP out of you." On the word CRAP he smashed his cane with a loud CRACK against the wall. It left a big black mark on the wallpaper.

I stood there frozen, staring at the black mark. I believed he'd do what he said. Daddy has a crooked nose; it's been that way since he was a little boy.

Mama told me Grandpa broke it for him.

"Well?" he said, bending over me, spraying me with his hot, sweet and sour breath, "well?" His eyes were red as the Devil's.

"Yes, sir," is how my lips went, but no sound came out.

"What did you say? What?"

Again, I couldn't find my voice.

"Just get the hell out of here," he roared, raising the cane again. I jumped, but there was no place to go. He blocked the only way out.

"Yes, sir, I'm sorry, sir," I said finally, shrinking into the wall as much as I could.

He opened his mouth to say something else, but burped instead. Then he whirled around and careened back down the hall into his room and slammed the door.

I didn't move. "Get out get OUT!" I was screaming inside me, but when I tried to back away from that wall it was like I was glued to it. It was like in a dream when a wild dog is chasing you and you're trying to run but you can't. My eye was on the door to Grandpa's room. I could hear him in there, heard him sit down heavily in his chair, heard him pouring something into a glass.

"Rose Marie," Mama suddenly called from far away, "what are you doing in there?" It was like a voice from heaven reaching down to me. "I hope you're not bothering your Grandpa," she said. "Get out here, right now, Rose Marie, do you hear me?"

Her words loosened me from the wall, and I shot through the hall, past Grandpa's room, around the corner and out the back door; I swear I didn't make a sound because my feet didn't touch the ground.

I never told Mama what happened, but I kept away from Grandpa after that. I learned to walk soft as a cat. And I never let him get between me and a door again.

Mama didn't want me to go to the funeral. I heard them arguing about it the next morning. "It's no place for a child," she said. "It's her grandfather," Daddy said. "Besides, she's got to learn."

Daddy won.

So Mama took me out to Sears and bought me a new dress. It had to be navy or black, she said, because that's what you wear to a funeral. It was especially important because we were the Immediate Family, and we'd be sitting up in the front pew at Blessed Heart with everybody watching and praying for us in our Grief.

After we got my dress, which at least had these neat little brass buttons I liked, we went to Ladies Wear. There I watched Mama try on every black dress on the rack. They all looked like different versions of the same old baggy black bag. We went to J.C. Penney's across the street, but we didn't have any luck there, either, not even in Better Dresses. Mama looked like she was going to cry. Time was running out; the funeral was tomorrow. As we left J.C. Penney's and walked down the sidewalk of the shopping center, we came to a small shop called "Elaine's." Mama opened the door to Elaine's and walked right in like she shopped there all the time. "Your father will want me to look good," she said to me for an excuse, though I wasn't saying anything. As soon as we came through the door, a sophisticated older lady, probably Miss Elaine herself, hurried up. She listened to Mama's story, making soft, soothing noises in the back of her throat, and led us into the back dressing room. We followed her behind a flowery curtain to a large, carpeted room with mirrors all around and a big, cushiony couch which we sank into, sighing. Then she disappeared to get some dresses.

The first one she brought back, Mama wouldn't even try on. "I'm going to a funeral, not a party," she said, frowning at the sequins all down the front. The next dress looked kind of like a party dress, too, but the lady convinced Mama to just try it. She left it in Mama's arms and slipped out through the curtain, slipping back in again just in time to zip up the long zipper at Mama's back. "There," she said, standing back, "just look at yourself!"

We stared at Mama as she stared at herself in the mirror. The dress fit her perfectly. It hugged her tightly, smoothing out her boniness into curves. Her pale skin looked creamy and rich next to the black material. Suddenly, she didn't look like Mama anymore. Suddenly, I could see her smiling and walking down the street on the arm of somebody like Cary Grant, or maybe just all by herself.

"Ooh, Mama," I said.

Mama closed her eyes a little. She looked like she was falling in love.

"It's perfect," cooed the lady, "elegant, appropriate for the Occasion, but just ever-so-slightly sexy. It emphasizes your fine bones and your lovely, thin figure."

"Oh my," was all Mama said.

The lady left us to think about it. Mama stared at herself in the mirror for a long time, turning around slowly to the right, then to the left. Then she turned all the way around and looked back at the mirror over her shoulder.

It was starting to get boring.

"Come on, Mama, buy it and let's go. I'm getting hungry."

That's when she looked at the price tag.

"Holy Mary, Mother of God!" she said."Do you know how much this little dress costs?" Without waiting for an answer, she started trying to wiggle out of it.

"Help me, Rose Marie, unzip it, please. And be careful, for God's sake!" I carefully unzipped the dress and watched her step out of it and hang it back on the hanger. The lady came back in, but Mama was already pulling on her own clothes, talking really fast in a high voice, saying, "I'm sorry, yes, it's really very nice, thank you for all your help but I just don't think so; not today, no, not today," and then she was hurrying me out the door.

Later that night, after we came back from the funeral home, Miss Louise brought over one of her old dresses. She and Mama stayed up all night re-making it to fit Mama. Daddy laid out his best suit and went to bed early, even before I did. He let me shine his shoes. When I was done I put them just outside his door. I waited a second, listening for his snoring, but couldn't hear a thing. "Daddy?" I whispered. There was no answer.

Mama let me bring my blanket and pillow into the living room where she and Miss Louise were working. For a long, long time I laid on the couch with my eyes closed, listening to their whispers and the familiar whir of Mama's sewing machine.

Next thing I knew, I was waking up in my own bed feeling sick from the smell of dirt.

It was a rainy morning, hot already; dank. I threw off my sweaty

sheet and sat up and took one look at the navy blue dress with the brass
buttons hanging on the door knob and decided I wasn't going to
Grandpa's funeral.

"Corn flakes?" I said at breakfast, staring down into my bowl of cereal. "Mama, you know I hate corn flakes."

"Don't start with me, Rose Marie. We're out of Cheerios. I haven't
been grocery shopping for a week. Corn flakes won't kill you." She was
talking fast and flying around the kitchen with a cup of coffee in one
hand and a bottle of spray starch in the other.

I groaned. "But you already put milk in it," I said. There is nothing
more sickening than soggy corn flakes.

"I don't have time for this, young lady," she said. "Now listen to me.
I'm going down to iron the hem of my dress. When I get back, I want
you through with breakfast and in the tub. You hear me?"

"Yes, Ma'am," I said.

She flew down to the basement, where the iron was heating up. I
took one more look at the soggy mass in my bowl then dumped it in the
trash.

I was eating my second piece of bread when Mama came up from the
basement. Her dress was draped over her arm, black and luxurious. She
asked me why was I just sitting there and didn't I know we had to be at
the funeral home in one hour?

"Mama," I said slowly, "I don't feel good."

"I don't care if you're on your death bed; get in that tub. NOW."

I didn't move. "I'm not going to the funeral," I said.

Before Mama could answer, Daddy came in. He was buttoning up a
new white shirt; it was so bright white it made me blink. He took one
look at me and stopped. "What's going on here?" he said to Mama.
"Why isn't she dressed?"

"I'm not going," I said again.

"What?" I really don't think he heard me.

Mama gripped the bottle of spray starch. "Stan," she said, "she really
doesn't want to go."

"Of course she's going," Daddy said, buttoning his top button. Then
he turned to me. "He was your grandfather, Rose Marie. You loved
him."

"No, I didn't! I hated him! He was mean!" The horrible words burst
out of my mouth like vomit.

Daddy's hand hit me hard.

"What?" he said, "what did you say?" For days Daddy had been going around like a robot, not hearing, not talking, off in his own robot world; now it was like he came back to life all of a sudden. In one second he was on me, jerking me up into the air by my arms and throwing me at the wall. I felt like a rag doll.

"Stan!" Mama cried.

"Get up," he said, standing over me. He was panting.

I got up.

"I will pretend you never said that. I know you didn't mean it." He kind of crumpled, then. His voice got very quiet. "I know you loved your grandfather," he said, leaning over, "and he loved you; he loved you so very much. I remember the day you were born, how happy and proud he was, how much love. . . . Don't you ever, ever say anything like that again, do you hear me? Do you hear me?"

I just looked at him. I didn't even try to open my mouth. It was like all the words were knocked out of me.

"Now let's get ready and get out of here. We can't be late," he said to Mama. Then he slammed out of the kitchen.

Mama, who'd been kind of crouched by the refrigerator, rushed over to me. She picked me up and hugged me to her and started to cry. I started crying, too.

"Are you hurt, baby?" she said, "I mean, besides your feelings."

I shook my head no.

"Your father didn't mean it, baby. He's just so upset about his Daddy. You shouldn't have said what you did, Rose Marie. It was very cruel. You know your father is upset." She wiped my nose with her hand. "Now it's time to get ready. The funeral is something you have to do. It's something we ALL have to do. It's time you grew up, Rose Marie; time you stopped just thinking of yourself and your own feelings."

Like a robot, I took a bath, got dressed and went with them to the funeral.

When I think of Grandpa Wojack's funeral, it's just a bunch of jumbled-up pictures and sounds and smells. Me and Mama and Daddy holding hands and standing over Grandpa's body for one last look; the awful snap the casket lid made when it was shut; marching behind the coffin up the aisle at Blessed Heart, trying to keep our steps slow and solemn and in time with the deafening GONG, GONG, GONG of the bells; Daddy's square shoulders; the hot, sweet smell of the incense burner as it smoked away during Mass; the shock of the ice cold holy water as the priest sprayed the coffin and everybody else with blessings; the long, slow, quiet drive in the pouring rain behind the black hearse out to the cemetery; the smell of fresh dirt when we got out of the car; the short prayers in the wet grass under the little tent; the deep, muddy hole that looked so small; how when the coffin was being lowered and the priest was saying his last prayer, the wind kicked up and it blew the cold rain sideways into our faces, like one last blessing.

After the cemetery, we all went over to Grandpa Wojack's house for a big party called a wake (short for "wake the dead," Denny said, which I think is really sick). Aunt Bertie and the Sodality ladies had spent the day before the funeral cleaning all the rooms on the first floor, setting out chairs they borrowed from the parish hall and cooking up a ton of food. When we got there, they were waiting for us; they skipped the cemetery part to get everything ready. Right away, Mama put on an apron over her black dress and helped them lay out huge platters of stuffed cabbage and kielbasa and fried chicken, giant bowls of potato salad and sour cream cucumbers, small glass dishes of sweet pickles, sour pickles, pickled beets, pickled onions and fresh ground horseradish, and a long cutting board piled with loaves of black bread. Daddy hauled a whole lot of bottles of vodka from the basement and started filling up paper cups, giving one to each guest as they started pouring through the front door. I got the idea they were going to drink a toast to Grandpa Wojack, like at Christmas. But soon, everybody got really noisy with eating and shouting and laughing, and I think they forgot about it.

There were no kids there except my weird cousin; rather than play with her, I helped in the kitchen. I also carried empty trays from the dining room back to the kitchen to be filled again and picked up all the little crumpled paper cups people kept throwing on the floor. I couldn't believe it; every time they wanted another drink of vodka, they got a new cup.

After a while, I got sleepy. The only place I could think of to lie down, though, was Grandpa's room, and no way would I go in there. Then I saw it had stopped raining. Without anybody noticing, I slipped out the back door.

Right away I felt like something was wrong. I looked around the back yard slowly. That's when I saw him, Daddy sitting on the grass. He was all by himself. He had his tie off and the shirt tails of that bright white shirt out and he was just sitting there with his eyes closed.

Next to him was Grandpa's axe.

Next to him on the other side, lying flat out across the grass, was the plum tree.

It looked a lot taller lying down than when it was growing up straight; its top almost touched the garage door. It'd been chopped off just a foot from the ground.

I stood there watching Daddy for a few minutes. He didn't move. Slowly, soft as a cat, I started walking towards him. My feet made squishy little sucking sounds as they sank into the wet grass. A couple of feet from him, I stopped. The front of his new shirt was all muddy.

He looked up at me. His eyes were tired and red. "I used to spend hours up in this tree when I was your age," he said.

I nodded.

"It was a good climbing tree."

I sat down next to him; the ground was cold and wet and soaked me to the skin. Daddy kept looking at the tree. I bent my head over the grass, combing it slowly with my fingers. No four-leaf clovers here.

Then Daddy wiped his face and reached over, brushing the hair out of my eyes. His hand was wet. "Listen," he said, "you want to work on your golf swing? I think I saw Grandpa's old clubs in the garage."

And that's what they saw, all the people at the house who wandered outside—me and Daddy taking turns hitting a golf ball around the muddy back yard, going in a big circle around the fallen plum tree. When Mama came out, she made everyone else go away. Then she pulled up a lawn chair and sat down to watch us.

❁

THE ARRIVAL
Joyce Kavanaugh

Everything looked the same, yet it was different. Everyone looked the same, but they acted different. She looked different and she acted different too. I didn't feel like myself at all. I wasn't sure who I was I just knew I wasn't me. Everyone was smiling but to me they all looked like their teeth were hurting. My sister and my brother kept shoving me toward my mother but neither my heart or my feet wanted to move so we didn't. Finally breathing one of her "Why me, Lord?" sighs, Susan pushed me straight toward my mother, who in self defense put her hand up to hold me off and ended up shoving her hand into my non-existent, some day soon, I hope not, but probably will be, forming breasts. I did a quick sidestep and landed on my Aunt Lou's foot, full weight, and got shoved off of her too. I was wondering where I would land next when my Uncle George, looking more like a raccoon than a human, planted a kiss, a wet one, somewhere between my eye and my hairline. Things went downhill from there.

Some homecoming, all for my mother's return. I didn't even want to know her nevermind greet her. But here I am trapped, with no escape in sight that I can see. It's all happening too quickly for me. One minute I am living my life the next minute she is back in it. No one wants her here, no one needs her here, she shouldn't be here. Look at Susie she is in her glory the more she has to do the happier she is and with all these nitwits filling our rooms there is plenty to do. She will probably stay busy for months just trying to clean up after these pigs. I can feel people staring at me, but no one is big enough to just come out and give me a dirty look, or even open their mouth and say what they are really thinking. Every time Susan looks at me I see the pleading in her eyes and that is really starting to get to me. Who does she think she is anyway? I do not have to do something just because she thinks I should. She always has to be the boss. Always doing the right thing, well I am not like her. I don't want to be like her either. Goody two shoes bullshit she wouldn't act on impulse it would kill her. That's probably what she would like to do to me kill me. She really hates it when I don't do what she wants she takes it personally very personally and she pays me back triple.

Look at this place it's hard to believe that two days ago I couldn't see the floor for all the junk all over. Now it looks like everything's wrapped in cellophane. Of course if anyone dares to open any of the closets they will be buried alive (that's where we hid most of the stuff we didn't have time to deal with) but of course no one is going into the closets, so we are safe. Sometimes I wish that you could fix up your insides like you can your outside. Life would be a hell of a lot easier. Taking a look around here makes me wonder if appearances aren't everything. To look at them you would think they are all okay but they are my family and I know better, a lot better.

Take Aunt Sandy, for instance, (please take her—no one else can). When you first meet her you think: this woman is smart and fancy because her conversation is mixed with foreign phrases and she speaks like she's on stage—clearly and carefully. After a couple of scotches I doubt that she could tell you her own name and if pushed she would call you any and every name you would rather not be called. Pushed in her book is anything from someone staring at her to not looking directly at her while she is talking. She could make a sailor blush and would consider it an opportunity not to be missed. She loves an audience and creates one wherever she goes. Of course most of them walk away (the smart ones) the others kind of fade out if you know what I mean. Of course that's just my opinion.

Then there's Uncle Jerky-Jack, he has two different color eyes; that is his claim to fame and fortune. He sure doesn't have anything much else going for him. He is not big in the looks department except to give them, much to his wife's disgust and the one he is looking at too. Brain activity 1000, result nil. The man is a moron, in his own words a man "born before his time" and destroying everyone else's. Then there's Aunt Jenna. She is instantly recognizable by the crocheting hook that is wedged between her fingers. I think she must have a hard time wiping, (it must be pretttty dangerous) that is if she has to relieve herself at all. She is no mere mortal according to her. Uncle Stanley, Aunt Alma, Aunt Jaclyn, Aunt Patrice each with their own horn to blow and plenty of air to do it. Alone as well as all together a crew geared for the funny farm, or electric shock therapy at least.

Uh oh, Uncle Ted is staring at me. If I don't move and fast, he is going to walk over to me and I am going to have to listen to duck, bird, and animal sounds for at least fifteen minutes. There must be a way out of this one. Aunt Betty! I'll go by her. All she does is turn her head around and smile a lot. I should be safe enough here. Anything more complicated than hello puts her into a state of panic and she gets these purple rings underneath her arms. My brother says it is because she is of royal blood but I don't believe him. Not just because he lies (which he does all the time) but because as a member of this family I find it hard to believe that there is any royalty here at all, except for royal pains in the you know where and no one has a market on that in this room, it's all up for grabs (no pun intended).

So, there must be someone else in here to examine, someone besides my mother. I still don't want to look at her. I can't. Where's Susan? There, standing next to my brother, the two of them beaming at me as if they have won the Irish Sweepstakes and they each own half the ticket. Some prize, having her back in our lives. It's a booby prize if you ask me but then no one is asking me. They only tell me they don't ask me. If I have heard it once I have heard it a thousand times. "Go hug your mother, she missed you terribly." "She looks great, go tell her how pretty she is." "I'm sure she'd like to know how much you missed her, go tell her." "You are her baby, the one she missed the most. Give her a hug." "Not just anyone could go through all she has, and look so good." "She is so strong, you must be proud of her." "You are lucky to have her for a mother, she is very special." "It won't be easy for her she has been gone a long time, try and be as good as you can be. You're a big girl now. Make sure you help out."

Lord help us. Who's done who wrong here? Certainly not me. She was one who got sick. She was the one who left. She was the one who stayed away for so long. She was the one who didn't call, didn't write, didn't visit, who just stopped being around. Not me. I didn't leave her. She left me. She left us. All of us. Tuberculosis or no tuberculosis, the villain here is her not me, not us. She is the mother, she is the one who is supposed to take care of us and she didn't do it.

Dumbass party, stupid homecoming, a lousy welcome that's what she deserves. Who ever asked her to come back? Not me. I don't care how happy they are, any of them. Even the two beauties. We were all right without her, we were fine. I am not happy and nothing they can say or do will make me feel that way. As far as I am concerned she can go back where she came from. We don't need her we got along just fine. She is the one who needs us. They are the ones who want her, I don't. Not now not ever.

Oh no! I should have watched my flanks—here goes everything. My mother next to me. Putting her hand on my arm, turning me toward her, looking me straight in the eye. She's hugging me. I am caught, I am held. I know her smell, I know her feel, I remember her, I love her, I miss her, I need her. Mommy, good grief, now I'm crying, no worse, I'm sobbing, just like a big skinny, dopey baby. And I might never stop it all feels so good.

Footnotes

[1] Ken Macrorie, *Telling Writing*, 4th ed. Portsmouth, N.H.: Boynton Cook Publishers, p.5.

About Writing "the Arrival"

As a child, I experienced the scene you have just read. I wrote about it in retrospect, as both participant and observer. Being the writer allowed me that privilege. Writing, for me, has several challenges which, when I'm successful, become advantages. The barriers of self-consciousness, anxiety, and fear of chaos are broken. Playing the creator frees me from the weight of remaining who I am, and encourages me to integrate how I felt with what I know, and with what is. Writing provides an environment in which words on a page lead to inventing images in my mind and exhuming responses I've buried. Intuition plays a part in how I write, what I write, and when I write by guiding me to a place, or a feeling, evoking a memory, and producing an awareness in me that was unknown before.

Intuition guides me to the "truth" that Ken Macrorie in *Telling Writing* talks about as being an important part of good writing: ". . . truth: not the *truth* (whoever knows surely what that is?) but some kind of truth—a connection between the things written about, the words used in writing, and the author's real experience in the world he knows well— whether in fact, dream or imagination."[1] Intuition not only helps me to find that truth, but it helps me deal with its complexities. Allowing a broad view of the paradoxes that exist with no room for doubt, the ambiguities that are in endless conflict, the emotions that threaten to overwhelm and devour, intuition is the overseer. It creates ways in which absolutes can coexist with possibilities, conflicts with resolution, and opposites can marry and produce change. The child who lived the experience exists in the woman who writes it, yet the writing is the melding of the past with the present that evolves into the future. In that sense both the child and the woman are parented by an uncontrolled force.

BEST FRIENDS
Laura Whiting

Cassie stood staring out of her bedroom window. She had a blank expression in her green eyes. Snow was falling in thick, white sheets. It was quickly gathering, sticking to whatever it touched. But Cassie saw none of this. On impulse she thrust the window open, allowing a blast of wind and snow into her room. She shivered and shut the window.

Cassie turned and walked out of her room. She turned the corner and walked down the steps. "Mom?" she called. She waited a minute, then called her again. No answer. Cassie sighed. Where is she? she thought, baffled. She walked into the kitchen and made a cup of hot cocoa. When it was finished, she went to the phone.

She dialed her best friend Sara's number and waited for her to answer.

"Hello?" Sara said two rings later.

"Hi, Sari, it's me, Cassie." Cassie smiled. She and Sara had nicknames for each other that they had used since they were six. Now, ten years later, they used the same names, never growing tired of them.

"Oh, hi, Cassie," Sara replied reluctantly.

Cassie was surprised. Sara never called her Cassie. Just as she never called her Sara. She began to feel uncomfortable. It sounded as if Sara didn't want to talk to her. "How are you?" she asked in a nervous voice.

"Um, I'm okay." Sara paused for a minute, then continued. "So I guess you're home," Sara said awkwardly.

Cassie frowned. "Yeah, uh, what are you doing?" She didn't like how this conversation was going.

"Oh, not much. I guess your mom's not there," Sara answered.

Cassie was shocked. She hadn't said anything about her mom's disappearance. She was about to ask her something when Sara continued, "I have to hang up now." Then, without even saying goodbye, she hung up.

Cassie was left listening to the dial tone. Her heart ached. Why had Sara been so cold? She searched her mind, looking for something, anything, that she might have done to make Sara act like that. Nothing.

Tears started to fill her eyes. Then she picked up the receiver and called her boyfriend. He answered immediately. Maybe Sara talked to Scott, she thought.

"Hi," he said, waiting for a response.

"Scott, hi. I was just talking to Sara and she was acting real strange. I was wondering if you had talked to her."

There was an unusual silence on the other end of the line. "Cassie?" he finally said in a quiet voice.

"Yes, is something wrong?" Cassie's eyes were wide with fear and her tears threatened to fall.

"I can't talk right now." Scott sounded hurried. He hung up the phone almost as fast as Sara had.

Cassie let out a low sob. She covered her face with her hands and fell to the floor. "Mom!" she cried. "Where are you?" Cassie cried until she was exhausted. Still lying on the hall floor, she drifted off to sleep.

When she awoke, the sun was setting, leaving gold and red light flooding through the window. She slowly stood up and stretched. Cassie walked to her mother's room. For the second time that day, tears filled her eyes. Suddenly, it all made sense. Her friends' hastiness to hang up the phone. Her mother's strange disappearance.

Her mother's room was empty. Nothing but the furniture remained. There was a note on the dresser. It read: "Dear Cassie, You deserve more than a mother that's never around. You would be better off living with your aunt. But because I can't bear living without you, I've decided to kill myself."

Cassie gasped and couldn't finish the letter. Her tears fell freely, forming puddles on the carpet. She couldn't believe her mother would kill herself. For the first time in her life, Cassie felt truly alone.

"Scott, I don't think she knows yet. What are we going to do?" Sara was frantic. She hadn't gotten the news of Cassie's mom's death yet, but she had her own problems to sort out.

"I don't think she *has* to know. I mean, we'll keep it quiet for a while, after I break up with her and give her time to heal. Then it'll seem like a decent thing we're doing." Scott tried to reassure Sara that they could continue their romance in secrecy. "Just don't act so nervous all the time."

"But I've betrayed her," she wailed, desperate for Scott's promise that what they were doing was right. None came. "Scott, I—I don't think we should see each other." Scott opened his mouth to speak when Sara put in, "Ever."

Silence. She waited for him to say something. She heard him sigh. "Okay. I don't really understand your decision, but if that's what you want. . ." His voice trailed off. He sat waiting for her response.

"I," she sighed. "Oh, Scott." It came out as a whisper. "I have to call Cassie. Goodbye," she said quietly. Sara sat there for a moment, then picked up the phone.

Cassie's eyes were red and swollen from crying. What will I do? she thought. The phone rang, interrupting her concentration. She cleared her throat and answered it. "Hello?" Her voice still came out sounding hoarse and scratchy.

Sara felt extremely guilty for the way she had acted. If only she could put her feelings to words. "Cass? It's Sara. I'm really sorry about how I treated you earlier. Will you forgive me?"

A wave of relief flooded over Cassie. "Oh, Sari! My mother. . ." Her voice cut off. Tears ran down her cheeks.

"What about your mother?" Sara asked, concern filling her voice.

"She—she's committed suicide! Oh, Sari, what will I do?" Cassie began to sob, and she tried to wipe away her tears.

Sara sat in shock. Cassie's mother had always been gone a lot, but she wasn't expecting this. "Oh, Cass," she said, finding her voice. But she didn't know what to say: *You're sixteen; so what that your mother killed herself and your father lives all the way across the country; it's no reason to be upset?* She sighed. "You should call your father."

"My mother left a note. It said I'd be better off with my aunt." Cassie stared out the window. The snow had stopped and was lying in a thick coat on the ground.

"Your mother hated your father. Of course she'd rather you live with your aunt. But she's seventy years old. She can't raise a teenager. I really think you should call him." Sara waited for her friend's reply.

Cassie thought it over. "All right. But will you come over?" Sara lived only three blocks away.

"All right. I'll leave now. Bye, Cass."

"Goodbye, Sari. See you soon." Cassie hung up the phone and smiled. It felt good to be able to rely on someone.

Sara walked to Cassie's house, her boots crunching in the snow. Her breath formed white puffs in front of her. She observed the houses she passed. They didn't appear too different from her neighborhood's houses.

Yet there was a strange calmness. It seemed as though it was a totally different world from her constantly active neighborhood. Finally, she reached Cassie's house. She felt a pang of sorrow for her friend. If only her mother had just gone out, as she frequently did. She always came back. Sara sighed and knocked on Cassie's door.

Cassie rushed to open it and smiled warmly when she saw Sara standing there. "Oh, Sara," she whispered and hugged her friend.

A tear ran down Sara's cheek. "I know," she said quietly. "Now let's go call your father."

They walked to the phone. Cassie slowly picked it up and dialed her father's number in Baltimore. She held her breath, waiting for him to answer. "Hello."

"Cassie, is that you?" Her father's voice sounded distant and unclear.

"Daddy, are you sitting down?" Cassie explained the situation while her father sat listening. Finally she said, "I'm really sorry, Daddy, I really don't want to live with Aunt Grace. I know you're really busy but. . ."

Her father cut her off. "Cassie, I'm never too busy for you. You're my daughter and I love you; don't ever forget that. I'd love it if you came to live with me."

Cassie was overjoyed. She talked with her father about travel arrangements for a few minutes, then hung up. She turned to her friend smiling, but her smile began to fade when she saw the sad look on Sara's face.

"Promise you'll write?" Sara said before she burst into tears.

"Sara," she whispered, "don't cry, please. I'm sorry, but I have to go." Cassie looked at Sara hopefully.

Sara managed a weak smile. "I know. You're my best friend and I'll miss you."

A week later, Sara watched sadly as Cassie boarded the plane that would take her away from her friends, her school, Nevada and her life there.

Sara's tears mixed with the heavy rain that was falling. As the plane took off, Sara knew that she was facing a new life, without Cassie.

Author's Note: Although Cassie moved away, Sara's life will still continue. Stay tuned for the adventures of Sara and her new-found friend, Anna.

❀

WANDERING HEART
Kate Lipper

That morning was like any other morning Gwyn had ever awakened to, though it was different. She knew it was different as soon as her eyes opened; she could feel it in the warmth of the sun's rays and how they fell into her home. She didn't actually know what was different, just that something was. She didn't even dwell on the subject, just accepted the fact and went about her regular routine.

After rising from her bed, she made her way across the room to light her beeswax candle. Then she changed into the sailor's shirt and pants that she had worn yesterday and every day before that.

She thrust a blue bandanna under and over her long wavy red hair, with an exasperated sigh at its color. Then she put a lone polished apple and a small jug of cider into a cloth sack and left.

Her path ran beside the cobblestone beaches toward the inn, a half mile away, where she worked. The land between was one full of solitude with several small cottages hidden behind sprouts of maple, oak and evergreen, mostly evergreen, which flourished all over the small island. These cottages were still dark and quiet with no signs of life except an occasional cat stretching.

But Gwyn did not notice these things as she walked quickly toward her destination. She was too intent on reaching it. Starting work early meant finishing quickly; that meant she would not have to walk home in the dark.

Before the coming of the old beggar woman, the walk home hadn't bothered her. Now, it did. The woman had first appeared several days ago on the road. Another beggar would not have bothered Gwyn; this one did. Gwyn understood why the woman bothered her. She realized that the woman KNEW. And the fact that someone else KNEW scared Gwyn. What might someone do with such knowledge?

No one had ever KNOWN before, except of course Gwyn herself.

But she had kept it concealed carefully, always wondering what some-one would think or do if she told them. The thought had scared her at first, but as the years passed, it had become only a vague presence, for-gotten. With the coming of the woman, everything changed. Now some-one else knew everything as well, and the only way, Gwyn thought, the woman could know was if she had IT too.

It had become one of Gwyn's most crucial goals to avoid the woman. If Gwyn walked home when it was light, there was no need to worry about a chance meeting. So Gwyn had been leaving her cottage earlier than in the past, for the innkeeper was a hard-to-please man and wouldn't think kindly if she did not do her share.

If you were to ask some of the village people about Gwyn, they would merely have smiled and left it at that. It was not that Gwyn was just a smile, but that they simply couldn't explain her. They had tried like many people will but failed. She was like a flower; one might get close to its beauty but not understand it.

As she neared the docks and sailors, her pace slowed a bit; the short journey was over. She scanned the faces, looking for her father, but could not find him. Normally he would be up and about his ship, but today the *Periwinkle* floated idly on the water.

Surely her father was all right? He had been fine yesterday, she reas-sured herself. Nothing could be wrong.

Gwyn had left her father's house several years before, which was quite young for a girl to leave her birth house. That had been when she first learned she possessed IT. Living alone, far from the village would be easier. However, her love for him was very strong.

"Pat!" Gwyn recognized the face of her father's young friend.

"Do you know where Da is? Surely he should be up and about."

"He's gone over to Abling for supplies on the ferry like he does each year. Didn't he tell you?"

"Oh!" Of course he had; just the day before yesterday he had asked her if there was anything she might need. Slightly angered with herself, she realized there was never need to worry about him.

"How you today, Gwyn?" Pat smiled warmly at her. "You're as beautiful as ever."

Gwyn blushed. "I'm fine, Patrick, and you're as blunt as ever. Haven't you better things to do than tease a girl?"

"I'm not teasing, Gwyn," Pat said seriously as he came to stand beside her. "You know I mean to have you as my wife one day."

Gwyn felt trapped; of course she had known Pat was interested in her but not this much.

"Just as soon as I have enough money, I'll ask. I'd best be getting back to work," Pat continued.

She watched him go, tall and strong. He was a few years her senior and had always been nice to her. Now their relationship seemed different. Gwyn was unsure how she felt about this change.

Gwyn continued along the beach path, already able to see the chimney of the inn through the trees. All across the island of Mermidon people were waking to begin the day. Mermidon was a bit different from the other islands, which were modern and busy.

The history of the island was known by all, taught to children from the time they were young until they were ready to leave their parents' houses. Mermidon, Abling, Chasire and Darnite were the four islands in the kingdom which had been ruled by the Montgomery family since the beginning of the kingdom. The family had been good to the islands, allowing them to flourish with low taxes and fair governing. The islands had been created by Mertholimule, the ancient wizard, as a place for life to prosper and grow for centuries. And it had. There had been no wars, only a few battles, and the only harm known to the people of the islands was the burden of life.

On each of the new islands, Mertholimule placed four different groups of people. Each was different from the others. The people of Darnite were large, solid people who fit well in their conditions that produced long, cold winters. The Chasire people were believed to have been elves; they were quite small and had elfin features. However as the years wore on they began to resemble humans more than elves, though even today they are a bit smaller than humans and have ears with pointed tips. Those from Abling were known for their brains and their dark eyes and hair. The Mermidon people were known as sailor people, able to navigate the waters better than anyone else. Today, these qualities had merged so that all the people were closer in appearances than they had been in the beginning.

The Montgomery family had come from Abling, the largest of the islands, where the palace was built; they lived in Trintian, the largest city. They had been chosen by Mertholimule to rule the lands because their ties with each island ran deep. No one opposed the rulers, and so the Montgomery family had been royalty since.

Mermidon was second to the smallest island, Darnite being half the size of Abling. There were only two villages which were placed on its shores: Satcorn, on the western banks, and Peascon, on the eastern shore where Gwyn worked. Peascon offered ferries to Abling, which was southeast of Mermidon. Satcorn had ferries to Chasire, in the west, and Darnite, in the north. There were several small communities scattered in Mermidon's boundaries, but none was any different from the others. Most families worked as sailors, as the people always had. Families passed down the heritage from one generation to the next. That was the way of life.

Upon entering the inn, Gwyn was immediately attacked by the innkeeper to begin work. It wasn't a highlight of Gwyn's life, but she would not always work at the inn, knowing that eventually a better job would come her way. Every woman had begun with a small, menial job and had worked up. Gwyn had worked in the inn a little over a year and had already been offered several other occupations, which she had turned down, knowing that an even better choice would come.

After several hours of work, Gwyn took her first break to go outside with Rachel and Martha, her two friends. The three of them worked at the inn. Martha was the oldest and Rachel the youngest, but no one was so much older or younger that it mattered. Martha would soon leave the inn for a teaching job in Robinside, a small community several miles away, and her presence would be greatly missed. The three talked for several minutes about this and that.

Then it was time to begin work again, work which they all despised.

Before lunch a guest came to the inn, causing many an eye to be raised. To begin with, a woman hardly ever traveled alone or had enough money to spend at an inn. Women traveling usually stayed with relatives. The woman wore a long, blue dress, and a black shawl covered her hair. Her face would always be beautiful; a face which grew even prettier as it aged. The woman gave no name and merely asked for a room that was warm. Gwyn was called to take the woman's bag up and show her where the room was.

Gwyn led the woman to the room on the second floor, set out the pitcher of water, made a fire and was about to leave.

"What is your name, girl?" The woman's voice was like music, silvery and light.

"Gwyn." She turned to go again.

"Gwyn is a magical name, is it not? I once knew someone named Gwyn." She smiled. "How long have you been working here, Gwyn?"

"About a year," Gwyn replied. She tried to say only what was necessary to say while being as polite as she could. The woman was rude to ask her such questions.

"How old are you, Gwyn?"

"Seventeen."

"Do you live near here?"

This was more than Gwyn could take, and she was about to say so when the stranger cut her off.

"I am in need of a young woman, about your age, to accompany me in my travels. I am, you see, a historian and travel the islands. But the years are passing, and so I am in need of help. I would ask of you to consider this job and perhaps have the answer in a few days' time. What time do you get off work here?"

"Five-thirty," Gwyn answered. So this was why she had known the day would be different! A thousand thoughts ran through her mind like a strong river. This stranger had offered her a job without even knowing her! To be an apprentice to a traveling historian was a job one only dreamed of being offered.

"Meet with me at five-forty-five for supper in the tavern. We shall discuss the job, and I will try to persuade you to take it. Now you must go. Until supper!"

At lunch Gwyn went down to the docks to watch the happenings.

Sailors shouting, gulls screaming, waves splashing—all was normal. The ferry had come back, and Greg McDowell was out in the *Periwinkle* working, but upon seeing his daughter, he came ashore.

"Hello, Gwyn, and how are you today? Still working at the inn, I see."

"Hello, Da. You went to Abling, didn't you?" While eating her apple, Gwyn sat waiting for the tale she knew was to come.

"Yes, and was it busy! So many people, one could get lost even if he lived there. Trintian has grown. I got you something." Greg McDowell's eyes twinkled, and his wizened face smiled brightly. He produced a small package wrapped in plain blue paper. "Found these in a shop, I did. They'll fit you nicely."

Gwyn quickly opened the package, girlish delight flooding through her. Inside were two combs of pearly white, made of shell. "Oh, Da. . . they're beautiful! I can't possibly wear them now though. Tomorrow! I'll wear them tomorrow." She reached over and kissed her father's brown cheek.

"Your mother wore combs every day, pulled her long red hair back with them." His eyes had a far-off look. "I received another letter from her, this one postmarked from some village in Chasire.

"She could never settle down, your mother. You know she looked so much like you. From Satcorn she was, met her on a ferry to Trintian. Oh, how I wish she'd come home; I still miss her, and it's been years. I always will. Well," he said with a strained brightness, "I must be getting back to work."

Finally five o'clock came; Gwyn began to ready herself for the dinner meeting. Rachel and Martha were leaving and wished her luck with the job. She finger-brushed her hair and put the new combs in it. Then she went into the tavern and waited.

After several minutes the woman appeared. The shawl still covered her hair. Gwyn guessed that it was full of tangles, and the woman did not want anyone to see it. They sat down in a corner, away from the smokers and drinkers.

"To begin with, my offer for a job is but part-time. Half the year you would spend traveling with me; the other half you may do with as you please. You are welcome to spend time here at your home or to live with me in Chasire, where I own a small cottage. You will, however, be paid full-time. I don't expect a woman of your age to wish to be away from home all the time, not with such matters as marriage ahead of you. You would travel with me to the four islands, doing such things as writing for me my notes, arranging all sorts of meetings and appointments, and so on. Let me assure you this job is a very interesting one, full of surprises."

The food came then. "Do you have any questions?" She smiled kindly at Gwyn.

"Yes." Gwyn said wiping her mouth with a napkin she was sure she had pressed. "What would you pay me?"

The woman, at this point, could have offered Gwyn a tiny price, and Gwyn would have taken it. She had always wanted to travel and now she had the chance.

"I am willing to pay you up to three hundred marks a week, considering you do all your work well and efficiently. During the time when you are not traveling with me, I will pay you one hundred marks a week. Is that all right with you, Gwyn?" The woman looked closely at her, and she had to try very hard not to laugh with joy.

Three hundred marks!!! Why, that was more than twice the amount she made in a month at the inn.

"That suits me well." Gwyn placed her words carefully.

"Good. I will be here several more days. If you could tell me in a day or two whether or not you want the job. . ."

"I can. I need to be going home now; there are some things I need to get done before I go to sleep. Thank you for dinner." Gwyn stood up and put on her coat.

"I enjoyed your company very much, Gwyn, and look forward to talking with you tomorrow. I, too, need to get ready for bed. Good night." The woman stood up and then looked sharply at Gwyn. "Oh! Will you be all right going home? It is quite dark outside."

Fear rippled through her. The beggar woman! How could she have forgotten? It was dark outside, and she would be there, waiting. Waiting for me, thought Gwyn. Then her fear was replaced with strained reassurance; possibly the woman wouldn't be there. After all, Gwyn hadn't seen her in a week. Everything would be fine.

"I'll be fine. There's no need to worry," Gwyn tried to smile. "Thank you for your concern, but I've walked the route day after day. You forget that this is Mermidon."

"Very well then. I shall see you tomorrow." The woman walked out of the tavern, in the direction of her room. Gwyn left.

The docks were quiet now, with only a handful of sailors sitting around smoking. One of them waved in recognition to Gwyn, then returned to the conversation. Soon the town was behind her.

The night was still, with a clear black sky and a bright moon which made it easy to see without the aid of a lantern. Still she was very much afraid that the woman would appear on the path in front of her, forcing a confrontation. But this did not happen. She arrived home without a meeting, sure the beggar was gone and would not be back. It meant that a huge dilemma was over, that no one threatened to reveal what Gwyn had hidden for so long.

Back in her tiny cottage, Gwyn set about packing the things she wished to take. She chose a box that was large enough to hold many things but was small enough to be easily carried. In this she placed two changes of clothes. One set was identical to the one she was wearing, the other, a plain blue dress. She also put in some books and a map of the kingdom. That done, she began reading in a book about the kingdom, its history and the lands. She sat up many hours reading all that she could before she finally blew out the candle and fell asleep.

In the morning she met briefly with the woman and told her that she would take the job. She was told to be ready to leave in five days' time, that they would be catching a ferry to Salcorn and then to Darnite. The woman wished to travel to the ruins of an old manor house in which a magician had lived.

She gave notice to the innkeeper, who merely nodded; workers were not hard to find, and some girl would take the place of this one. Then she told Rachel and Martha of her plans.

"So soon! My, you are the luckiest thing in the world; how I envy you!" Martha laughed gaily. Gwyn knew, as did everyone else, that Martha hated traveling. "I'll be leaving for Robinside next month, so we'll all be apart. How I'll miss you both, though I can't say the same for my job. We'll keep in touch; I promise."

"I'll be left all alone working at this miserable place," Rachel mumbled glumly. "You two have all the good luck."

"Good luck will come to you." Gwyn sympathized with her friend. No doubt, she had several more months of work here before a new job would be offered. "You'll get one soon enough."

At lunch she went down to the docks. She knew that she had to tell her father about the new job and the trip. Yet something deep inside of her did not want to tell him; it would hurt him, she knew, that his daughter had become a traveler just like the wife he had lost. He wouldn't stop her from going, but he would not understand.

However, instead of seeing Greg McDowell first, she saw Pat.

Gwyn had thought about Pat these two days, despite all that had happened. She had finally come to the decision that she didn't feel for Pat what he did for her. However, she had also resolved that, given time, she might. After all, Pat had been her closest male friend during the past few years; he possibly knew more about her than anyone else. He had not learned from her words alone but from the all the times they spent alone. It was Pat who introduced her to poetry, something she had never been interested in before; it was with him that she took long evening walks. And so she knew that there was a good chance that she could come to love him.

"You have been offered a job." He studied at her a moment, then looked away. "A traveling job, one that will take you all over. Perhaps I should feel glad for you, but what will happen to me when you leave? What am I to do?"

"How do you know already? I've told hardly no one and yet you do."

"Rachel told me and several others of the job you had been offered. So it's true then. You are going."

"Yes, but it is only a part-time job. I shall be leaving in a few days but will be returning at the end of the week. Does Father know of the job?" She was afraid that he did, that she would not be the first to tell him.

"I don't think so. He was on the boat when Rachel came. No one's told him; I've been the only one out with him, and I figured you would want to tell him yourself. A week isn't too long; you promise me you will be back? I have heard how your mother broke your father's heart. I don't want you to break mine."

"I'm not going to. Pat, I don't love you, but give me some time. Then we'll see. I've got to talk with Father now." She had seen her father coming nearer. "I'll talk with you before I go."

The father and his daughter chatted about nothing for several minutes. It was Gwyn who monopolized this conversation, leading it slowly toward where she wanted it to go. Finally she let it out.

"I've been offered a job; this one I've taken. Da, it's a traveling job; I shall be the apprentice to a historian. I know it's not the one you would like me to have, but the pay is good and it's only part-time." Gwyn waited, looking at her father's face intently.

"So, it's happened; I feared it would. Someday, Greg McDowell, I told myself, your daughter is going to start to travel; someday she'll be just like her mother. It must run in the blood, I suppose. The cycle has begun again.

"When I first met your mother, friends who knew her advised me to let her be. Already she was a spunky character and loved to move about; I thought she was just full of life and would settle down once we were married. But there was nothing that could stop Marian, not even me. You know your grandmother was a traveler and her mother was too. It's just like the McDowell men and sailing.

"You see, I don't mind the job; it's just that you're becoming like Marian, and I don't want to lose you too. You know, there's no reason why you must be like her, and if you don't like traveling, then come home. Well, Gwyn, you've made your decision; I must be getting back to work."

The man headed back to his boat, leaving Gwyn speechless. She had thought that it would be her father who would be uncertain; instead it was her. Was it true? Had she no control over her life? Must she travel because of her blood? So many questions ran through Gwyn's mind. Unsure and worried, Gwyn headed back to the inn.

Gwyn had decided to work late the next few days, so that she might have enough money to buy some cloth. With the cloth she could sew herself one more set of clothes for her trip. She had realized that the two sets she had were old and worn.

In the evening Gwyn visited with the woman one more time, just to run over any last details. They would leave Peascon early in the day and travel by wagon to Satcorn. From there, ferry tickets would be purchased. They would spend the night in an inn and leave for Darnite the following morning. The lady also inquired about why Gwyn was at the inn so late. Gwyn explained, a bit embarrassed, but the woman seemed lost in thought and did not really hear her.

As Gwyn left to continue with her work, the lady stopped her, reached into a bag, and found some money which she gave to Gwyn so that she might be able to get cloth.

"It is not good for a young woman to be out so late at night," the woman said. "Whether or not Mermidon is safe, one must get sleep. Take this and get the cloth you need. You can pay me back later with the money you earn."

It seemed to Gwyn that the woman did not care if the money was returned to her or not. This woman, who still had not offered her name, was so kind to Gwyn that she could not help but feel kindly toward the woman.

It was close to ten o'clock when Gwyn left the inn. The night was still, and there was hardly anyone at the dock, just a few sailors who were drinking. The air had a chill to it, but Gwyn was fine, wearing her old wool coat. She could see easily by the moon's bright light. Gwyn walked on towards her home.

She was half-way there, in the middle of nowhere, when suddenly she was aware of someone approaching her from the other direction. Her blood ran cold as she realized who the person was, the beggar woman. The old beggar was shuffling towards her, smiling crookedly. She was not pretty to look at, and Gwyn would have preferred to look away except that her eyes were locked with the woman's. When they were a few feet away from each other, the two stopped. Slowly the woman pointed a gnarled finger at Gwyn.

"You." The woman laughed, a wicked laugh. "You are in trouble. I KNOW. I KNOW all about you. You are in trouble."

"Leave me alone," Gwyn choked out. "Just go away. I don't want to talk to you."

"You are like me; you will one day look like me. Won't that be nice?" The woman cocked her eye at Gwyn, daring the girl to look away; she did not.

"You are afraid of me and what I am about; I can see it in your eyes. Don't you know why we have IT, don't you? We are demons, placed on this earth to do our craft. We are evil; only evil people have it. You are evil." Gwyn shook her head vehemently.

"Yes! That is what we are; you have no choice. You were a mistake, child, not meant to be. The history tells it so; any child that is a mistake will bring wrong to the land. Your parents did not want you. You are a demon," the woman spat out. "You have no choice in the matter. I know all about you, I do. Why do you think your mother left? It was because of you."

"I-I won't lis-listen to you. I shall not be-believe you," Gwyn was crying now.

"You will listen to me, and when I am finished, you will believe me. Your mother, Marian McDowell, never wanted a child; she did not want you. When you were born, you were a surprise. At first she pretended that she wanted you; such was not the case. Finally the strain of you drove her away. You were a mistake! Because of all this, you got IT; you have the gift right now. You must come with me; I will teach you how to use it. Let us go now!"

"I don't, I don't ha-have anything, nothing."

"YOU HAVE THE MAGIC OF THE DEMONS!!" the woman screamed.

"No!"

"NO!" Gwyn and the beggar turned to see where the voice had come from. "She is no demon. Leave her be, Medra; leave her be."

There in the moonlight stood Gwyn's employer wrapped in a blue cloak which waved in the breeze. The determination in her voice made Gwyn feel somehow safer. She glanced at Gwyn and smiled reassuringly. All would be fine now that the woman had come. The beggar seemed to shrink back away from the other. There was fear in her eyes, as well as hatred.

"Go away, you-you witch!" the beggar woman spat out.

"Don't reprimand me, Medra. I'm here because I wish to be, and there is nothing you can do about it." Gwyn's employer spoke with firmness. "You know that my magic is greater. Leave the girl be."

"How dare you come here, Marian? You've ruined everything. You too are a devil. You too—" But the beggar broke off as the woman stepped forward into the moonlight, her long grey-red hair streaming down her shoulders. Then the beggar woman was gone.

Gwyn stood in the night calming down. She had been frightened and was horrified thinking about what would have happened. What had the beggar called her? Oh yes, Marian. Marian? Marian. . . . .

"Mother!" sobbed Gwyn as she ran into the woman's arms. It was like coming home to a home she had never, yet always, known.

❀

THE ROCKPEOPLE
(from *GIFTS*)
Janet Calico

Chapter One

When the squeezing of her belly began, Sarra was proud they let her come to Centerfire. Although it hurt terribly, she felt safe among the others. The fire burned bright and warm, and Rue was by her side with weedbroth to dull the pains. But when the baby was born, she regretted not staying near the edges of the cave—for the others saw the infant and wanted to throw it in the fire, like they did those with the wasting sickness. This was the first baby born alive in many seasons, the first baby not grossly misshapen, and Sarra was going to keep it.

"Don't hurt, mustn't burn! It's my baby!"

Sarra bit Rommy when he tried to take the baby. She screamed and hit, and struck Fitch with a burning stick from the fire. She huddled over the baby, covering it in creeperskins and holding it close to her breast, letting no one but her mother Rue come near. And the others, following Jobo's lead, backed off. Rue was Weedwoman. No one wished to offend her. Sarra sang the baby a song of a distant time and nursed it. Her breasts would make plenty of milk. She would love this baby and keep it with her always. And because Rue was there, the others left Sarra alone.

Sarra called the baby Em, and she grew. Covered in old skins she wasn't noticeable among the people, some without hair, some with bright red flaky skin, no noses. She fit in. Following Em, Sarra had other children. Nexxie was squat and broad-faced and couldn't think well. Mella had no fingers, which was worse. But Sarra and Rue fought for each child and would not allow Jobo to put any of Sarra's children on the fire. People forgot and praised Em for her tufts of hair and long and perfect arms, her legs that carried her about on errands, her pleasing face. Covered in creeperskins, the fleshy additions on her shoulder blades were not noticeable.

But as Em grew, so did the projections, as if they wanted to fan out from her shoulders. Sarra bound them flat with strips of creeperhide. In the darkness of Maincave, away from the fire, she felt the pale skin of the folds. It worried her. Something was growing within, not bone but like the solid part of her own nose or ear, and this something was stiffening and extending the flaps.

There came a time during Weedbloom when Em began to grow breasts, and the bindings felt too tight. Loosening them for comfort, she couldn't re-tie the skins herself, and Sarra was not there. Someone saw.

On the beach Sarra could hear Jobo hollering, and she ran, hearing Em cry out, but was not fast enough, big-bellied as she was. Jobo had torn Em's covering from her: the additions leapt up in an arc above her head and hung down her back where she crouched. They were bigger than Sarra had thought, almost covering Em's body, but they offered no protection from the blows the people gave. Conn held Sarra back and beat her when she tried to reach her daughter. The loss of fingers, legs, noses could be tolerated. But an addition was new and horrifying. They said such a person was not human. Em wasn't the girl they had known but a thing foreign, a thing strange, a thing to be put on the fire.

But Rue had died, and Sarra had her power. She shouted, "If you burn this child, I'll gather no more weeds! Let her go!"

Jobo looked at Sarra closely. They needed the weeds Sarra found; no one else understood their uses. "We won't burn this one," he said, and stepped back from Em. "But she can't live here among people."

They wouldn't let Sarra give Em food or wash the blood from her body; they certainly wouldn't let Sarra go with her. So she stayed with Nexxie and Mella and was the Weedwoman of the Rockpeople like her mother Rue, and before her Dina, who had learned from Cara, who'd been taught by Vonda. And like these women, Sarra found yet more weeds of healing and would teach one of her daughters. Sarra tried to forget Em, dying alone and afraid.

*   *   *

Em lived off in the forest on whatever she could find. Misery and loneliness filled her, but she dared not return, knowing she would be cast into the fire. She scavenged unfamiliar forest foods, longing for lumpyshells and smoothshells, for sandscuttlers. Instead, she stuffed herself with redgrass and greycaps when she found them and other times went hungry. Her arms and legs lost their nice roundness, and her bones jutted out from her skin.

Sometimes she felt she was losing herself. As she pulled bladeroot, the green stems and pale roots would suddenly blur and dim; she would begin to sob uncontrollably. Tired and listless much of the time, Em had to force herself to gather food. She had built herself a nest, taking downed branches and jamming them into the limbs of a longtree, covering the whole with sandreeds plastered with mud to keep them from blowing down. She formed a little cup shape to sleep in, and it looked like the sloppy nest of a spottyscolder. But it was still difficult to sleep. She could hear largecreepers padding in the darkness beneath her nest. She needed fire.

Em searched for many suns before she found a large flatshell wider than her two hands. She returned to the caves, slipping silently through the trees, to steal burning embers when most of the people would be in the fields tending the grain. From the edge of the trees she could see only the woman Loo, watching over a few small children.

Em wanted to turn back to the safety of the trees, but she knew fire would make her life easier. She had to get it. She stepped forward. Loo looked at Em and then looked away, but the children watched her wide-eyed.

Holding out her flatshell, Em said, "I've come for fire."

Loo acted as if Em weren't there, lowering her eyes to where her hands scraped a runnerhide.

"Loo, it's me, Em. I need fire."

The woman kept scraping and didn't look up, but one of the babies toddled over towards Em, smiling, with arms outstretched. "Marka, come back. No one is there."

The baby stopped, turning from Em to Loo.

Loo continued, "No one's there, so how can I stop no one from getting fire or using a pot beside the fire to take dried runner that hangs in the tree beyond? We've been lucky, and Dunn has killed a runner, so we have lots of meat. More than any can keep track of."

Gratefully, Em squatted to scoop embers into her flatshell and then filled the pot with strips of the dried meat. Loo addressed the toddler again. "I'll remember to tell Sarra I saw her child in my sleep, and she is fine." Loo did not look up from her scraping and did not see Em's smile as the girl slipped in among the trees to work her way back down the beach.

Now Em slept in the base of a tree uprooted in a storm and forming an earth hollow, her fire keeping the largecreepers at bay. She enlarged the hollow, stuffing sandreed among the exposed roots to hold dirt from trickling down on her, and layered the floor with yet more sandreed. She carried broken limbs and leaned them across the front of the hollow, slowly stacked rocks and earth against them to cover the front of her hollow, except for a small slit. Here she kept her fire burning constantly. With her pot and with fire she cooked redgrasseed which she crushed between rocks, and this sustained her. She ate and slept better, and the tearful outbursts decreased, leaving an endless sadness.

Despite the hardships of her life, watching the flyers was a thing that pleased her. She would miss them when they left for the Coldtime, all but the scolders. They would still be around, their raucous voices waking her every sunrise, their glossy dark bodies strutting around her treecave, looking for scraps and keeping her company. One spottyscolder, a distinctive white splash under its chin, grew bold and would come quite close, until it was almost tame. Em talked to this flyer. It would tip its head to the side, listening, and its bright eyes looked at her with intelligence. She tried to lure it closer so she could touch it, but the flyer always remained just out of reach.

The scolders had raised their young of that season, but the chirpers still had babies. Em watched the parents darting back and forth and could hear the peeping cries coming from the tiny nests secreted in fissures of rock on a bluff not far from her treehome. Em decided to steal one. Then it would be used to her, and she could play with it. The bluff was not as steep as some, and she thought she might just be able to crawl across the face of it. She found a downed tree and dragged it to the bluff to lean against the rock. Climbing up its branches, she got high enough to reach close to the lowest fissure.

From there she crawled, her fingers and toes gripping the crack, towards the spot where she knew there was a nest. It had looked closer from the ground, but it wasn't difficult going as long as she went slow and kept her body against the rock. The slant of the rockface was not as steep as she had worried. When she reached the nest, a frightened flyer, in an explosion of feathers, launched itself straight into her face.

Startled, Em reared back and lost her balance. She skidded on her knees down the rough rock, and in surprise she threw out her arms and extended her projections. And the projections automatically spread to cup the air, slowing her skid; she had time to swing her legs out in front of her as she slid down the rock and so land on her feet.

She abandoned the idea of capturing a flyer. Perhaps her projections could act as wings. Then she would be her own flyer. She began to study the flyers and watch how they leaped into the air and the wind caught their wings and they lifted, how they tilted at turns and caught the warm winds to ride.

Em would stand on the cliff and inhale, and as her lungs filled, the muscles around her rib cage and across her back would lift her wings. Exhaling, the sound of her breath was echoed in a downward swooping behind her. She could feel a faint tug on her body; the overcast sky beckoned. But like a hand, gravity held her.

Was she a winged thing not meant to fly? She raged at her weakness, standing on the cliff face with the up-draft catching her wings, flapping and flapping to make them strong. Her shoulders ached with the effort and she would curl in her hollow to sleep, covered with scrapes and bruises from her attempts. She dreamt of flight.

Em practiced three, four, five times a day, preoccupied and annoyed with her body's need for food, so she had to stop and search for bladeroot and wideroot, greycaps, curlyleaf, sweetreds in the woods, streamscuttlers lurking under flat rocks. She could not be objective and see progress, as her wings had more growing to do, her body had to lengthen and lean. Yet somehow, her heels lifted from the ground. She pulled the sky closer.

And in the Scoldermoon, there was the whoosh of air from her wings behind her and beneath her, and gravity was broken. She only partially saw the rock disappear and the fast approaching yellow stubble, as she concentrated on holding out her wings, then went limp with surprise to land with a crash and a cry across the way from the cliff.

Her legs and hands were skinned. She sat unmoving, her wings draped back and a leg twisted uncomfortably beneath her. The world had spun and jerked to a stop, never to be the same.

*   *   *

Gradually Em grew in strength and in skill. She learned to breathe with her wing strokes, to become a part of the wind. She flew with the flyers and went farther over the land than any of the people had been, and farther out over the sea. Food was easy to find. She could fly at dusk to the far edges of the fields where the people were growing stumpy breadgrass and fill a creeperskin bag with seeds. She trapped and strangled smallcreepers in the shortgrass meadows further up the mountain; she learned to be like the barehead and grab chirpers and redflyers from the sky.

Knowing her earth hollow would not be enough protection to survive the coming Coldtime, Em decided to seek out a cave. Carrying Loo's pot filled with coals, she flew farther from the area, flying down the beach Away from Brightstar. Here the land jutted out into the sea and up into the air, and she wanted that bulk between her and the Rockpeople. She found a few shallow caves in the dark rock, but after sleeping through the dark in one, she knew it wasn't what she sought. She flew on, and around the foothills she found a tiny bay where a stream came down from the mountain. Here was fresh water, and she was far from the Rockpeople; after several suns' hunting, she found a deep and dry cave high in the cliff above a marsh.

The entrance was small and unseen from the ground, but after a slight drop down, it opened into a long and narrow room. Em was well pleased, for in this place she felt safe. A small fire would keep this place warm. She flew up with the largest rocks she could carry, to heat in the fire so they would radiate their warmth. With an angular rock, she chipped away at the grey cave walls where streaks of darker stone were soft and crumbling and made several narrow ledges to hold her food out of the reach of smallcreepers that crept from the back of the cave at night. Here she kept rolled leaves of dryfood: sweetreds, greycaps, whatever she did not need right away. She was worried about the coming Coldtime. She carried armfuls of grasses and sleepingleaf up to the cave, like a spottyscolder building a nest, and brought up all the broken limbs of seekra bushes and longtrees that she could manage. She tried to make torches like the Rockpeople, but hers burned too fast and were soon gone.

Locating smallcreeper nests and digging out the day-sleeping creatures was easy, but skinning them was tricky without a blade, and preparing the hides correctly was beyond her skill. There was no skintree nearby. And she feared going close to the Rockpeople to gouge out the bark she would need to make the pelts soft. She scraped and scraped with the thin, sharp-edged rock she called Blade and sand-rubbed the skins, but they never became soft and supple. She shivered and starved through the first Coldtime.

The next Coldtime found her better prepared, with more dryfood on the ledges and more and softer creeperskins to huddle under. She built a windscreen of piled rocks and branches by the cave entrance to keep out most of the wind; she no longer had to fly out in the worst of Fireside to gather branches, but knew how much wood she'd need and kept the back of the cave filled with branches gathered in the Warmtime. And all this flying and carrying, weighted with wood and rocks, made her strong.

During Creepersleeping she practiced weaving, for her baskets and nets were never as sound as the Rockpeople's, but fell apart with use. Sometimes she longed to be back with Sarra, curled tight with Nexxie and Mella to sleep. She missed the voices of Conn, Rommy, Jobo and the rest, talking together late at night. But she knew she was lucky that it was Loo who saw her when she went for the hot coals; another would have put her on the fire. Even this cold loneliness was preferable.

*   *   *

Coldtime was followed by Warmtime, and followed by Coldtime and yet another Warmtime, and a restless, relentless feeling moved Em. In the early sunup, she sought out the Rockpeople, hiding and watching from concealing trees, until she saw a man, alone on the beach in the faint light. She knew what to do, having seen the women of the caves. She lured this man from his swimmering and inside her to calm this feeling— the desire for skin on skin and hardness inside of her softness. And the feeling was calmed for a time and then returned, stronger than before. She sought out another man, always choosing one alone at sunup or sundown, away from the other Rockpeople, and later she sought out another.

The pregnancy was easy. Her belly increased but a small amount and she could still fly, compensating for the shift in her balance, until near the birthtime. The birth itself was frightening, but she had seen Luta have a baby, so she knew what to expect. She collected some of the weeds Sarra had used and managed to do well for most of the labor. But as the coming baby pushed harder to appear in the world, Em writhed in pain, rolling about the cave floor, strewing her leaf bedding about her, calling to Sarra to come help. But rather than Sarra, a screaming, thin, slippery baby appeared, and in the joy and wonder of no longer being alone, Em forgot what she had just experienced. Em loved this child, and she flew, gently cradling him against her breasts. He had tiny stubs of wings, and she named him Firsson.

Flight came easily to Firss; he seemed more at ease in the air than on land. Before he could walk he flittered around Em as she went about the tasks of wood and food gathering. Em had to purposely work with him, holding him steady on the ground so he could learn to walk. He laughed and bobbed under her hands on his shoulders, and achieved a light-footed stride, seldom falling, for his wings were ever extended to catch him.

The next pregnancy was harder. Swollen to a huge size, only with difficulty could Em lift herself from the ground. Despite Firss, she felt lonely and spent days in the cave hating the world without flight. The lightshells, filled with smallcreeper fat and waxberries, burned so much quicker than those made by Sarra, and Em used them sparingly. Even the cheerful Firss, who had seen four Coldtimes, became somber. Earthbound and depressed, Em waited in semi-darkness, and Teecher was born with a struggle she felt would tear her apart. She had learned from the earlier time and brought in a big pile of dry grasses to absorb all the liquids from the birth, but it was nowhere near enough. Firss cried at seeing his sibling bursting forth, covered in blood. There was no joy, simply relief the baby was out.

He was massive, with heavy bones and thick flesh and no wings. But Em loved this child too and nursed him, flew with him close to her breast and Firss flittering beside. Teecher was more serious than Firss, who approached everything lightly. Teecher would hold a stick in his pudgy fingers and study it intently, his brow furrowed. He walked, with many falls and sudden sittings, and spoke slowly, each word given careful thought. When he could toddle, Teecher would feel his shoulders and scream his red-faced rage, "Me too! Me too!" He would push Em away when she tried to comfort him, bruise himself jumping off high rocks. Firss was kind and played with Teecher, but it wasn't enough.

And finally Teecher asked, "Where are my wings?" Em was not a thinker but a flyer, and unsure what to say, she told him, "You have a different gift."

"What is it?"

"I don't know." And Em, feeling as if she might be telling a lie, said, "It is something you will grow into."

Em worried about Teecher. Neither of the children spoke much, but Firss returned her glance with an open, joyous smile that told her what she wanted to know. Teecher was different. His silence held secrets.

*   *   *

Teecher was filled with a bitter longing. Watching Firss and their mother play in the air above him, practicing swoops and dives, he felt cheated. Em carried him in flight, but this was not enough; he wanted to soar out on his own, to chase Firss and catch flyers as they streaked past. Once, watching them above, he picked up a palm-sized rock and held it tense in his hand. He could see Firss tumble from the sky in pain, and the thought made him glad. Frightened, he dropped the stone and ran into the trees, wanting to run from his envious self. But he couldn't and finally stopped in a small clearing to let his breath catch up to him. Leaning on a downed tree, he still felt the desperate need of some special thing of his own, a craving like hunger, but in his chest. He gathered small spotted rocks, rooting them out of the vines growing around the log, and clustered the rocks in a semicircle about the clearing. He jumped up on the log and began to instruct.

"My mother is your mother. Her wings carry us. She flies to find us food. She shows us how to catch smallcreepers, shows us what to pick to eat. She gathers weeds for us. She takes us over the treetops to places we could never go alone. And loving her makes us happy."

Teecher wanted to tell the assembled rocks more, but lacked the words. So he stood and gestured speechlessly, telling them of wonders that had not happened. Pretending the rocks looked at him and listened to his non-existent words made him feel important. With the admiration from the rocks, it didn't matter that he had no wings. Satisfied, he dug under the log until he unearthed a smallcreeper tunnel. He jammed rocks into each opening, and cast about for further tunnels, blocking them when he found them. Then he opened the round nest and strangled three of the confused creepers to take back for dinner.

Teecher could descend the cliff below the cave by climbing and sliding, but the sheer walls prevented his return on his own. Em, her strong arms under his, her hands locked across his chest, had to fly him up to the cave. Now there came a time when Em could not lift Teecher as easily, for she was growing round with another child, and Firss, although he tried, was unable to lift Teecher. Teecher grew panicky at the thought of being trapped in the cave, and losing their moonlight flights. Em had always carried Teecher when they flew over the sleeping people Em had come from. Firss and Em were preoccupied with flight, but Teecher was fascinated with the fields of the people. Each time they flew over, the fields extended slightly further up the hillside, the scrubby weeds and saplings replaced by geometric patterns of growth. Now he would not be able to see what was happening.

One dark of the Treemoon, Em told stories of the multitude of creatures gone long before her time, stories Sarra had told her. And Teecher thought of all his unanswerable questions, for Em would rarely speak of the Rockpeople and then only with scorn. He began to conceal handfuls of breadgrass that his mother had gathered and hid it on a rock shelf deep in the cave. He caught swimmers; most he shared but a few he dried in the sun and hid with the stolen grain. He studied Em's tasks. How she ground the seed between smooth rocks, picked through it to get out the tough hulls and ground it again, the muscles of her arms and back bunching, her wings moving in sympathy. He had her teach him, and he learned to form water and ground breadgrasseed into flat loaves, and bake them on the heated rocks.

When Firss and Em were out flying, looking for greenfruit, Teecher ground the pilfered breadgrasseed to make five small loaves and wrapped them with the dried swimmers in bannaleaves. He wound the bundle tight, knotted it with creepergut and cast it out of the cave as far as he could. It landed in bushes below and luckily sank out of sight.

In the darkness while Em and Firss slept, he slid and scrambled down the cliff. He felt in the bushes, and after an impossibly long time his shaking hands located the bundle. Largecreepers had been at the swimmers and bread, nibbling. Teecher set out up the beach, walking in the shallow waves to conceal his prints and hoping the largecreepers would stay under the trees. Suntimes he had to abandon the shore, as once Em and twice Firss flew over, calling. The terrain was rocky, the ground choked in vines; the hills and cliffs much harder to walk than to fly over. He finished the food but kept walking in the direction of Brightstar. Em had said his gift was something he would grow into. He had to find a place where he could grow.

The Birth of the Novel *GIFTS*

My writer's group was invited to give readings at an event called Future Visions, and although we were excited, none of us had any writings about the future to read. Margaret Blanchard, a member of the group, arranged a meeting with Eugenia Pickett, a therapist specializing in Guided Imagery with Music. Eugenia had us lie on the floor and relax, and then guided us to find a place where we felt safe. She began to play a piece of music. First I visualized myself in the mountains, but felt unsafe there. Then I tried the seashore, up a tree, in a cave. No place felt safe. I became panic-stricken. I curled like a baby, seeking safety, and tried to fit back into the womb. Unsafe! So I cast myself forward, to a time following a nuclear holocaust. Here, the worst I could imagine had already happened.

An entire landscape unfolded, a seashore, caves in the towering cliff face, an overcast sky. People appeared. I watched a young girl with wings being beaten, then driven away from the caves where these people lived. I watched her struggle to learn to fly; I watched her give birth to babies. I was astounded. These scenes were so real, and I felt I somehow knew this young girl. Following the Guided Imagery, we all sat and wrote. Words flowed effortlessly. When I got home, it was easy to continue writing. And each time the story faltered, I did a Guided Imagery with myself, and there the characters and landscape awaited me, seemingly eager to show what happened next. A history evolved that felt as if it had been waiting for me to discover it. Two different cultures appeared, and it was my conscious task to integrate them. Then, as I worked, a third culture emerged, and hints of others beyond these.

I had tapped into my unconscious in a very direct and powerful manner, and couldn't have been more surprised or delighted. The story told itself; my task was to get it into words. And each time I sat in front of my computer, the screen would blur and fade away as this other world opened up before me, expanding beyond the boundaries of myself and my room, beyond my house and neighborhood, spreading out to cover the edge of a continent and its offshore islands.

Reflecting back on the book, I can see that it is a metaphor for my own psyche. An integral aspect of the plot is the divisions that arise between people—how events can make groups separate from each other. The challenge of the novel was how to merge these disparate groups. Each culture had both skills and ways of seeing the world that others lacked, and when brought together could complement one another and make for a more complete way of life.

This was an echo of my own internal process. There were parts of myself cut off and seemingly lost that I subsequently needed to discover and integrate into my waking being. There was yet another vast internal world, peopled with these parts of myself I had lost or denied in the past. After the novel was completed but for minor revisions, I began doing Guided Imagery with Music as therapy.

These lost parts, once acknowledged and reclaimed, brought me new skills and world-views that made me a more total human being. I wrote a novel, and it launched me into the realm of self-discovery. I wrote a novel and discovered who I truly am.

❀

DIRT FROM HOME
Nora Nellis

In *The Art of the Possible,* Dawna Markova tells the story of her grand-mother who always kept a carved walnut box which she had brought from her native Russia to New York. Inside the box was a handful of dirt. When she asked her grandmother where it came from, the older woman replied, "Home." She had sprinkled a pinch of its contents be-neath her feet to make a friend of alien ground (Markova 1991, vi).

The desire for one's own soil, I concluded, is what moves people to spend their entire lives searching for the missing parts of themselves—birth parents, long-lost relatives, children given up for adoption. Perhaps this desire is basic, instinctual, the spirit which moves so many to make ancestral journeys of their own.

I began my own quest when I inquired about my paternal great-grandmother, a woman whose demeanor, appearance and metaphorical way of expressing her faith strongly suggested Native American heritage. My father proudly proclaimed his Indian roots, but the rest of the family denied them. There was something about the vehement denial that was, in itself, silencing—especially to a child of eight. I set aside any thoughts of seeking information about my ancestry. The insidious part of effec-tive silencing is that finding out the truth no longer seemed important to me.

As a mature woman, returning to college to study for my master's degree in writing and women's studies, I selected women's silencing as a major part of my thesis. Gradually, I reconnected with my sense of loss and longing for knowledge about my heritage, the great-grandmother I remembered, but had never really known. Only now all those who could possibly give me the information I needed were gone—my great-grand-mother, all of her children, as well as my father (I later discovered that even her own children had denied their Indian blood). In order to begin my search, I returned to the street where my great-grandmother lived during the last forty years of her life. I recalled snatches of family stories and relied on childhood memory to write a poem about her:

I'll Wait Here

They said
Grandma always slipped away
when people came
she ran and hid
stayed in that room
no matter how dark it got
stayed until company left
and even now
long dead
she slips away
from me
And I wait and wait
for her to come out
of that room
where she hides
but Grandma
I'm not going
I'm not company
I'm family
I'll wait here
until you're ready

In September 1991, I wrote in my journal: Always a voice said, "That is not all." I felt unexplainable stirrings brought on by loneliness and being close to nature. When a breeze gently rippled the water or a forest animal came close, I felt as though I had been in this place before, remembering what I never knew.

I sense that my great-grandmother has messages she wishes to convey through me. I will try to discover all that I can about Marancy Akey, a young Indian or part-Indian girl who married a French Canadian. Whether the story unfolds through facts or becomes partially a creation, I know my great-grandmother will speak to me:

AKWE:KON*

Grandmother
you have been sleeping
since you died
forty years ago
only sleeping
while they sold your home
denied your birthright

I heard you say
she is the one
child of dark eyes
and long braids
who watches plants grow
and speaks with animals
this child will give me
back to my people

Yes, Grandmother
I am coming
I speak for you
for them
for me
Akwe:kon

*Akwe:kon—Mohawk meaning "all of us"

By October 1991, the genealogical portion of my ancestral search was well underway. Marancy Akey LaJoy's death certificate verified that she had been born in Peru, New York in 1847. The truth remained hidden as it had for so many years while I proceeded with other portions of my graduate studies. Nearly a year passed before I made the trip to Peru to search for clues to my heritage.

I planned the day, the first in some time which guaranteed sunshine. I trudged through several graveyards without finding a single family stone. I contacted an Akey family member who could not meet with me that day and gave no indication of a more convenient time when we could discuss my questions.

The Catholic church had records dating back to the 1840s, but I was told they did not get involved in genealogy because it was too time consuming. I told the receptionist that when I was doing research in the Mohawk Valley on the Nellis family line, the Lutherans gladly opened church records dating back to the 1700s. That fact did nothing to sway their decision, and I left, feeling frustrated that "ordinary people" could withhold information which might be the key to solving the mystery of my heritage.

As I left Peru, I decided to make one final attempt to connect with my past. I placed an ad in *The Press Republican*, Plattsburgh's daily newspaper. It read, "Seeking genealogical information, Marancy Akey LaJoy, Born 1847, Peru, NY."

When more than a week passed without a response, I was not surprised. I was hoping to obtain information about a woman born nearly one hundred fifty years ago. The chance of connecting with someone who was related to or knew of her was remote. The following is an excerpt from a journal entry dated September 17, 1992:

When I answered the telephone, a woman's voice said, "I saw your ad in the newspaper, or rather my mother saw the ad, and we wondered what your connection to Marancy LaJoy might be."

"She was my great-grandmother," I replied.

There was a long silence before she said, "She was my great-grandmother too."

Following a conversation during which we exchanged family information, we agreed to meet in Plattsburgh in early October. She planned to invite her sister, as well as her mother, who is my great-grandmother's granddaughter. Even after we had established a time to meet, we continued discussing long-forgotten details as though neither of us could believe we had found this link to the past.

October 4, 1992

It is a bright and glorious morning as I begin the trip to Plattsburgh. The foliage colors gain intensity as I head north. There is little traffic on the Adirondack Northway to interfere with my thoughts. I have with me the portrait of my grandfather, Sidney, and a picture of my father, as well as one of my son; with my presence that accounts for four generations of this family. Perhaps one of the relatives will have a photo or some memento of Grandmother Marancy. Plattsburgh is quiet on a Sunday morning, and I find the house easily. It is situated on the site of the former Platte Estate, named for the founder of the city. From the front porch of the home there is an expansive view of Lake Champlain. Our meeting is warm and friendly in a way that feels very familiar. Over coffee, at the kitchen table, we four women, newly introduced relatives, exchange photographic offerings, peel away years. Grandfather Sidney's large portrait dominates, as Josephine, who remembers many of my great-grandmother's siblings, remarks, "Doesn't he look like my brother, Walter?" The comparisons and reminiscences continue most of the afternoon. We visit the Plattsburgh cemetery together where we see the graves of several other family members. The whole day has about it a dream-like quality, and we part, vowing to stay in touch and to continue the research we have begun.

> We are four women
> one granddaughter
> three great-granddaughters
> meeting this first time
> at the grave
> of our common ancestor
> we are gathered
> in this cemetery
> knowing much more lies
> beneath carefully sculpted words
>
> We walk row by row
> grave by grave
> hoping answers will emerge
> as corn from the soil

October 30, 1992

As I continued the search for details of my paternal great-grandmother's Native American connection, more and more information developed: that my great-grandmother on the maternal side was also Native American. "I thought you knew," my mother told me. My mother, who said the Indian ancestry in my father's family was something which should be denied, informed me with pride that my inheritance is greater than I ever suspected. Several of my mother's nieces and cousins verified that this was true. I believe this is a search which will continue long after the program for my degree has ended.

November 1992

I heard from my relatives in Plattsburgh. They found deed records which indicate property where my great-grandparents lived in the 1880s. There is some evidence that my great-great-grandmother's name may have been Carle, rather than Carroll. They also discovered that Marancy had several brothers and sisters. They indicate the name Akey may have originally been Aka. I had obtained all the factual information I could for now. I began to seek more intuitive answers through my poetry.

> Grandmother
> you are not the storyteller
> you are the story
> you are the dust
> that is part of me
> you are the wind
> that is part of me
> a storm that brews
> beneath my surface
> sun that shines too seldom
> winter that lasts too long
> my feet tap to drums
> my feet stay close
> to Mother Earth
> Tonight
> I hear your story
> you Grandmother Moon and I

Sometimes my rational mind sought to understand the emotions, longings and occasional lapses into a dreamlike state. I remembered the words of

Eunice Baumann-Nelson, the first Penobscot Indian to earn a B.A., M.A. and Ph.D., and whose mother was the seventh daughter of a seventh daughter. In the book, *Profiles in Wisdom: Native American Elders Speak About the Earth* by Steven McFadden, Baumann-Nelson speaks of a process she calls anamnesis, something within us which goes all the way back. She theorizes that since we inherit our DNA from our ancestors, we carry memories back to creation. Past lives, she postulates, become the recollection, through DNA, of the life of an ancestor, with intuition being part of the theory. She notes that anyone can retrieve this memory, bring it into consciousness and experience a change in feelings toward other persons and nature (78, 79).

My words, my great-grandmother's words—it no longer mattered who spoke, nor did I need to separate fact from fiction. What mattered to me was that the silence had been shattered, veils lifted, messages received. It was not just what I learned through fictional spirit visits with my great-grandmother, but the value and clarity of the words of many wisdom keepers.

> Old Woman watches
> this child grow
> watches this child
> in sunlight
> in twilight
> ever at the edge
> of fog
> of storm
> of dreams
> which swirl around her
>
> Old Woman is quiet
> holding close
> those stories
> she will not share
> for silence is her choice
> is her power, her essence
>
> Without a word

> Old Woman guides this child
> through inner journeys
> and the young one believes
> the stories she tells
> are her own creation

During a session with a transpersonal psychologist, I spoke to my great-grandmother's spirit. I asked her why she had remained silent about her heritage and never shared the stories of her elders. Her answer, coming from my own lips, surprised me, and I was initially confused by a reply I had not anticipated. She said, "Silence was my choice and so it was my power and my essence."

Silencing by oppressors and women's self-silencing formed the basis of my studies. The power women could claim as a result of silence by choice was an alternative I had not considered.

Among female ethnic groups whose roots are not discernible to the casual observer and for lesbians attempting to blend into their communities, invisibility might serve as a kind of "protection." Silence I assumed was part of that defense. But what of those who could not "pass" or chose not to do so? Why would women who were identified or declared themselves part of a marginal group maintain silence?

Magda Gere Lewis views silence as much more than avoidance, calling it a discourse aimed at telling a different story, a counter language useful even in political and social transformation (1993, 35).

For individuals or groups who speak the language but are not "heard" when their words are misinterpreted or not believed, silence becomes a powerful tool. When two or more share knowledge but choose to withhold it from others, power is achieved through selective exclusion.

I thought of my own search for the truth about my great-grandmother's life, the possibility that she was Mohawk. For reasons of pride I wanted it to be so. A woman in her day who was half, or even less than half, Native American carried the label "half-breed," placing her and her family at risk of prejudice and even physical harm.

Mohawk writer Beth Brant described the agony experienced by her great-grandmother when her children were taken away and placed in government school to be civilized. They were given new names and not allowed to practice their religion or speak their language:

It will make them civilized the agent said. I do not know civilized. . .a picture of my son and daughter being lifted onto the train. . .all of the girls dressed alike. . .my son, his hair cut (1984, 100-106).

Brant recounted her great-grandmother's response to letters received from her children, signed with new names—Martha and Daniel:

There is no Martha. There is no Daniel. She tore the letters into scraps which she buried, and her own people called her crazy as she howled at the moon in mourning for her lost children (103).

Always Remember

his mother said
how important
your hair is
braid it
clean it
comb it
tie it

at government school
where Indians learned
civilized ways
he was washed
clothes burned
disinfectant poured
braids cut

Remember
his mother said
when you go out to pray
your hair
must always be
in braids

as he silently
remembered all
his mother had said

His mother wove
one eagle plume
into his black braids
and said
always remember

One Indian boy
two shiny braids
one eagle plume
the property of
the U.S. government
and his mother
had no say

"So you were unsuccessful in tracing your great-grandmother's lineage," a Native American acquaintance remarked; "you cannot claim the heritage you so greatly desired. You all want to claim it now, but then—in olden times," she shrugged. "It is good they left no traces."

She misunderstood the purpose of my ancestral journey. Communication with my great-grandmother was part of a concept I needed to grasp—the importance of the wisdom of the elders. Oh Shinnah advises, "If you don't have a grandmother or a grandfather around you, then go and adopt one because you cannot understand the cycles of life unless you have old people around you" (McFadden, 158).

It was not just what I learned in fictional spirit visits with my great-grandmother, but the value and clarity of the words of many. Amylee said, "Take all the baskets you've been given and inherited, fill them with the gifts of the grandmothers, sow the seeds, give the contents away" (McFadden, 182).

Works Cited

Brant, Beth, ed. *A Gathering of Spirit: Writing and Art by North American Indian Women*. Rockland: Sinister Wisdom Books, 1984.

Lewis, Magda Gere. *Without A Word: Teaching Beyond Women's Silence*. New York: Routledge, 1993.

Markova, Dawna. *The Art of the Possible*. Berkeley: Conari Press, 1991.

McFadden, Steven. *Profiles in Wisdom: North American Elders Speak About the Earth*. Santa Fe: Bear and Company, 1991.

✿

IV. HEALING, TEACHING, SOCIAL ACTION: COMING TO LIGHT

In this final section, "Coming to Light," we see how intuitive languages have been used for healing, teaching, and social action. Intuition's capacity to assist healing, to make whole again, is evident in Vicki Gabriner's powerful image for healing from abuse; Virginia Holmes' eloquent descriptions of personal and professional treatment of pre-verbal abuse through symbolic language; and Dottie Menard's intuitive method of empathic body work through breathwork and massage.

Intuitive teaching is described by Tania Kravath, who explores interactions between her own processes as an artist and high school art teacher; by Bernice Mennis in poems which explore the magic of intuitive learning, its fragility in the face of scorn and judgment; and by JoAnna Allen, who reflects on the intuitive role of mentor in experiential learning.

A synthesis between healing and teaching is explored in Sherry Kaufield's insightful description of intuitive diagnosis and creative process with children, and in poet Harriette Wimms' intuitive process of teaching creative writing to inner-city children.

Moving toward social action, Margaret Blanchard and S.B. Sowbel share intuitive exercises for solving problems, on both personal and social levels; Lisa Blackburn describes a moving international community art project which helps feed the hungry; Sandra Churchill, using collage as an intuitive metaphor for ethical thinking, explores questions about validity when narrative and holistic methods are used as bases for theorizing; and Norma Bradley describes the inspiring process by which she creates quilt designs from earth materials for political action and environmental education. Finally, Margaret Blanchard's poems recording voices from an ancient oracle bring us full circle by reminding us of our intuitive roots.

Vicki Gabriner, who lives in Brookline, Massachusetts, was an activist in civil rights, anti-Vietnam war, feminist and lesbian politics. In the late seventies, an internal voice cried out for quiet; the wounds of sexual child abuse, never forgotten but equally never dealt with, moved to the front burner for the decade of the eighties. Recently her heart has been in her Bat Mitzvah preparation, for the moment of being called to the Torah with her lover and seven other adult women, and in her deepening connection to her Eastern European Jewish roots.

Virginia Holmes was born and grew up in Maine. She lived in Minnesota, Chicago, St. Louis, Edmonton, Alberta, and Portland, Oregon, before settling back in Maine in 1983. Her experiences include anti-Vietnam war activities, early women's movement organizing, being a social-feminist lesbian, being a bar dyke, teaching kindergarten, working in a collective day care center, driving a wheelchair van, and bookkeeping for various social service agencies. In 1987 she earned a master's in psychology at Vermont College and in 1992, a doctorate at the Union Institute. She works as a child and adult psychotherapist.

Dorothy Menard, a licensed massage therapist, specializes in integrating energy balance with body work. Dottie is a trained REIKI practitioner and has been practicing Vipassana meditation for over 13 years. Both of these practices are important influences on her dynamic body therapy. Of French Canadian descent, Dottie lives in Rhode Island and in upstate New York.

Tania Kravath was born in the Bronx in 1943 of first generation Russian/Jewish heritage, with a large network of aunts, uncles, and counsins. Educated at City College, she has been an art educator in the NYC schools for 25 years, painting and sculpting throughout, traveling, exploring and feeling blessed to be a woman in this time.

Bernice Mennis lives in, wanders through and loves the southern Adirondacks. She teaches literature and writing in Vermont College's Adult Degree Program and Skidmore College's University Without Walls Prison Program. Her students, nature and friends continually teach and inspire her.

JoAnna Woo Allen teaches physics for Baltimore County Public Schools. Her undergraduate major at Mount Mary College in Milwaukee was chemistry, with a minor in mathematics. A period in the Peace Corps in Malaysia determined her career path in education. She earned an M.A.T. from Harvard and a M.A.S from Hopkins. An introduction to adventure and outdoor education led JoAnna to experiential education, in which she earned her Ph.D. from the Union Institute in 1992.

As a mental health specialist working with children, **Sherry Kaufield** has served as a crisis counselor for the State of Illinois; a senior counselor in an acute care psychiatric hospital; a therapist in a child psychiatrist's office and in her own private practice. She has written extensively about children's mental health wellbeing, including a workbook *Child Therapy Groups for Children*. Her M.A. in counseling psychology is from Vermont College. Sherry teaches at Rock Valley College and works as executive director of a community mental health program.

Harriette Wimms-Cutchember has been writing poetry since she was ten years old. By day she is a special accounts manager for a human services publisher in Baltimore, Maryland. By night and weekend, she is a graduate student in bibliotherapy, a support group facilitator, a creative writing teacher, a women's bookstore volunteer, co-owner of a tea party catering company, and full-time Mom to her dog Ariel Blue (Canine Extraordinaire).

Lisa Blackburn is a co-founder of the Imagine/RENDER Group, a non-profit organization dedicated to social change through the arts and art education. Lisa also co-founded the Empty Bowls project, an international grass roots effort focused on using ceramic arts to raise awareness and money to fight hunger. Lisa's B.S. degree is in botanical illustration and her M.A. degree is in art, social action and service learning. She is a workshop leader and artist/educator currently teaching children four through fourteen at Upland Hills School in Oxford, Michigan, and children and adults at the Detroit Institute of Arts.

Sandra Churchill loves to think. She prefers to think in the company of other women who honor their deepest, most complicated sense of self. Using intuition as companion to observation and analysis is her favorite form of thinking. Sande grew up in Arkansas and lived in Tennessee before settling in North Carolina. Officially she is a feminist philosopher of culture. She studies gender and patriarchy as these affect the rhetoric of professional discourses.

Norma Bradley is an artist who was born in the Bronx to parents who were forced to flee from Russia in their teenage years. In NYC, a matrix of different cultures and classes, Norma studied art at museums, galleries, studios, the Art Students League, on city streets and in colleges, and was active in installing environmental sculpture in the city. In 1980 she visited the place of her dreams, the mountains of North Carolina, and stayed. In 1986 the Department of Energy decided to construct a high level nuclear waste repository in this community. Her protest, along with others, stopped the destruction and gave birth to the Earth Quilt project, which she has taken to schools, rehabilitation centers and campuses, inviting others to join her in the creation and installation of

Earth Quilt Gardens.

Poet, photographer and stained glass artisan, **Margaret Blanchard** is the author of *The Rest of the Deer*, and with S.B. Sowbel, *Restoring the Orchard: A Guide to Learning Intuition*, and a book of poetry and paintings, *Duet*. Her poetry has been published in *Unlacing*, *Linking Roots*, *The Atlantic Monthly*, *The Word*, *Women*, and *Sinister Wisdom*. She has edited a national women's magazine, a community newspaper, a book on teaching, a union newspaper, a book on cancer. She teaches in the Graduate Program of Vermont College. She lives in a hut she built in the Adirondacks. When she wins the Publishers' Clearinghouse Sweepstakes, she plans to fund publication of the work of all contributors to this book, and then some.

❀

Bernice Mennis

JoAnna Woo Allen

Virginia Holmes

Sherry Kaufield

Harriette Wims-Cutchener & Norma Bradley

Sandra Churchill   *Margaret Blanchard*

Not Pictured: Vicky Gabriner, Dorothy Menard, Tania Kravath, Lisa Blackburn

THE GOOD FAIRY
Vicki Gabriner

Finally, from the corners where the silence still remains came the urgency to go to a mountaintop and scream out the whole truth. For starters on that trek, I offer you this story/image, and I offer it to you under my own full name, for the first time. It danced out of my head one night at the meditation center. I had not started meditating. I was eating a bowl of soup. But when the mind gets quiet and knows it is in a receptive space, it speaks the truth.

* * *

I sent out a prayer to the Universe—it's too painful, I can't take it—and she came to me, the power of my mind, the Energy of the Universe, in blue like the Good Fairy in the Wizard of Oz, waving a wand. I sat cross-legged on the floor of my bedroom, looking up, about five years old. She said, Sweetheart, here's the deal. There's too much going on here, and I don't have the power to make it be gone, to make it be okay or even to help you cope with it in a way that's not going to cause you some pain. What I can do, sweetheart, is help you get through this time now, help you forget it as it is going on, so that it will come back, but it will come back to you at a later time when you're able to handle it. So I said, okay, because I can't take it.

She waved her wand and said, I'm going to send things that are happening into different parts of your body, and they are going to hold them for you like a treasure chest, like a dowry. I am going to have to tie up your pelvis and have it lock in a lot of your sexual feelings because you think they're getting you in trouble. And your belly and pelvis will feel dead, and they will also hold in your rage and a lot of your fear. I'll also have your thighs be very tight to hold in the energy coming from your vagina and genitals. And your heart, your heart is broken, and I'm going to have to let your rib cage close in around your heart and let your heart constrict so that you don't feel the pain of your heart breaking.

And I'm going to really tighten up your neck and let it be a fortress with very thick round walls so that what you're feeling doesn't get up to your mouth and you can't speak the words you can't cry out for help you can't scream out in rage you can't breathe too deeply to feel what's going on in your body. And that fortress will keep the knowledge of what's happening in your body from connecting with your head so that you will not be fully conscious of what's going on. And I will tie up your ears so that you hear but don't take too much in.

I want you to be fairly still as a child and not very athletic so we don't interrupt what we're going to put very carefully in place. And it will stay this way. You will have trouble feeling and being close to people, but it will be your way of surviving. And you, my darling, will be a fairly functional human being in spite of all this pain because you have a strong mind and you can hold this all in. And I will be helping you. You will not forget everything. You will remember just enough to always know that this happened. I will leave a voice inside of you that will urge you to reconnect with your whole self, to find this person who you are now who is calling out for help and whose heart is totally breaking. It may not be clear it's a voice. It will manifest as an urge inside of you, but it will be me speaking as I can through your frozen muscles to come back and find yourself.

At the time of your second Saturn cycle, you will begin to open up. It will be a very long process. It may take you as long to heal as you've been in pain and the frozen place. Finally around forty, your muscles will no longer be able to hold all this in. They will begin to give way, you will feel an urgency to do physical work, and that will begin the process of really unwinding your body and releasing what it will have been holding all these years. There will be physical as well as emotional pain in this process. But by then you will be strong enough and old enough to bear the truth, and you will have a network of friends around you, mostly women but some men also, who will hold you as you find yourself again. You will not be a very physical person for most of your life; you will have come to accept the frozenness and rigidity of your body. As it begins to unwind you will struggle to re-learn the language of your body/mind and come back together wholly. But you *will* do it because you are a strong person full of love. I don't know exactly how it will unfold but the Universe will move you through it. You will have to be very patient very brave very courageous, but it will be your training, your firewalk, your healing. And when you are through it, you will be a whole person:

new but still the same.

Now I want you to go to bed. I will wave my wand and you will go to sleep and when you wake up you will forget I was here you will forget you asked for help you will forget your daily pain. This is the only way I know to get you through this. You are a beautiful child. I don't all the why's of how something like this comes to pass, but I do know that I love you and the Universe loves you and you will have to love yourself enough to heal so that the last half of your life will be strong and power-ful and full of light; the pain will be there but it will all be in proportion. One day you will have it all again. Until then and for always I love you.

❁

FINDING THE WORDS
Virginia Holmes

Over several years in the 1980's I went through a process of trying to come to terms with what seemed to be memories of pre-verbal sexual abuse. I did not know if these memories were factually accurate, but I did know that something major was going on for me. As I was going through a therapeutic process, I stood back and watched and recorded what I was doing. In my reparative process I found that I was frighteningly without words for much of what I was experiencing, even though words were my natural medium for working through personal issues. Paradoxically, I chose to write, to put into words what I could not find words for. My initial writing was chaotic and groping. Often I wrote the same words over and over. Sometimes I could only write, "I have no words for this." As I moved along in my process, I eventually wrote a narrative. Much of that story came to me in whole paragraphs, words falling together and coming whole into my head. Using writing and listening to my dreams, I slowly came to be able to organize my experience, making meaning out of what had been chaos. Writing the narrative was only a beginning, but once that organization was there, I had the material and the tools with which to grapple with what I experienced and then to change that experience and myself. Throughout this process there were times of clarity when I could stand back and see what I was doing; those flashes of understanding brought some rudimentary theoretical ideas about the particular damage resulting from pre-verbal sexual abuse and about the reparative process.

I was working as a child therapist during this period and also conducting an exploratory, descriptive study of six other women who were also working with memories of pre-verbal sexual abuse. Each strand of my work—the research, the clinical work and my own therapy—illuminated and enhanced the others. My observations of my own process gave me a framework through which I could imagine exploring others' process. My clinical work with one child in particular stimulated me and encouraged me in my belief that pre-verbal memories of abuse can be worked on therapeutically.

This child was a severely damaged five-year-old girl, whom I will call Misty. She had been badly abused, both physically and sexually, before the age of twenty-two months, when she was taken into foster care. At that time she was seriously developmentally delayed and did not talk at all. In many cases of child abuse, it is extremely unclear what trauma has taken place during the child's pre-verbal years. In Misty's case there was documentation in the form of police and medical records. Misty had fallen out of a second-story window; she had been badly burned with scalding water; she had been restrained by securing her legs with duct tape; and there was physical evidence that she had been sodomized, probably more than once.

Misty's adoptive family had not told her the story of her abuse or about her adoption. She came to therapy with severe symptoms of post-traumatic stress disorder and some suspicion of multiple personality disorder. She sometimes acted like an infant, curling up and sucking her thumb, and at other times was overly-mature and fearless. She had times when she would be completely out of control, screaming, swearing, jumping up on the furniture and assaulting adults if they tried to restrain her. She was unpredictable—sometimes tractable, sometimes running away, sometimes fighting back violently.

In the first months of therapy, Misty's play involved themes of fire, accidents, hospitals and death. She discovered a set of anatomically correct dolls in my office and obsessively inserted her finger in every available orifice. She and I discussed amicably whether this would hurt the dolls or either of us if someone did that to us. Misty thought it would not. Having ascertained that bodies and sex were an acceptable topic of discussion, Misty moved on to penises and showed me how they go up and down. One day Misty suddenly commented to me that someone had hurt her a long time ago. She listened intently when I agreed and told her that I was sorry that had happened to her. Later in the same session she told me, "I know a little girl who doesn't cry when people hurt her."

The next week I talked with Misty about her adoption and how her other mother had not been able to take good care of her. We did not discuss abuse at all. Misty followed this up quickly in the next few weeks by telling me about how she had a little girl in her back. She introduced me to the little girl, who wanted to talk to me about "that other mother." Soon Misty was calling her birth mother on the toy phone and scolding her for not taking good care of her.

After several months, Misty came in and announced that there was a monster in her back. She said that he was hurting her, and uncharacteristically, she displayed some distress about this. She began to growl and bark and play out both the monster and herself. The monster turned into a bear, and the little girl in Misty's back tried to fight him off. Misty called to me that the little girl in her back couldn't win, and I suggested that she, Misty, help her. Misty stopped dead, looked astonished and then pleased, rushed in to help, and together they vanquished the bear. When Misty's mother came in at the end of the session, Misty recounted this play enthusiastically in narrative form.

One day Misty came in and told me that she had had a bad dream. When I encouraged her, she told me the whole dream in detail:

> There was a big bear. He came at me with his big hands. He had a tail. (She looked confused, turned to look at her back, then decided that it had been on the front, even if she was calling it a tail.) It stood up straight—like this. (She suggested an erect penis with her hand movements.) He put his tail in the hole back there, you know? (She showed me the rectal area.) And he put it in and out, in and out, in and out. (Her eyes got bigger and bigger with each "in and out.") My mother (she stopped and looked at her adoptive mother, who was in the room, in confusion). . .not this mother, you know that other one? (I nodded, yes). . .that mother, my mother, she said I made the bear do that...

After telling me the description of her dream, Misty was very calm. We talked about how scary that bear was and how her mother was wrong, that Misty had not made the bear do that with his tail.

The following week Misty did not act out in school. She was impulsive and hasty, but there was no violence. In therapy she continued to talk about the bear, reiterating how big his tail was and how it went up and down, up and down. She verbalized being afraid of her birth mother.

Misty's play in therapy turned to rescue fantasies. We would save babies from bears and "bad men." We chased the bear out of the office and locked the door. We did this play over and over. Misty began to have time in therapy when she would ask to "be a baby." She would suck on a bottle and ask to be held and rocked, though she could only tolerate that for a few minutes. She began to have sessions during which she did fantasy play with no abuse in it.

One day Misty played with my tape recorder as her mother and I talked at the end of a session. There was a moment's quiet and then I heard Misty telling the tape recorder slowly and carefully with pauses in the first sentence while she thought out what she really wanted to say,

> I know. . .I believe. . .that I am Misty. I am six years old, five years old? Six years old. I go to school and then to therapy. . .

I was incredibly touched by this careful, halting pledge to her identity as one person with a life in the real world. Misty made that statement in May; she had started therapy the previous August. She continued over the summer to make statements to me about her self and her history:

> Remember that bear?. . .the one who hurt me with his tail? Some boys hurt a baby's back. . . The little girl in my back is a baby; her mother didn't take good care of her. The little girl in my back is scared of men.

These comments did not terrify her; they seemed more to be nice little tacks that held her to her reality. She wanted to make sure that we still both knew what had happened. She and I were holding this story between us; she needed to have me hear it.

Misty and I are still working together, though on a much less intensive basis. Most of the time her behavior is more "normal." She has begun to have the space and energy to do some learning. She occasionally acts out in school, but now the acting out is more voluntary, not out of control. Now she pushes limits and boundaries and needs help to settle down, which is quite a different proposition.

Misty was an incredible steadying force to me as I did my study of the reparative process of survivors of pre-verbal sexual abuse and as I did my own therapeutic work. Working with Misty has given me faith in myself, faith in her and faith in the reparative process that can follow pre-verbal abuse. She has told me the same story that the six co-researchers in the study told me, the same story I have told myself. She has shown me that she has pre-verbal memories, in the same inchoate way that the co-researchers and I have them and that she is able to work with them now and to produce change and growth out of a process of telling a story, organizing chaos and making meaning.

Armed with the corroboration of Misty's therapeutic process, and stimulated by the rudimentary theoretical ideas that had evolved out of my own experience, I designed an interview format for a study of survivors of pre-verbal sexual abuse. My hope was that I would be able to discover a pattern to this reparative process and describe it coherently. It seemed to me that there was particular damage from early sexual abuse, damage that was somewhat different from the damage created by later sexual abuse. I was curious to see if there were common threads in both the experience of that damage and in the reparative process. I was especially interested in what the reparative process looked like. For me, it had been a matter of slowly and arduously putting words to my internal experience, making a story of it, making sense. I thought that the process of narration had been crucial for me; I knew that it had been crucial for Misty; I suspected that similar kinds of organization of that experience could be done in other ways as well. I began to think in terms of symbolization as the key to helping the survivor of pre-verbal sexual abuse organize her experience. Over time I came to believe that the process of symbolization did not complete the picture; it was the process of symbolization in the service of organization and communication. The symbolization could not just symbolize; it had to communicate and narrate as well. There had to be some communicated story that was told through the process of symbolization for the reparative process to be successful.

The clinical question, it seemed to me, was not "what really happened." The clinical questions were how we go about the process of constructing, or re-constructing, pre-verbal memories of sexual abuse when we are involved in a reparative process, and what this process looks like as we go about repairing the damage of such abuse.

This was the main question that I was trying to answer as I examined both my own experience of that process and that of the six women whom I interviewed. It was both simple and not simple at all to say that I was not going to concern myself with whether these memories are "real." It was simple in that I never found myself silently questioning the memories of the women who did the interviews with me. We did not involve ourselves in "proving" anything, and that was a pleasure. On the other hand, I think that we were all aware that the re-construction of early memory is not a simple matter. There were many questions about the construction of memory and experience that surrounded and informed my thinking and my work throughout the study. I was excited to find that these were not just my questions; they were questions my co-researchers shared.

Some of these questions were: What are pre-verbal memories? Are they experienced differently from later memories? Can pre-verbal memories be retrieved or re-created? What is the difference between memory retrieval and memory re-creation? Is there a difference? How can each of these processes be best facilitated in treatment? How can memory retrieval or memory re-creation be experienced in treatment as a healing process rather than a retraumatization? What does it mean to try to reverse the development of language acquisition in retrieving or recreating these memories? Can this work with pre-verbal memories be done verbally? What is the role of the use of symbol and metaphor in the work that victims/survivors do with memories, particularly pre-verbal memories?

I expected to find some answer to my main question: what does this process look like? I did not expect to find answers to all these questions that surrounded my work. I expected them to keep me in touch with the complexities of the material. I expected that if I kept these questions in mind, I would not find myself sliding from the simplicity of taking each of the co-researcher's experiences for what it was to thinking about pre-verbal memories in simplistic ways. I wanted to think about this process in complex ways. All these questions would help me do so.

In planning the unstructured interviews, I pulled themes that reappeared again and again in my own writing. The following themes were echoed by the co-researchers:

> doubt;
> no feeling of ever having known safety or security;
> repeated nightmares of death, dismemberment and
> > violation;
> a sense of No Words/CHAOS;
> a sense of always having been fighting to survive;
> circles of feelings of trauma that include rage, terror,
> > despair, powerlessness;
> coming to terms with one's own responsibility in the
> > present;
> telling the story.

I took the extensive interview material from the six co-researchers and organized it around these eight themes. This information became the material that fed my thinking about this particular damage of pre-verbal sexual abuse and the reparative process.

I began pulling these threads together by looking at the pattern that underlay the descriptions each co-researcher gave me of her experience. I combined the visual images with the descriptions of feelings that the co-researchers described working through over and over. I related that pattern to my own thoughts about circles of trauma and about the process of moving out of circles of trauma. I looked at what helped these women move out of the circles and why it might be helping. I found that I was thinking about this material in very complex ways. The task was to pull all the strands of my thinking together. To do that, I needed to think about infant social development, neurochemistry, memory and symbolization and narrative. I began with the circles of trauma.

Almost every co-researcher saw her process as looking chaotic or haphazard, but believed that this was only its appearance, that in essence, her process was ordered, progressive and, above all, hers. Each co-researcher described in some way what I think of as the circle of trauma, in which there is a cyclic path through a particular set of feelings. These feelings may be accessed anywhere on the circle. The feelings within that circle are pain, powerlessness, terror, rage, despair, loneliness, and guilt. Chaotic feelings of powerlessness and terror can be brought on by re-living the memories or by being reminded of the abuse. The possible paths can then be best shown in diagrammatic form:

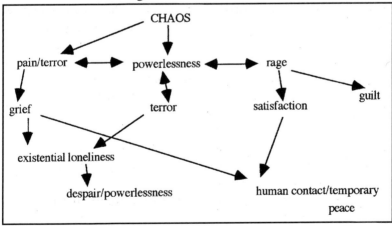

The sense of chaos can lead to a renewed sense of pain and/or powerlessness. The sense of powerlessness can lead back to pain and terror or to rage. The pain and terror can lead to an increased sense of powerlessness or to grief. The feelings of rage and anger can lead to guilt, to a sense of satisfaction or back to a sense of powerlessness.

When the survivor experiences the grief that comes with the pain and terror, she may move to a sense of existential loneliness or she may make human contact through her grief and achieve temporary peace. If she does not make human contact, her feelings of existential loneliness will lead her back to powerlessness and despair, which may lead her to terror or rage all over again. If she makes human contact through her anger, she will achieve a temporary peace as well. If she does not make human contact through her anger, then that anger may lead back to guilt, terror or a sense of powerlessness.

These are what I think of as the circles of trauma. It is quite possible to circle for some time through cycles of pain, terror, rage, loneliness and chaos. Each one of these feelings begets some of the others. In this construct, one way out of circling back over and over is to achieve human contact. Each co-researcher described in some way how human contact helped her break through and continue with her movement forward.

Often, whether the survivor achieves human contact through her grief or through her anger merely depends on how available that contact is for her at that moment, and that of course may depend on whether she has created a support system and has learned to judge what will provide a safe and appropriate contact at those moments. If safe, appropriate human contact is not available in those moments of grief or anger, then the survivor will probably cycle back into the circles of trauma until the next opportunity arises for leaving the circle.

Achieving human contact does not necessarily give one a definitive way out of the circles. Notice that I have labeled it "human contact/ temporary peace." This is the place that allows the survivor to regroup, to regain strength to go back into her chaotic and painful memories and to rest in a state that allows the possibility of imagining living outside the circles of trauma.

This movement and pulling out of the closed circle is connected to the images the co-researchers described: images of spirals and helixes. Each circular part of the spiral can be seen as one of the circles of trauma. Each time that the survivor pulls out of the closed circle, she moves along the spiral to the next "circle." The co-researchers describe going back over the same material, ending up in the same places and yet moving steadily forward as well. Thinking about that image led me to research that has been done on learned helplessness. The movement described by the co-researchers reminded me of Seligman's experiments on learned helplessness (Maier & Seligman, 1976), which provide a model of response to inescapable shock, both behaviorally and biologically. In the experiments once a dog has entered the state of learned helplessness, in which she no longer believes that she can escape the shock, even if she easily could, then she needs training to help her rediscover her ability to escape. This seems to me to be what is happening in the therapeutic process for the survivor of pre-verbal sexual abuse. The survivor of pre-verbal sexual abuse is in a state of learned helplessness. Her only perceived options are to move from painful emotion to painful emotion following the circles described. The spirals enter when the survivor makes complete human contact in a safe context and experiences that contact outside the context of attack and defense in which she lives internally. Each time the survivor allows herself to step outside (or be dragged outside) the circles and feel safe while in relation to another human being, she moves forward along her spiral. She will, no doubt, re-enter the circles of pain and terror and rage, but it will be from a slightly different perspective internally. She is moving along in her spiral. Therefore, she will continue to fall into the chaos, the abyss, the terror, the pain, the rage, whatever piece she uses to stand for her experience of the world. There will continue to be terrible times, but each time there is a slight progressive movement.

How is this any different from the experience of the survivor of later sexual abuse? The key is in the absoluteness of the sense of chaos. The memory itself may be the chaotic feeling, the sense of dropping into an abyss. The survivor of pre-verbal sexual abuse cannot necessarily help herself move out of these terrifying places by remembering what happened to her; chances are what happened is that chaotic feeling. Why?

To answer that question, I had to look at some of the work that researchers have done on the brain, on memory and on infant development. It is possible that part of the reason is that memory before the acquisition of language is different from memory after we can talk and symbolize our experience. Our brain development is incomplete when we are still pre-verbal. At that stage of development, memories are processed and stored in the hippocampal area of the brain that does not fully develop until somewhere between eighteen and thirty-six months (Grotstein, 1991; van der Kolk, 1987). The quality of the memories is apt to be quite different from memories that are processed by a fully developed hippocampal area and stored in the cortex. Early hippocampal memories are based upon sensual experience—smell, taste, feel and

202 • FROM THE LISTENING PLACE

sound—particularly if there is considerable stress. Later, memory is stored in the cerebral cortex and tends to be more organized spatially and temporally and to be structured by language (Grotstein, 1991; van der Kolk, 1990). This makes sense in terms of the co-researchers' experience. They all described their pre-verbal experiences in sensory terms.

Another strand I examined is infant interactional theory. Lynne Murray, a researcher studying attachment at the University of Cambridge, says that the infants in her studies really know when there is something wrong in the interaction between the infant and her mother. They expect a certain pattern of responses, to which they are well able to respond, and when those responses are not available, they become disoriented and distressed and show dissociated responses, described as averting and unfocusing the eyes and staring away (1991). This is true even when the mother is doing all the "right things," but not particularly in concert with the infant. Murray experimented with video-taping infant/mother interactions in such a way that the infant could see the mother and the mother could see the infant, but only through a monitor. She took the tape of the mother's responses that had been part of a healthy, satisfying infant/mother interaction (and which had been satisfying and pleasurable to the infant even through the monitor) and played it to the infant at another time, so that the mother's responses were no longer synchronized or responsive to the infant's part of the interaction. The infant reacted as though the mother were now having all the wrong responses even though the mother was, of course, still doing all the "right things" that she had done before in an appropriately interactive way.

The implication is that infants are not easily fooled. They know when someone is not truly in interaction with them, but is instead acting at them, and they respond with distress and disorientation. Similarly in an incident of sexual abuse, the infant should indeed have a sense that something is wrong; this adult will not be responding in an appropriate dyadic fashion. Instead, the infant finds herself lost in a sea of chaotic sensations, since the interaction for which the infant is prepared developmentally is distorted or does not happen at all. What is happening interactionally loses all meaning and organization. According to Murray, in normal healthy infant/parent interaction the infant will move actively to attempt to bring the interaction back to its dyadic form if the adult's attention slips away and the responses become inappropriate. An infant who is being sexually abused is not going to find that her attempts to return to appropriate dyadic infant/parent interaction are going to be effective. Eventually she is going to give up and may experience herself as unable to act upon the world. She may experience herself as not in relation to others at all, particularly if this abusive interaction is repeated over and over. Later in her life she may find herself "remembering" that sensation of chaos and of the world becoming a meaningless mass of sensory impressions when she is confronted with a reminder of that abusive incident—a certain smell, color, texture or perhaps the presence of the abuser him/herself.

Another researcher whose work helped my thinking process was Robert Marvin. In Marvin's study (1990) small children who had severe cases of cerebral palsy and could not move away when they were frightened (as infants cannot) were given strange situation attachment interviews. The point of the study was that you don't have to be able to move away from strangers physically in order to experience and express attachment. However, an interesting side finding was that every single child, when confronted by a stranger from whom she could not escape, dissociated as a way to avoid the situation. Each child went into a trance when she wished to move away from the stranger but could not physically do so. This response is very similar to the avoidance techniques in infants that Murray describes in which infants averted their eyes, stared away, etc.; it is also similar to the response of many people to inescapable trauma.

What all these researchers seem to be in agreement about is that infants do know when they are being interacted with in inappropriate, non-interactive, objectifying ways; they try to rectify that situation, and when they cannot, they protest, withdraw or dissociate.

Other research that seems to illuminate what might happen to an infant who is being traumatized is that of Mary Sue Moore from Boulder Mental Health Center in Colorado. I heard her present at a conference, describing the research of Ashley Conway from Charing Cross Hospital in London. Conway is looking at the flow of blood within the brain during dissociation. Moore states that Conway has found that during dissociative episodes, the blood in the brain flows to the right hemisphere and is cut off from the left. The right hemisphere produces and accesses sensory impressions and fleeting intuitive recall rather than organized memories surrounded with language and narrative images.

Moore states that when a traumatized person remembers her trauma, she does not remember that event in the same way that we remember less disorganizing events. When we remember a benign event, we remember it in a symbolic way—with words or images that tell the story of the event. If we are unable to organize and surround our memories with symbols, as Moore and Conway are suggesting is the case with traumatic memories, then when we remember a traumatic event, we are unable to separate the memory from the event itself. We have no buffer of symbols to represent the event. We are reliving the past event in the present rather than remembering it.

Other work being done on traumatization and change within the brain is by Bessel van der Kolk and his associates. What van der Kolk is finding is that during traumatization there is a depletion of norepinephrine and dopamine, chemicals in the brain that affect emotional states and functioning; he and other researchers (Anisman, 1981; Redmond & Krystal, 1984; and Kolb, 1988, e.g.) are suggesting that there is a permanent alteration in the central neurotransmitter systems, leading to physiological hyperarousal. In other words, the production and reception of these brain chemicals are affected. Van der Kolk's suggestion is that the alterations happen both in terms of output levels and receptor levels in the noradrenergic system, resulting in a hypersensitivity to threat or other arousal. The result is that when a trauma survivor is reliving the traumatic event, neurochemically she is experiencing the same arousal and feelings of terror that the original event inspired and that this "neurochemical potentiation provides a neuro-physiological analogue of memory" (van der Kolk, 1987, p.70). Van der Kolk is providing a neurochemical basis for the experience of reliving trauma.

The question that arises from van der Kolk's work (as well as from Conway's) is what is to be done about these alterations in brain functioning. One obvious direction is psychopharmacology,or treating psychological states with drugs, which van der Kolk himself is certainly very interested in. However, he also speaks of the use of therapy and suggests combining the two treatments (1987, pp. 75-76).

Considering what these researchers have brought to light, I found myself thinking about the long slow process for both myself and the co-researchers of learning to pull ourselves out of the state of response to inescapable shock—to pull ourselves out through symbolizing, through moving arduously from the right brain to the left when all the physiological functions of our brains are making that incredibly difficult. Learning to organize, name, contain and control our response to traumatic memories seems to me to be a process of coming to use symbols, or language—learning to use left brain functions. For survivors of pre-verbal sexual abuse this is particularly arduous; it is a matter of coming to use symbols to name and contain something that had no organized basis in the beginning. It is not a matter of recovering those symbolic skills or applying them to this particular set of memories; it is often a matter of learning completely from the beginning that there is the possibility of using symbols at all to keep from becoming overwhelmed by the sensations that these memories bring up.

Symbolization is one of the ways in which we create boundaries and distance ourselves from input. It is also how we come to create, construct and control our responses to that input. Without the ability to use symbols, it is difficult to imagine options in terms of response. There are no options; there is no thought; there is only response. An example would be that before I had learned to organize my responses through language, I often found it very difficult just to hear the word *infant*. That word conjured up a sense of physical vulnerability and violation that was so immediate and complete that I would find myself in a state of arousal and would respond with sensations and emotions without any intervening thought.

This difficulty is seeing symbols for what they are—symbols and not the event itself—and thus in using symbolization, seems to me to be a crucial piece not only in thinking about the damage done during traumatization, but also a crucial piece in thinking about repair. Learning to reclaim the ability or, in the case of pre-verbal abuse, to create the ability to use symbols may well be the crucial "way out" of the circles of trauma that my co-researchers described so eloquently. In fact, through trial and error, most of them had come upon the use of symbols through creative endeavor in their attempts first to describe and then to contain their experiences.

How did I get to these thoughts about the circle of trauma and about symbolization from the information that the co-researchers gave me? When I examined the eight themes that the co-researchers and I had explored, many of them were descriptive of the reality or inner state of the survivor of pre-verbal sexual abuse. The recurring themes described the damage and in some instances defined the particularity of the damage of pre-verbal sexual abuse. The five that described the damage were doubt, the feeling of never having known safety, horrific nightmares, the sense of no words/chaos and the feeling of having always been fighting to survive.

There were three themes that did not describe the damage; these were themes that led out of that damaged state: 1) the methods of access and soothing; 2) telling the story: finding words or other symbols to express having no words; and 3) taking responsibility for one's pain and one's self. In examining these themes, I was not just looking at what the co-researchers had answered to specific questions around these themes. I was listening throughout the interview for how each woman described herself and her experience of abuse and recovery. What methods of access to feelings or memories each co-researcher used was important information, but I was also interested in how she talked about those methods. How able the co-researcher was in using words or pictures or motions to describe her inner state and how important that was to her was part of the answer to how much she was succeeding in symbolizing her experience.

This level of listening allowed me to hear how, in talking about the methods of access and soothing, co-researchers sometimes described a particular method as soothing and then later as a method of access to internal information without even seeming to notice that the focus had changed. A method such as drawing, for example, could sometimes soothe and sometimes provide information from inside.

One of the things I began to notice was that some co-researchers focused more on soothing than on access, and vice versa. Listening to them and then thinking about my own process, I came up with some interesting speculations about the process that might be involved. I came to think that there was some kind of flow involved, that the process involved flowing back and forth between soothing and accessing in order to move forward. Soothing was necessary as a tool in order to continue coping, then accessing could happen again and then soothing again, and then accessing and managing.

It is my belief that one of the skills involved in learning management of trauma symptoms is learning not to over-medicate oneself with soothing methods and not to over-stimulate traumatic memories and responses with accessing methods. Part of learning that management involves coming to a balance between soothing and accessing, between the passive and the active, between allowing oneself to feel all the chaos and learning to manage it. The survivor acquires feelings of control and power over her own responses and experience through achieving that balance. Those feelings are crucial in the work that is required in coming to symbolize one's experience and in taking responsibility. She also acquires more than a feeling of control; she acquires some actual control over how re-traumatized she is going to be when she accesses memories or feelings. When she can moderate her own traumatic responses somewhat, then her work on symbolization does not have to be as difficult. That balance makes it possible to do the subsequent work. However, that balance would not necessarily be achieved before the symbolization begins. The work probably proceeds all at once, but as the balance between access and soothing falls more into place, working with the accessed memories and feelings moves more easily.

The next piece that I was listening for was the way in which each co-researcher used, or did not use, symbolization. Did she have some process of symbolization—words or pictures or movements—that circumscribed and described her experience, both the initial abuse experience and her subsequent experience of the trauma and the reparative process? And crucially, had she been able to use those words, pictures or movements in a context of communication? There seemed to be a connection between the use of symbolization and the moments of human contact that the co-reserachers described as moments when they were able to step out of the circles of trauma. It seemed that the symbolization must be shared, that it must be communicated, that human contact was necessary in order that the symbolization become complete—what was said must also be heard. All the co-researchers had in some way described not only how human contact was important, but how in that contact it was someone understanding what they were experiencing that was important. We had discussed human contact as a soothing method and as a support while accessing. I came to believe that it was even more crucial as a necessary piece in completing the process of symbolization.

Symbolizing the experience seemed to contain the experience and, at the same time, give the survivor the ability to control the feeling of chaos and falling into an abyss. Communicating using those symbols with another human being and feeling understood seemed to solidify the sense of containment, organization, and control. The use of the symbols of language or drawing or dance gave the co-researchers distance, as it had me. That distance seemed crucial. Without distance, when we came in close to our experience, we would slip into chaos. The distance created by symbolization allowed us to think and communicate about our experience without re-traumatizing ourselves. We needed distance in order to tell the story. That ability to symbolize was required in order to use narrative in ways that moved the reparative process forward. The use of language, drawing and dance were all forms of narrative. No matter what the symbols, the purpose seemed to be to tell the story. Telling the story takes the experience from within the inner world and sets it out-side, however temporarily. This may be a different process for the survi-vor of pre-verbal abuse from what it is for survivors of later abuse. She may have no detailed story to tell. And yet her task is to take that sense of chaos, that sea of sensations, and to construct a narrative that makes sense of it, that creates meaning.

A sense of responsibility for oneself seemed to be a crucial part of the reparative process. My impression was that this work of symbolization and narrative preceded that sense of responsibility. Although responsi-bility was one of the themes that I explored with the co-researchers, only one of them had much to say about it directly. She spoke about respon-sibility and taking control of her life and getting freedom and power in return. It is possible with my small sample that most of the co-research-ers had not yet reached that part of the process in a very conscious way. As a result, my thoughts about the role that taking responsibility plays in the reparative process are mainly speculative, based on my own experi-ence and the way in which the one co-researcher's experience seemed to back that up so clearly.

My own experience was that the more responsibility I assumed for the management of my own trauma response, the less importance I at-tached to the details of the narrative. The story still was important; it made sense out of what I was experiencing, but issues of fact and fantasy, of what really happened, fell away, and the focus moved to what I was going to do to change my present reality—how I managed trauma symp-toms, but also what I was going to do with this material that I had come to believe about my own experience, how I chose to relate to people, what I chose to do with my life in both a daily and a long-range way. I could never have reached a point at which I could comprehend that present reality and responsibility if I had not first acquired control of the responses that flung me back into the abyss and chaos and kept me in the circles of trauma. I acquired that sense of management and control through a gradual process of symbolization and narrative—through making the story and thus making meaning for myself out of chaos. Taking respon-sibility for oneself is the only part of the reparative process that seemed to come at a particular point in the process; it could not happen until after much of the other work had been done. The process of symbolizing and naming and creating narrative seems to go on throughout the re-parative process, to happen again and again, getting more refined each time. Then the real sense of control over oneself and one's reality comes when there is sufficient containment of the traumatic responses to make that possible. Part of learning to take responsibility requires letting go of dualistic thinking.

My growth toward taking responsibility probably began with the struggle around dualistic thinking about dependence and independence. Several of the co-researchers described themselves as being independent children; many of the co-researchers also referred to learning to trust or depend on their therapists. I certainly had to learn that there was such a possibility as dependence; I had never known trust that allowed such a thing. At first, however, I leaned one way and then the other. I was either dependent or independent. I had not learned any flow between these two, any balance. I could categorize the first part of my therapy as learning to and agreeing to be dependent. Then I could say that I eventually discovered that it didn't matter if I would agree to be dependent, that my therapist could not save me from myself.

But the crux is more complex than that. What I had to learn was that I could need that contact, that support, that love perhaps, and get it, and still I was on my own, still I was the only one who could save me from myself, and that neither of those things cancelled out the other. I had to have them both at once—dependence and independence—responsibility. Dependence does not imply taking care of oneself; independence does not imply relatedness and contact. Responsibility is both together, balanced and in process with each other.

There are other dualities that are involved in the changes that become taking responsibility. Good and bad is one. As long as I was focused on who had done what to whom, I was thinking in categories of good and bad. Unless I saw someone outside me being "bad"—the abuser—then I must be bad. In order to make sense of the chaos and the pain and the body memories, I had to come to understand what had happened to me. In coming to understand what had happened to me, I came to symbolize that experience and to make a narrative of it. That process requires understanding and labeling a victim and an abuser. But after that part of the process is satisfactorily completed, then there is another move that must be made, a comprehension of the impossibility of dividing the world into good and bad. Until that duality can be broken down, the survivor is left with the possibility that she is, in fact, the bad one. She will either have to hate herself or the other. Coming to know that the abuser was wrong and that one was a victim is a beginning, but it is not enough. It is a mistake to blame oneself for another's misdeeds, but it is also a mistake to blame that other for all one's subsequent actions. The survivor must take responsibility for herself. Giving up good and bad is one of those ways.

By this I do not mean that we should never hold others responsible for their actions. Of course we should. But after we have done so, we are, in the end, responsible for our own actions. Their reprehensible action does not create us. It is merely an action that we can judge and then move on to our own actions and our responsibility for them.

A third duality that must be dealt with in some way in this process of taking responsibility is the question of real and not real. This question is at the heart of many of the struggles of a survivor of pre-verbal sexual abuse. The survivor of pre-verbal sexual abuse has even more doubt than the survivor of later abuse about whether the abuse really happened. She must come to learn to trust her own experience, her memories and her internal reactions. At the same time she does not know if what feels so right to her is an actual memory, or if it is a memory that she has created in order to make sense of her world. Initially, she will experience much distrust of her experience. She will think her memories are "not real." Later as she comes to trust herself and her process, she will know that they are "real." Still later, there comes the question of what to do with these memories. Does she confront her abuser? Does she try to convince others that she knows what happened to her? At this stage the question of real/not real memories becomes much more complicated. It has stepped out of the therapy room and into the world. In my process, part of coming to take responsibility was to let go of that duality. What I was coming to know about myself was real, but that somehow did not have to be a repudiation of the idea that memories were also something I constructed to make sense of my experience. I didn't know how "real" they were. I did know how much sense they made, in every way. That wouldn't have been much good in a court of law, but when I let go of the idea that "real" and "not real" were somehow mutually exclusive categories, I came closer to coping more with what was happening inside me than worrying about what was "factual." Without the splitting of good and bad, and real and not real, I do not spend energy looking outside myself for blame or reality. The work becomes naturally a question of what now? What do I want? What do I do next? Taking responsibility.

So the learning to take responsibility had something to do with letting go of dualistic categories. It had to do with understanding about the present, knowing what was mine now. That was a prerequisite to thinking about where to go with it, to taking responsibility for myself. Ultimately, it didn't matter who did what to whom. Ultimately, for me, it was a question of who I was and what I did now. I came to that realization when I understood that reliving traumatic memories was actually happening in my own brain (reading van der Kolk and understanding about neurochemical reality did that for me). Understanding that appealed to my desire for ownership of my own experience and led me to responsibility. I suspect that each person's trigger for understanding that she is ready to take and can take responsibility would be different, but that before that point, she will have done work untangling her ideas and feelings about dependence and independence, good and bad, real and not real.

Taking responsibility is one of the final steps in this process. I suspect that each person will find her own form for taking responsibility. Pulling together all the work that I had done was my form. Tying together the story of Misty with the stories the co-researchers told me, understanding their stories with the framework I built out of my own therapeutic process and struggling to weave a comprehensible whole out of all the strands—that was my way of taking responsibility.

I began with the story of Misty. Misty is now nine years old. She tells me sometimes that the "bear" has gone away, sometimes that the bear has turned into a good bear, who is a friend to her neighbors. She says mostly that the neighbors have moved away, though occasionally in stressful times she will mention that she misses them and that they have come to visit. Actually, there is no sign that Misty's neighbors ever take over now. They have taken on the form of imaginary friends; they are not Misty's constant companions. Misty is much more able to cope with the social requirements of the world. She has some behavioral difficulties in school, but nothing like the problems she had when she was five and six years old. I don't think that Misty is finished with her reparative process. There are major gaps in her development. However, she has been relatively free to proceed on a more normal developmental path for the last two years, and at some point she may be ready to do more of the work on the damage resulting from her pre-verbal abuse.

I also began with my own story. Doing the research study and writing it up was part of that story, as was my own therapeutic work. I used that work and my thoughts about it to structure my exploration and the way I listened to the interviews with the co-researchers. In writing about my own experience, I said, "I found myself frighteningly without words for much of what I was experiencing." In my reparative process, I had struggled to find words; I had moved from chaotic, almost meaningless writing to writing and publishing a short story that described my experience in an encapsulated way. In working on the research study, I had taken what I knew in an inchoate way about my own reparative experience and struggled to put it into words. I took that experience and enclosed it clearly enough with words to shape the interviewing process. I talked with and listened to the co-researchers. I discovered that what I was perceiving as my process was not mine alone. And then I sat and worked to use words to describe and explicate that reparative process in a way that drew not only upon personal experience, but upon clinical thought and experience. I went beyond trying to describe the experience of pre-verbal abuse, or trying to describe what I was experiencing during the reparative process; I came to try to describe more structurally what it was that I was doing while I was going through that reparative process. Each step is a little more distanced, a little clearer, a little more in communication with others. Each step uses a more sophisticated form of symbolization as language and communication in my attempt not only to clarify my experience, but to put it in a form that might be useful to others. As Misty came to be able to do, I am thinking about my experience now, not just re-experiencing it.

In some way this also has to do with responsibility. This is a responsibility to myself. I knew something. No matter how obscure and inchoate and unclear that knowledge was, it was there. I was clear with myself that I knew it, but I was also clear that I could not communicate what I knew to others. That was the need I felt. Taking the responsibility to do the work that would tell the story to others in a way that they might comprehend would round off my process. I needed to give myself the gift of taking seriously what I knew and trying to shape it with language until it could be communicated. That was my responsibility to myself—to think hard and clearly and put into language my experience, so that it would exist outside myself.

References

Anisman, H., Ritch, M., & Sklar, L.(1981). "Noradrenergic and Dopaminergic Interactions in Escape Behavior." *Psychopharmacology*,74,263-68.

Conway, M.(1991). " In Defense of Everyday Memory." *American Psychologist*, 46, 19-26.

Grotstein, J.(1991). "The Infantile Neurosis Revisited: Toward an Integration of Psychoanalysis and Infant Observation." Unpublished paper.

Maier, S. & Seligman, M.(1976). "Learned Helplessness: Theory and Evidence." *Journal of Experimental Psychology*, 105, 3-46.

Moore, M.(1991). "Implications of Disturbed Attachment: Understanding 'Disorganized Infants' and 'Controlling Children.'" Unpublished paper.

Murray, L.(1991). "A prospective study of the Impact of Maternal Depression on Infant Development." Unpublished paper.

Redmond D. & Krystal, J. "Multiple Mechanisms of Withdrawal." *Annual Review of Neuroscience*, 7,443-478.

Van der Kolk, B.(1987). *Psychological Trauma*. Washington, D.C.: American Psychiatric Press, Inc.

Van der Kolk, B.(1988). "The Trauma Spectrum: The Interaction of Biological and Social Events in the Genesis of the Trauma Response." *Journal of Traumatic Stress*, 1, 273-290.

❀

DYNAMIC BODY THERAPY
Dottie Menard

As a massage therapist, I have discovered in my practice that whether I do a basic massage or one with breathwork, intuition helps deepen the therapeutic benefit for the client. It guides me to a more dynamic level of reality.

An Everyday Massage

I begin massaging by using conventional Swedish massage strokes. As my thumb sweeps across the body, I feel small or large adhesions. Adhesions are generally healed tears in the tissue caused by physical or emotional traumas. They feel like small lumps. I bring my awareness to that particular area. I imagine the spot on my body. How would I work it? What strokes would make it feel good? I use different strokes on the area until I feel the "right" stroke. I feel the sensations from the stroke on the client's body as if it were on my body. As my focus intensifies, there is a sense of merging with my client's body. The merging is brought on by experiencing only the sensations—thereby dissolving the illusion of two separate bodies.

After finding the "right" stroke, I begin to probe deeper into the tissue. I "see" (feel) many levels of striations. Working down into each striation sometimes requires new and different strokes. As I get closer (deeper) to the source of injury, the client may either experience an image of the injury/trauma, a memory or simply a feeling not accompanied by a story. I may get an image or a feeling, such as sadness or unshed tears. If I get an image or feeling before the client does, I'll share it with her. When the trapped energy (memory/injury/trauma) is felt/remembered (brought to consciousness) in the body, it is usually released.

Breathwork With Massage

I worked with the client on extensive breathing techniques until she entered into an altered state of consciousness. This state enabled her to open to the pain in her body via the unconscious. Not having previously worked on her body, I had no expectations as to how her healing process would arise nor about my part in her healing.

She began experiencing pain in the heart chakra area. I simply placed my hands on her chest and did Reiki to help the energy move. I became aware of the energy shift when she indicated that the pain had now moved to her head. I began to massage her head—simply flowing with what was comfortable, using strokes from differing healing modalities, such as massage therapy, reflexology, facial massage, holistic headache techniques. The pain decreased and moved to her groin. (She had been gang-raped as a child. She had not, as yet, fully regained all her memories of that trauma. Her body was holding onto the memories. The trauma (energy) was trapped in her muscles. Until she could "relive" the rape, the pain (memories=trapped energy) would remain, calling out to her.)

Intuitively I sensed that her body would have refused deep massage work at this point. So I placed my hands gently on her groin muscles and did Reiki. A light touch was indicated because the body was experiencing deep pain and was frightened that more pain would be inflicted. The area of pain began to pulsate. I felt myself shaking all over. Clear and vivid memories of her rape assaulted my psyche. The memories passed, the vibration decreased and I found myself gently massaging her muscles in the groin area. The pain had decreased and shifted from psychic pain to body pain. I felt the muscles which had retained the memories of her rape did not know how to function. I intuitively guided them, stroked them, until I sensed they knew how to once again function as healthy muscle. I worked this way with every part of her body. Wherever the pain called, I answered with Reiki and massage.

After her treatment, I shared with her the images I had received. They were the very memories she had just experienced!

❀

TEACHING AS ART
Tania Kravath

Wandering the studio
seeking a solution
        for a problem in design
problem solving
focusing on spatial relationships
        size and shapes
        proportion and aesthetics
experimenting
as mental images become tangible
as the art teaches the way
answers revealed
        in the laws of nature
art as teacher
        teaching.

Strategies in the arrangement of
  forms
enticing the collective
modeling of images
        of bees and nectar
creating the atmosphere
motivating to focus
lighting a spark
transmitting information
pollinating into the unknown future
relying on the organic
        nature of nurturance.

Providing the opportunity
        for new growth
organizaing
        shapes for maximum flow
cans * jars * colors *
        rules * scissors
accessible.
Bouncing energy
calmed by order
taking steps through skills
methodical order
until the skill takes hold
        and the vision flies.

POEMS
Bernice Mennis

The Pond's Edge

I stand at the pond's edge
and watch the still sun suspended
above the mountain's graceful curve.
The ice moves darkly and deeply under me.
At this moment I do not know
if the thundering growl
means a hardening into or a
melting out of form
if that sun is moving up
into the warmth of summer day
or setting slowly into winter night.
At such times we look for instruments
to show us our bearings
to watch a compass a calendar
to tell us whether to carry
the heavy woolen sweater or leave it
behind or if we should even
begin such a long journey at all.
Yet I have felt a tender breeze
on a February night that has
warmed me more than summer's sun.
And quick darkness and unwelcomed
cold have brought me where I
could never have chosen to travel
so deeply so richly.

The Door

That bird that glided
into the golden blue wind
took me under its wide wing
even though my feet stayed locked
into this earth.

Today it is very different.
The winds howl in gray slates of ice.
I sit inside and think about the bird
moving somewhere in that cold sky
beating its huge wings.
It's December. I wrap
myself in sweaters and blankets.
Even when a breeze blows warm
I know the cold of what is coming.

What lets me go out into
that cold wetness is the faith
that I can come in
again and again.
(Is it faith, knowledge, or illusion,
I do not know.)
To be able to open and close a door,
to have such a door.

And if that door in the mind or in fact
would disappear like Elijah
we would have to fly through the
icy gray for miles and miles
the stretch of years
buffeted in mist
with no knowing.

And where would that knowledge
that has no knowing take us?
To what other faith?

We stand on our own isolated island
shivering as we gaze on the surface
of the endless blue green sea
no way of seeing the distant boats
that circle around the island
offering thin translucent lines
floating on the waves.

To follow that cord we cannot see
means moving in gray storm
refusing the shelter that stands only
inches from our path offering us
warm food and rest till the sun comes.

The door—
the knowledge of it the belief in it
the need for it the desire for it
the prayer for it the entering into it.
The door whose keys lock out
the golden sun the silver flight.

A Knowing

There is a knowing that knows
and there is a knowing that needs the long way
and maybe it needs the long way because it is already lost
  and that now is the only way.

We look for cairns in the dark flashlights focused
  because there is no moon
  because our feet can't feel the way.

The ancient Hawaiians blinded the children
   who were to be the seers
   taught them the chants to move
   through miles of monotonous waters
   to find the way home.
The way is to sing the way
to not look for what will deceive.

But if we cannot remember the chant
   or know the breeze that touches our skin
   and what it means then our eyes strain to see
   the small island in the immense sea
   and only sometimes we find it after years
   of gazing at empty miles.

Can you imagine what we will become
if we embrace all that we are.

That long route home awkward humbling
   tripping over the debris of wasted passageways
   to find our simple thirst and direct hunger.

My friend will be happy.
I have found bananas and papayas
after all these years.
And they are good.

The Spinning

   I almost missed it
   except for the thin curled branch
   the faint arc of light
   the speck moving.

And even looking closely
the angle of sun made the web
disappear into air until I moved
and tilted my head a certain way
looking sidewise in order to see.

She moved quickly clockwise
completing the small inner circles
using all her legs/arms to spin
her web. Using everything she had.

There was an order a regularity
she knew the space between lines
the rhythm of movement. But still
it was a leap of faith that first line
of light woven from her body and flung
between two distant points of earth.
How did she know the second would be there
and that she could reach it?
Yet she had to do it.
It was her hunger the knowing of hunger
and the movement of her body in her from her.
It was all she had.

Something so fragile in such immense space.
So much inattention walking by. Not conscious
malevolence but the inability of others to see
what your hard labor has created all those long
hours. The threads of light that keep you
and your children in body.

The complex weave of gossamer lines
which is really the art of poetry.

You spin words out from your body's gut
into that thin and lonely air and you

wait. And mostly it is not seen at all.

But sometimes for no real logic or reason
you see it there total the whole world
and what was done is known.
She has taken you there.
You are trapped
and sit
stunned and silent.

Myths and Knowing

There are no myths to grow by.
Every myth I know keeps one small
trapped by a mouth whose words
shape a cage more real than life
a mire so heavy that the small feet
sink deeper each time the child
tries to move with her own two feet.

And he said, "If you take away someone's illusions you kill them." And
I thought, "It is the illusions that kill. The tearing leaves room for
new births."

This is a collective poem to rip apart
the illusions that strangle our possible births
to name the myths, to say them aloud,
to exorcise their power over us.

For example, this room is only a small
plain rectangle with tables and chairs
and a group of middle-aged and old women.
Empty except that one feels at times
a fire that casts light and shadow
in strange patterns and warms with
irrational intensity. At times the
words take one through dark caves

across fields dotted by sunlit grass
and you find yourself—who knows how—
in some unknown meadow filled with
columbine and wild iris
at a sumptuous picnic
and you wonder how everyone knew to come here
carrying their intricately
woven baskets from which they slowly
remove delicately wrapped parcels
which they place tenderly on
a silken tablecloth of rich green grass.

And it is true that an observer might see
only a room full of tables and women
laughing over nothing
crying over nothing
and sometimes we ourselves—sitting around
that silken cloth—begin to question the
rich and luscious food that rolls around
our own tongues and moves down our bodies
and with that questioning we begin to choke
to feel hungry
to be ashamed.

But the magic is real here.

I remember an African tale of a man who laughed when he looked
into his wife's basket, the basket he had sworn never to touch, never to
open. His laughter greeted her when she approached. He laughed, he
said, because the basket was empty.

The woman slowly and carefully
picked up her precious basket
and left the laughing man
to join her sisters.

❀

INTUITION AND EXPERIENTIAL
EDUCATION
JoAnna Woo Allen

If experiential education is key to understanding knowledge which can't be told, then intuitive teaching is at the heart of experiential education because intuition guides us through this "tacit dimension."

I have long believed that anything learned is best learned experientially. A favorite saying is, "Tell me and I forget. Show me and I remember. Involve me and I understand." It's so much more fun and interesting to be actively involved than being handed words on a page or collecting them from the vibrating air molecules of a lecture hall. I like being taught experientially because I'm physically oriented, a doer, and I tend to fall asleep when sitting still too long.

I now realize that some lectures can be experiential, that too much experience in my teaching can be as bad as too little, and that a good educator uses all sorts of ways to reach students. Doing is not necessarily experiencing. A little experience can go a long way if reflection on it is skillfully facilitated. But I also know more fully than ever that there is *knowledge which cannot be told*, which can be shared only by helping someone else have an experience which will teach that knowledge.

Seeds for this insight were planted by Polanyi's statement that "we know more than we can tell." (1972, p. 4) Polanyi calls this facet of knowing which is not communicated through language the "tacit dimension." How then can we share that knowledge? Through a process he calls "indwelling," similar to empathy. "When we make a thing function as the proximal term of tacit knowing, we incorporate it in our body—or extend our body to include it—so that we come to dwell in it." (Polanyi, 1972, p. 16)

Such experience with a piece of the world leads students to tacit understanding. Through what they sense, the outward expression of something, they come to know the being of that thing. A connection is made within which they understand. This understanding cannot be communicated by telling it to another. The actual event or object, or one related to it, must be experienced by the other learner.

Experiential education is not "experimental education." As a movement, it has its roots in John Dewey but as a professional field it is relatively new. I believe its rise relates to the growth of democracy. As we evolve from the other-directedness of authoritarianism toward self-direction and self-education, we demand more freedom to learn in individualized ways. The democratic ethic empowers us to take the lead in our own self-actualizing processes.

Experiential educators are not, therefore, distributors of knowledge but facilitators of learning. "Where there is teaching, there is not always learning. Where there is learning, there is not always teaching." Experiential education is learner-centered, with the learner having a large role in determining the path and style of learning. Educators help bring about understanding and meaning, often in ineffable ways. This ineffability requires intuition and trust from both facilitator and learner, an openness not only of mind but also of the inner self.

The field of experiential education is composed of three groups of components: outdoor (adventure education, environmental education, outdoor recreation); indoor (service learning, adult education, community-based education, apprenticeships and internships); and classroom (cooperative learning, the project approach, writers' workshops, whole language). A learner-centered approach which celebrates experience as pivotal is the common ground.

Learning experientially is very empowering, but we can get fooled by planned activity we call experience. Experience involves the whole person, mind and emotions. "Doing" in the classroom can involve people physically while cutting off internal processes of thinking and feeling. Such learning does not last. In experiential learning an internal change takes place (Cell, 1984) because the whole person participates. As a result of authentic learning, there is a change in attitude or perception, a "eureka" effect, an enlightening. The person after the experience is different from the person before it.

To structure a situation so that genuine learning occurs takes skill. Challenge, apprehension, uncertainty, exhilaration, conflict, either external or internal—all help "doing" happen deeply enough to become experience. Inductive reasoning and simulations allow more permanent learning of scientific laws or facts of history. Such strategies encourage real understanding, not just temporary knowledge of definitions and information. In matters like understanding oppression, which require empa-

thy, experience through a classroom simulation is crucial to genuine understanding. Sometimes an experience will mean sharing another's passion for something until it is absorbed and understood.

Mentoring

Let's focus now on one way of learning experientially, apprenticeship
and its related process, mentoring. However the Greek tutor for whom
the process is named did his job, I imagine it was deeply integrated with
intuition and experiential education.

Take, for example, a master craftsperson, a woodcarver, who takes
on an apprentice. Both understand at the beginning the apprentice seeks
to learn from the master a skill which must be practiced under the master's
supervision and watchful eye. There will be demonstrations, advice, cor-
rections and adjustments during the apprenticeship's development.

The mentor in turn works beside the apprentice. S/he does not simply
hand the apprentice a book although much can be learned this way initially. The master shows the apprentice, involves him/ her, and most
importantly lives and models the art in his/her presence. Untold subtleties are communicated in nonverbal ways.

If the apprentice is to become a true artisan, s/he must strive to learn
what cannot be told. This can happen only in the presence of the master.
What lies within the intuition of the master—the holistic, aesthetic understanding of the craft—is what separates the master from ordinary
woodcarvers. The status of being a master comes from recognition within
the profession that s/he is highly developed. This knowledge which the
master has attained cannot be told; it is ineffable. It can be learned only
in ways beyond language. With a beginner's mind the apprentice must
be open to an inner grasp of the whole understanding of the master, to
connect experientially with the unspoken messages which can only be
felt and sensed.

The apprentice experiences woodcarving by practicing it and being
allowed to make mistakes. The master knows when to let the apprentice
alone and when to project just the minimum of an encouraging hint.
Such timing comes from the mentor's experience and intuition. Provided the mentee is patient and persistent, the mentor trusts that the skill
will emerge and develop in its own good time. While the master has
grasped the whole of the craft, the apprentice must begin with pieces.

In experiential education learners must be allowed to take their own paths within a framework, to bring their own experience to their learning. Learner and mentor must be open so they can "dwell within" each other. While it may be agreed that the learner is subject to the teacher's influence over content or curriculum, the learner must be respected to make the connections in his or her own way. The outcome of an apprenticeship depends on how well master and apprentice relate to one another. Can their presences meld in harmony and insight so that the apprentice takes on some of the being of the master and the master is also changed by the apprentice? Such a merging of spirits results in ineffable common understanding.

This is experiential learning at its fullest, a far evolution from the more mundane "learning by doing." Such a model can only be shared by those who understand intuition. Certainly, more empirical models of experiential learning such as hands-on classroom activity, math manipulatives, discovery science or mock trials, are ones which traditional educators accept and practice. Any good teacher recognizes the value of active learning. But experiential learning will not only improve but transform mainstream education if this deeper intuitive level is reached.

Intuition in Teaching

Teaching is called an art and a craft (Eble, 1984 and Rubin, 1985). Intuition is integral both to the craft and to the training of the craft people, teachers themselves. Certain skills such as lesson planning, classroom management, and assessment are learned by all teachers. The added quality of the outstanding teacher is an intuition for when and what to do next. This sense, like the aesthetic sense of the woodcarver, might be inborn or trained. Most often, it develops through actual experience and apprenticeships under master teachers.

> Artist teachers. . .differ from ordinary teachers in that they function with consummate skill. Some, blessed with natural gifts, rely principally on instinct. Others, less intuitive, cultivate equally impressive artistry through practice and effort. In so doing, they often borrow insight and confidence from the methods of those whose talent is innate. (Rubin, 15)

This artistry in teaching describes experiential educators I have studied. Most artistic teachers, Rubin writes, are characterized by four attributes:

First, they made a great many teaching decisions intuitively; second, they had a strong grasp of their subject as well as a perceptive understanding of their student; third, they were secure in their competence and expected to be successful; and fourth, they were exceedingly imaginative. (Rubin, 17)

What stands out in Rubin's work is his frequent mention of intuition, perception, taste, instinct, hunch and sensitivity. The good teacher hones her sense of timing and quick decision-making so she can adjust to the individual or situation, to the teachable moment. Intuition rises to the occasion at these times rather than prolonged deliberation. This ineffable artistry in teaching comes from a feel for knowing when, how and what to do during an unpredictable moment. It arises from the reflective practice and creativity of an intuitive teacher.

Artist teachers. . .use insight. . .to get at the heart of a matter and sense what will work. They not only prefer to obey these instincts but are uneasy when, for some reason, they   must disregard them. Such teachers find instinctive knowledge exceedingly useful, readily accessible, and an effective shortcut in reaching conclusions. (Rubin, p. 61)

Real learning comes through reflection on an experience, however long it takes. Anyone facilitating such learning by encouraging the learner to look back and glean meaning is an experiential educator. One does not have to structure the experience to be such an educator. An instructor may provide a unique setting for team and confidence building, as in adventure education; a teacher may use curriculum, texts and her own background to set up learning activities, as in classroom education; or a therapist, without structuring the events in a client's life, may guide her self-reflection so she can heal wounds she may not have been aware of before this examination of her life. In each case it is facilitation of debriefing, the reflection on the experience which brings about new understanding.

Without necessarily setting up activities or arranging emotion-filled events, classroom teachers can be experiential educators. Students bring their own worlds into classrooms, sometimes yearning to describe an important experience, needing deeply to process it—knowledge to be clarified from a recent vacation trip, the tragic loss of a friend through drunken driving, a nerve-shattering racial incident, or the pleasant occasion of winning an award. To facilitate this kind of learning, to give permission to students to bring their outside worlds in, is part of the artistry of teaching experientially.

This art involves a polished ability to facilitate a discussion so that a door to learning from an experience is swung open. Timing, sequencing of structured events, sensitive response to individuals, with the right amount of restraint, brings about optimal learning. Tuned and aware of who and where the learner is, what next step is needed for light bulbs to flash on, for learners to construct their own learning, the experiential educator must have a honed intuition to skillfully and effectively facilitate learning.

I believe artist teachers are best made through apprenticeship with master teachers, just as the apprentice woodcarver learns from the master. Artistry is not learned from books or lectures, helpful as they are for teaching theory and skills; artistry comes from praxis, a reflective practice which questions continually whether and how students are genuinely learning. Natural teachers with a gift for seeing the whole child and the whole class have highly developed intuitive senses from their first days of teaching and attain the master level more quickly than others.

Persons on their way to becoming artist-practitioners, woodcarvers or teachers, eagerly embrace learning situations. They are not set back by disappointments or mistakes. They work on themselves, gathering experiences as steps to wisdom. This way they develop their intuitive faculties, the ability to make right decisions without long deliberations, to grasp teachable moments, to understand students. There comes a point when they just do it, without being sure what they are doing; the artistry is part of their being. Such knowledge is not attained through books or lectures. It enables them to teach through experience those things which cannot be told.

References

Cell, E. *Learning to Learn from Experience*. Albany, NY: State University of New York Press, 1984.

Eble, K.E. *The Craft of Teaching*. San Francisco: Jossey-Bass, 1984.

Polanyi, M. *The Tacit Dimension*. New York: Anchor Paper, 1972.

Rubin, L.J. *Artistry in Teaching*. New York: Random House, 1985.

❀

HELPING CHILDREN HEAL
Sherry Kaufield

Nothing prepares counselors for working with children. Everything prepares counselors for working with children. When I make these two statements to classrooms of college students considering a career in the therapeutic field, they look at me with polite, sympathetic indulgence and not a little disbelief. How, in a field of work where psychological theories abound, where preparation and education are intense and ongoing, can either statement be true, let alone both be true at the same time?

Nothing prepares counselors for working with children because every child's mind is a gift to be opened. A surprise. We can learn therapeutic language, a helping demeanor, a theoretical base, but we can't really prepare for the flesh and blood child in front of us—not if we stay open to the whole of who this child is. If we form definite conclusions about a specific child from circumstantial knowledge—family, teachers, friends— we give up parts of that child. Like the blind men touching different parts of the elephant, sometimes we choose not to learn more than we already think we know, no matter how near and obvious lies the conflicting evidence. When we work with children, we can only prepare ourselves for a gift. We know the sun will come up, we know where we can expect to see it and the time sunrise will occur, but we know nothing about its colors and patterns and shades until it's there before our eyes. So too with children.

On the other hand, everything prepares us for working with children. All that we know, all that we are, all that we expect and yearn for colors our perception of an individual child. In fact, the child before us is, in many ways, the total of our own experiences, not hers. From infanthood we distinguish between self and non-self, me and other than me. As we grow and learn we constantly compare what we know and don't know, categorizing and sorting information according to fields of personal experiences, values and beliefs. When some bit of information doesn't fit into one of our knowledge fields, we create new fields—and we learn. When we work with children, we bring with us the personal treasure of ourselves. Everything prepares us for working with children.

This book is about intuition. How is intuition part of the therapeutic process? When I counsel children, intuition can help make the contradictions make sense. Intuition lets me know which bits and pieces of information to gather, when to gather them, and when to wait and allow information to build and grow. It can make the crucial, qualitative difference in choosing a diagnosis, developing interventions and even in knowing when therapy is complete. For me, intuition isn't an "a-ha," a sudden realization of truth or a mystical revelation. It's that time when all that I know and don't know about a child begins to make sense. I use that sense to help children heal.

When a child suffers emotionally, the people who care about her are desperate for answers. With heartfelt intensity, they pour forth an effusion of facts, behaviors, conjectures and questions about the child, hoping someone can quickly wade through it all and offer some insight and understanding into their child's emotional distress. I learned very early in my therapeutic work to contain these emotional floods as soon as possible. While a child's family and community relationships are irrevocably bound into her being, and those people who are significant to her are valuable information resources which should never be minimized, the child is her own best storyteller. And I have questions of my own to answer.

What does this child want me to know? What is she terrified that I might find out? What does she need from me and from herself in order to tell her story and begin to heal?

Information gathering is, for me, a nebulous, intuitive process. Information comes from everywhere; from seeing, hearing and feeling the whole of a child through all of her communication. In fact, this wealth of information always provides more answers than questions, more perceptions than categories in which to sort and examine them. Patient, careful listening and watching, joined with a sense of wonder, curiosity and empathy, and balanced with absolute respect help shape a fertile crucible in which the child's answers can grow into healing knowledge.

Without a doubt, the choice and use of language determine the quality of the questioning and the information gathered. How do I choose the "right" words and know when to use them? Training in therapeutic communication helps, but at some point, often very early in the therapeutic process with a child, training falls short. Why? Because training, whether based on abstract theory or reinforced with specific examples, begins to fight with instinct and intuition when a child's personal story is being told. I find that if I trust my sense of the child from our very first interaction and if I pay attention to that knowing, this sense will guide my communication. I rely much more heavily on the intuitive use of language than on what might be theoretically "correct." At some point in our work together, the wholeness of the child emerges, real and imagined, seen and unseen, spoken and unspoken. The questions which need to be answered are answered, and healing begins.

Effective interventions with children are almost always heavily experiential. Since our environment contains metaphors for virtually every human emotion and behavior, interventions are basically a matter of matching a child's need (my goal in working with a child) with a useful metaphor and then using age-appropriate materials in an experiential treatment process. For instance, if a child says, "I *never* do anything right" and this is a belief which causes real problems for the child, I might have him collect his toothpaste tube, tennis shoes, jacket, shampoo bottle and a stick of gum. Without telling him why, I would ask him to humor me by removing and replacing the caps from the toothpaste and shampoo, zipping and unzipping his jacket, tying and untying his shoes, and then unwrapping and chewing the gum. Can this be a child who never does anything right? He gets it. Once we prove that "never" is way out of line, we can begin to narrow down the child's specific concerns and deal with them realistically. The process described here: isolate the therapeutic goal, identify an everyday metaphor and create an intervention to help reach the goal.

Here's another example. A child is so easily frustrated that she gives up without really trying new things. She basically has weak problem-solving skills. The goal then is to strengthen her skills when she's confronted with a *new* situation. What would be a metaphor for "newness?" I might give her an infant doll and ask how the "baby" could get what it wanted—food, for instance— gradually comparing that to how the child gets what *she* wants. With constructive guidance she might end up with something like this: "First I think about what I want, then I see what there is to eat, I check with my Mom, then I just get it." I would reinforce this throughout counseling as *her* four-step process for new situations: 1. *Think about it*; 2. *Look at it*; 3. *Ask for help if needed*; 4. *Do it*. Her problem, a useful metaphor, her solution. It works.

I've often been asked how I "just come up with" interventions. I think it's a combination of several things. First, I rely heavily on intuition—

just letting answers flow from all the information available. Once I know the goal or where we need to go in therapy, I open my thoughts and feelings to a metaphoric example of either the stated problem (the first example above) or the solution (the second example). Second, I cultivate creativity. I use a metaphor in whatever way it will address the issue. And third, I continually update my training and skills. Keeping abreast of what's going on in the field gives me a wider view of my own work by comparison and provides me with valuable resources from others.

The following informal case study demonstrates how all of this comes together, how having a sense of one child translated into therapeutic intervention and, in this case, guided the healing process. While this study is based on an individual child who was hospitalized in a psychiatric hospital, at times she becomes a synthesis of other children with whom I have worked. All identifying information about "Sara" has been changed to protect her right to confidentiality.

Patient
Sara is a 10-year-old female.

Chief Complaint
Sara told the intake counselor that she was hearing "voices" and that one of the voices had told her to kill herself.

Brief History
Sara stated that her parents were divorced when she was seven. Shortly after the divorce, her father remarried, and her mother allowed a boyfriend to move in with her. Sara lived with her mother at that time. Two years later, Sara's mother died of an overdose of drugs. Sara said that shortly after her mother died, her mother "came back for a few days at a time and stayed with me in my head." She said that when her mother went away, she left a number of "good and bad voices" to help Sara take care of herself. Recently one of the bad voices had told her to kill herself.

Brief Family, Social and Medical History
Sara went to live with her father and stepmother following her mother's death. She was enrolled in the fifth grade in a local elementary school. Sara hated her stepmother, often acting aggressively towards her and defying her openly. She said her father was always angry with her and that he always sided with her stepmother against her. Her father stated

that Sara attempted to control much of what went on in the family—mealtimes, including what was served, television shows and entertainment, the bedtimes of all family members and even what types of clothing everyone should wear. They often let her have her way in order to avoid conflict.

Sara blamed her mother's death on the boyfriend, stating, "He killed my mother; he made her take drugs." Sara believed her mother was perfect, that she was forced to take drugs and that Sara's life was "wonderful" before her mother died. Sara described one occasion of having been locked out of the house by her mother's boyfriend and her mother helping her "sneak back in through a window."

She used this as an unfortunate example of how much her mother loved her and had taken good care of her. In fact, Sara did a great deal of caretaking—shopping, fixing meals, doing laundry and helping her mother when she was "sick" on drugs.

Sara said that she had twice been sexually fondled by her mother's boyfriend, but she had never told her mother. Penetration had not occurred.

Sara's father offered very little information regarding her medical history except to state she had been diagnosed by her family pediatrician at age five as having Attention Deficit Disorder (ADD), was not presently on any medication, had no known allergies, and was in good health.

Crisis Events

In the recent past on separate occasions, Sara had ingested hair spray and furniture polish and had taken prescription medication that was not prescribed to her. Each time, Sara's father took her to an emergency room, and staff referred them for psychiatric help. Unfortunately, he neglected to follow up. He finally called a local social service agency because of Sara's talk about the voice which was telling her to kill herself. The agency recommended that Sara be brought to the hospital for an immediate assessment.

Mental Status

Sara was cooperative during the assessment process and talked easily and at length. She seemed generally relaxed, focused and oriented to reality, though she matter-of-factly claimed that she heard the voices as cited above. She was also very concerned about how she was answering the questions and asked anxiously several times, "Am I doing all right?"

At the time of her assessment and subsequent admission to the hospital, Sara was considered at high risk for suicidal behavior due to her recent attempts and the destructive voice she was hearing. In addition, Sara stated she had lots of problems at school, including failing grades, physical and verbal fights with peers and defiance of her teachers. Sara was admitted with the provisional diagnosis of severe depression.

Admission and Treatment

I became Sara's therapist and care coordinator on the Child unit in the hospital. When Sara arrived, she was open and curious about the other children and her environment. She settled into her room by following the directions I gave her, listened carefully as the rules and structure of the unit were explained to her—"This is how we do things here"—and was then included into the therapy group taking place on the unit. Sara was cooperative during the group and remained so throughout her first few days on the unit, but she responded superficially to questions related to her feelings. When asked, she always felt "fine." She showed little hesitancy in matter-of-factly talking with staff about her "perfect" mother and about the good and bad voices her mother had given her. At times she would appear tearful and sad, but would deny feeling anything but "happy" or "fine."

Psychological tests and assessments began as quickly as possible after Sara was admitted to the hospital, but results would not be available for several days and in some cases, for almost two weeks. In the meantime, treatment had to begin.

From observing Sara, I noticed significant, persistent incongruities between her demeanor and her verbal responses and between what was actually going on in her environment and her emotional experience of it. She would look sad and depressed and say she felt happy, or she would see other children in emotional pain and appear calm, happy and unaffected. It was confusing and disorienting to watch. A therapist's response to a patient often mirrors what a patient is feeling regardless of the patient's behavior. Was Sara confused and disoriented about her feelings? We couldn't begin to understand Sara until we could understand how she felt and experienced her life.

With this goal in mind, I planned a series of groups. Since all of the children on the unit would be involved, the groups had to be general enough to meet some need in each of them and specific enough to be useful for Sara. My objective was to give Sara and the other children an opportunity to identify the feelings which were important to them, to understand the reasons for their importance and to express them in a realistic and useful way.

For this first group I handed each child a card with a feeling written on it—Love, Hate, Anger, Happiness, Pain or Fear. They were instructed to hold their cards so all could see, read everyone else's card and then one by one if they wanted to, trade their feeling card for one they wanted more. The only rules were that if someone wanted a feeling no one could refuse to trade and each child would have only one turn to initiate the trade. Sara had initially been given "Pain" and had traded it for "Happiness." However, when a peer took a turn, Sara ended up with "Fear." During the ensuing discussion each child was to tell when he or she had experienced the feeling represented on their card. Sara insisted she was not afraid of anything because her mother had given her a voice to comfort her and protect her from fear. I asked, "Are you ever afraid the voices will not be there for you?" She said, "I'm afraid people here will try to make them go away." I told her it was a *good* thing for her to be afraid to lose some of her voices because they had been useful for her in a lot of ways. I reassured Sara that only *she* had the power to decide whether her voices should be with her, and that we would help her discover other ways to take care of herself too. She would be the one to decide which way was best for her.

On another day, using the same feeling cards, I planned a second group. This time I gave each of the children one of each card; they all had *all* of the "feelings." I read a story and asked the children to raise the appropriate card when they thought one of the feelings on their cards related to something they had heard in the story. Sara had great difficulty in this group. She raised her Happiness card almost continuously, even when very sad things were taking place in the story. She could not understand, or refused to accept the explanations the other children gave for feelings other than happiness. She seemed agitated and nervous. Why? I asked Sara if she thought it was important for people to always think she was happy. Sara revealed that a counselor at her school told her she should *always* smile no matter what she was feeling "because nobody likes to be around unhappy people." This message had been reinforced with her for over two years. No wonder Sara was conflicted in the way she expressed herself. She would need to learn to give herself permission to have and show her real feelings.

With this new knowledge about Sara, my objective in the third group was to help Sara and the other children understand that it is all right, and even good for them to have all kinds of feelings and important for them to communicate these feelings to others.

I gave each of the children two index cards and asked them to write the "worst" feeling they could think of on one card and the "best" feeling they could think of on the other card. They were not to show one another their cards. The children and I then sat in a circle on the floor and all of their cards were placed face down in the center of our circle. Each child by turn drew a card, read the feeling and told the group when he or she had felt that feeling. If a child said he or she had never felt that way, any other child in the group could respond. In this group the children actually had the experience of sharing their best and worst feelings, heard other children talk about them and most important, understood that all feelings were all right. I had seen Sara write "Hate" on one of her cards and wondered if she would say anything when that card was drawn. She interrupted the child who had drawn the card and said, "I hate my mother's boyfriend for killing my mother and for hurting me." Sara began to cry, saying over and over that she wanted her mother and wanted to kill her mother's boyfriend for making her mother take drugs.

Following this group Sara began to share her feelings more and more each day. She was offered a great deal of positive feedback for this, and she began to accept and like herself better. Her question changed from the anxious, "Am I doing all right?" during the intake process to a more self-validating, "I'm doing all right, aren't I?" It was still a question, but she was moving in the right direction.

Sara's test results had been received by this time. All of her physiological tests were normal except for the P300—an indication that she did have ADD. Sara frequently had difficulty concentrating for any substantial length of time. In groups, I had been gently reminding Sara to focus on what was going on, had changed activities frequently and had moved groups along with deliberate speed. Based on the test results, his observations and reports of Sara's behavior, her psychiatrist ordered a trial of a stimulant medication. She had a very positive response: her attention problems decreased almost immediately. I continued to facilitate groups in the same way in order to accommodate other children with ADD but found I had less need to refocus Sara's attention. Other staff working with Sara made the same observation. ADD became part of Sara's diagnosis.

Sara's psychological profile provided interesting information about her. The psychologist reported that Sara had made numerous attempts to control the testing experience, wanting to make deals in exchange for providing information. When this was not allowed, Sara became sullen and uncooperative for a time. It was noted that Sara had a high need to have control whenever possible—over interactions with people, her environment and her emotions. This was consistent with information offered by Sara's family during the assessment process.

The testing also revealed that Sara did not want to live in the present. This fit with the relationship problems Sara was having with her father and stepmother. Sara could stay close to her mother by remaining emotionally isolated from her present family, focused in the past. Consequently, Sara had not developed a sense of identity with or investment in her family. Paradoxically, she complained of feeling ignored and unloved by her father and stepmother and felt betrayed by her father for having remarried. Sara's attempt to *defend* herself from feeling outcast and unloved was to outcast and isolate herself from the family even further, which *fed* her feelings of being outcast and unloved.

While all of the test results helped me understand Sara better or confirmed what I felt I knew, there were still a lot of unanswered questions. Because of Sara's voices, some staff were convinced that Sara had a true dissociative disorder, an inability to stay oriented in reality. Others thought she was just severely depressed.

I agreed that Sara was suffering from depression; she certainly had good reasons to be depressed! But I felt that Sara knew intuitively what she needed in order to feel protected and had created her voices with "magical thinking." It was extremely useful for Sara to create the controls she needed to feel safe when she couldn't find safety within her environment. Her mother's good voices provided her with a sense of love and protection. Could the bad voices be Sara's developing maturity fighting with her prepubescent magical thinking? Could the voice that told Sara to kill herself be the only way of relieving the confusion and frustration? We still had a lot to learn about Sara.

At this point Sara's treatment became focused on three areas. First, we continued to provide activities and experiences and planned interventions which would help Sara continue to express her thoughts and feelings in healthy ways. Second, based on her academic test results, we set clear expectations for Sara within the hospital school program to provide opportunities for her to be successful in a school environment. And third, because of what we knew about Sara's relationships within her present family, we planned family therapy sessions directed toward helping Sara, her father and her stepmother learn to understand each other and communicate more effectively.

In addition to Sara's emotional estrangement from her family, her need to control them was interfering with their ability to parent her; roles were confused and undefined. I decided to give each family member the task of writing a description of their family role—father, stepmother, daughter. Sara gave herself many of the parenting, caretaking and controlling functions she had assumed while living with her mother. In *her* belief system, Sara had parental responsibility. Family therapy focused around redefining and practicing family roles appropriate to her present family. This was difficult and frustrating for Sara because her fragile identity was so tied up in her parental role, but I felt it was crucial in helping Sara establish positive and useful relationships with her father and stepmother. Sara was not a happy camper. And in her eyes, it got even worse.

On the unit, Sara would "parent" the younger children, often to their distress. They complained that Sara wouldn't leave them alone. I asked that Sara's interactions with the younger children be restricted in order to keep her focused on her own needs. Sara became very angry with this and often swore at me and the rest of the staff when she was redirected to remove younger children from her lap or when she was asked to let other children speak for themselves. She began to kick chairs and throw toys and other objects when she was confronted and began to need time away from the group in order to regain control. As difficult as this was to watch, it was *good* for Sara. She was giving herself permission to express her feelings openly and honestly. After all, she had every right to feel angry. She was not only a motherless child; we were forcing her to be a childless mother. We were exquisitely patient, though unwaveringly consistent in our expectations of her. Sara was forced to deal with her own feelings and needs. And day by day she did.

Since Sara was becoming emotionally stronger, we approached her with the idea of directing a personal psychodrama. Sara's psychiatrist supported the intervention, suggesting that Sara communicate symbolically with her mother and her mother's boyfriend. Sara excitedly agreed to participate. I felt that psychodrama would be a very useful tool for Sara. I still held the "magical thinking" view and felt if we could collapse that thinking into her present reality, an integrative healing would begin to occur. At the least, I knew Sara would reveal and learn more about her personal map of reality by acting it out and felt she was strong enough to deal with what might come up as a result. I also felt that it was time for us to carefully and delicately address the truth about Sara's "perfect" mother. If Sara's mother wasn't perfect, Sara could have less investment in the destructive voices her mother had "given" her.

Sara was given control over who would play the parts in her psychodrama. She asked a male staff member to be the mother's boyfriend and asked me to play the part of her mother. Sara would play herself. In a quiet, private room we sat on chairs facing one another.

Sara was asked to tell the boyfriend how she felt about him. She began with little emotion, very calmly stating, "You killed my mother and I hate you for doing that." She became louder and more angry as she accused him of taking her mother away from her. At one point she yelled, "It's your fault I'm alone and my mother is gone. If I could kill you I would; I would stab a knife in your eyes, then you could never see your mother again either." Sara began to cry and repeat, "I want my mother, I want my mother." I reached over to where Sara was sitting and said, "I'm here, Sara." Sara rushed over from her chair onto my lap and put her arms around my neck. Sobbing, she said "I want you to come back. I want you to take care of me and read me stories and be here when I come home from school. I miss you so much." I said, "I miss you too, Sara. I didn't want to die. I wanted to be with you always and take care of you. I shouldn't have taken the drugs." Sara pointed at the "boyfriend" and said, "It's not your fault, he made you take the drugs, he killed you." I said, "I had a choice, Sara." Sara said, "No, you didn't, it's his fault." I said, "I took the drugs, Sara, I made a mistake but I never wanted to leave you. I didn't want to die." At that point Sara stopped talking and just cried. I rocked her gently and patted her back and stroked her hair. Sara sat with me for about twenty minutes more, slowly regaining control. Then without a word, she stood and moved back to her own chair.

To end the session, I suggested that the players describe to Sara what we had felt and thought when she was talking to us during the psychodrama. I thought it was important to bring Sara's feelings into the present in an analytical way to reestablish the purpose of the intervention and to leave Sara *thinking* as well as feeling. The staff member told Sara he could tell how much Sara hated him as the boyfriend and how strongly she blamed him for her mother's death. He thought Sara truly believed the boyfriend had forced her mother to take the drugs which had caused her to die. I told Sara I felt how much she loved and missed her mother and that she did not want to believe that her mother had a choice in taking drugs. When asked to talk about what it had been like for her, Sara said she didn't know, that she just felt confused. We finished with hugs and a lot of positive feedback for Sara "for having worked so hard to understand things better."

Several days later, we arranged an additional psychodrama session for Sara at her request. We each played our former parts. This time Sara began with gory, detailed descriptions of what she would do to her mother's boyfriend if she could. She looked at the "boyfriend" and said, "I hate you for hurting me," referring to the sexual abuse. She looked at me angrily from her chair a few feet away but said, "I know it's not your fault." I said, "I'm so sorry you were hurt, Sara. I didn't know. I never wanted you to be hurt. I made some wrong choices about the way I lived my life and you were hurt. But I always loved you and I never wanted to leave you." Sara looked at me quietly for several minutes, said she didn't want to do this anymore and walked out of the room. Rather than dealing with the sexual abuse that Sara brought up (which was continuing to be addressed with Sara by her psychiatrist), I felt it was important to stay with the issue of Sara's mother's behavioral choices. It was a tough call; Sara was in a lot of pain.

During the week that followed this psychodrama, Sara was noticeably quiet and thoughtful. She began to ask questions about drug addicts and drugs. At times she held the dolls we had available, at other times she wanted to be held and rocked.

When a younger patient was admitted to the unit, I asked Sara if she wanted to help him get used to things. She said, "I'll show him around and then I'll bring him back to you." She stood and looked in my eyes for a few more seconds, smiled a huge, joyful smile, took the new little guy's hand and walked away. I knew Sara was going to do just fine.

At this point Sara had been hospitalized for five weeks. Her attention deficit symptoms were stabilized and her depression was lessening. She was responding very well in the school program. She was dealing well with her role expectations on the unit and cooperating in family therapy. She was clearly oriented in reality. The treatment team agreed that Sara's voices, while psychotic in nature, were not evidence of any deep-seated, pervasive psychosis. They were, in fact, helping her cope with the loss of her mother. The bad voice which had told Sara to kill herself had gone away. She was no longer talking about or acting out suicide. Added to her diagnosis of ADD was Major Depression, Single Episode with Psychotic Features. Though her work would need to continue for some time, Sara was ready for discharge from the hospital.

Sara continued to attend aftercare groups and to work with her psychiatrist. She and her family also continued with outpatient therapy.

I planned the final group in which Sara would participate while in the hospital. The children were given a long sheet of white butcher paper to place on the floor and an assortment of crayons and markers. They were told to arrange themselves on one side of the paper in any order they wanted and then they were each to draw one car of a long train. They were told that all of the train cars needed to connect together in some way. In their train car they were to draw themselves and a person they would like to have with them and then to decide where their train car would be going. Sara began to direct the other children to positions along the paper, deciding who should draw the engine and the caboose. She looked at me, smiled, and said, "I'm doing it again, right?" I told Sara to check that out with the other group members. When she asked, two children said they felt bossed around and didn't like where Sara directed them. She shrugged, asked the others where they thought *she* should be, took that place and began to draw. Early in her treatment, Sara wouldn't have recognized that she was attempting to take control and would have become *very* distressed at giving it up.

Sara drew a lumber car as her part of the train. She said that she didn't know why, but "people build things with wood and I like that." Perhaps Sara recognized that changes were building in her life, and allowed the train car to become an unconscious metaphor for her own growth. Also, building things with wood is a future action and indicates future possibilities and plans. I suggested to Sara that maybe she could see herself building something good for herself and that it didn't really matter what that turned out to be. She just smiled.

Sara connected her train car to those on either side of her with colorful rainbows. She said she drew them because rainbows made her feel happy. When I asked her what else made her happy she said "knowing I can have friends and other people to talk to." I knew with support and encouragement that time, growth and experience would continue to move her forward in healing.

Finally, Sara drew a picture of her father in the train car with her and said she would like her train to go to Disneyland. She said, "Everybody can pretend all they want there."

I believe people are self-healing. They may need guidance and support, but in the end, they find the answers and make the decisions that enable them to heal their own lives. Sara made many decisions that helped her healing process. She still has difficult times ahead as she continues to adjust to the idealistic and physical loss of her mother, to acceptance and the building of relationships within her present family and to her own multi-layered abuse. Though the bad voices were gone, Sara still had voices with her when she left the hospital. She said she told her mother to keep all of the bad voices away from her. "The good ones can stay for now." She said her mother had not answered like she used to but Sara believed that her mother had heard her. She said, "Maybe my mother has other things to do now like I do."

About three weeks after Sara was discharged, she called the hospital from a pay phone during lunch hour at school. She said things weren't perfect, but she was still going to outpatient counseling with her family and working on getting along with them. She said she really just wanted to say hello and that she missed us. Then she said, "And you know what, Sherry, I'm all right!" I remembered all the times Sara had questioned herself, looking for others to tell her she was worthwhile. I told Sara I had never doubted that for an instant. Now she knew that for herself.

What did this child want me to know? What was she terrified that I might find out? What did she need from me and from herself in order to tell her story? Questions now both crucial and irrelevant. Answers from an intuitive openness to the wholeness of Sara.

❋

If telling your story is like dropping a pebble in a pond and watching its effects spread out in ever widening circles, imagine what it would be like if a group of people stood around the edges of a pond and simultaneously dropped pebbles. Each one's widening circles would intersect, without disruption, the circles of the others until eventually they would all form one large, encompassing circle—for one moment.

From *The Rest of the Deer* (Blanchard, 1993)

DRAW ME PICTURES WITH YOUR WORDS
Harriette E. Wimms

In late spring, 1993, on an afternoon that was even more stress-filled than most at my office, the receptionist buzzed me.

"Yes," I snapped, before I could stop myself.

"You have a call from a Penny Potter. I know you're busy. Do you want me to take a message?"

First I answered yes, then for some reason I changed my mind.

"No, Joanne, never mind. I'll take it."

Ms. Potter, the director of the Baltimore Mayor's Advisory Committee on Art and Culture, was calling to ask me if I'd like to work on a project called BrightstARTS. BrightstARTS contracts artists in Baltimore city to conduct art workshops in different disciplines, including story telling, pottery, jewelry making, music, drumming, portrait drawing, and puppetry. Ms. Potter had heard of me through a writing therapy project for battered women that I was putting together and thought I'd be perfect for the BrightstARTS writing workshop—a creative writing workshop open to Baltimore city students between the ages of 7 and 15. She wanted to know if I would like to teach the classes for February and March.

The left side of my brain screamed, "You can't do that. You're a marketing rep in a publishing company. What do you know about teaching? What do you know about kids? What child is gonna want to come to school on a Saturday? Tell her No Thank You!" The right side calmly answered Penny's question. "Yes, I'd love to do it. It sounds like fun."

I spent hours researching teaching techniques, writing structure and the fundamentals of group facilitation. I pored over children's book after children's book. I combed through education journals and magazines with pages and pages of "instructional aids." And then I stopped. I sat down and remembered what I liked to read when I was younger. I tried to remember my favorite classes, my favorite teachers and what had been the difference in those classes. I tried to remember how it felt to write my first poem, to show my first poem to anyone. . .and then I put all of the books and journals and articles away. Somewhere inside of myself I knew how to teach this class.

With copies of poems by Alice Walker, Lucille Clifton, Maya Angelou, Langston Hughes, T.S. Eliot, Ntzoke Shange and May Sarton I walked to the building where the class would be held. With cassette tapes of music that was "mad, happy, or sad" and pictures cut from magazines that illustrated the same feelings, I made my way down the dim stairway of an old community church to the drafty basement room that would soon become my classroom. I was TERRIFIED.

The class was comprised of two groups of ten people. The morning group consisted of children between the ages of seven and eleven who lived in urban areas. The afternoon class—the same demographics, but with an age range of twelve to fifteen. One by one the kids walked in, letting me match their faces with the names on my roster. With each face and each smile and each pair of eyes, I became more calm.

At four o'clock that evening I opened the door to my house, falling through it and collapsing on my sofa. I was completely exhausted, experiencing absolute overdrive; I had an even greater appreciation for teachers, and I had learned something about myself: I *could* teach! My background in the study of the intuitive process allowed me to **not** approach this teaching assignment as the person with all of the knowledge and research and answers. I was able to stand back and assess the situation as a whole. I approached my students as my partners. We worked together to express our collective creativity.

BrightstARTS classes met on four consecutive Saturdays in the early spring. With this in mind, the structure had to be different from that of a typical classroom. I encouraged free speaking (as long as one was respectful of others), answering questions without raising hands, reading aloud and sharing if moved to do so while stressing the option to pass without guilt or explanation. I did not focus on extensive grammar and spelling correction. I praised each child for expressing her or his feelings—for getting the message across. The shock on the faces of my students was almost comical when I informed them of my classroom rule #1: It's fine with me if you lie on the floor and scream, as long as you get up when you're done and write about it.

In the middle of each class we stopped to play a game related to the topic we were discussing (example: During the nature module we "made a rain storm" or during the city life module we imitated movements and sounds that one hears in the city). The primary requirement for these games was they had to require a lot of movement and a lot of noise. The children got a charge out of being encouraged to yell in a classroom.

I created a study plan for each class and each group. However, I also followed the clues my class gave me. Many times my curriculum was "thrown out of the window" to address the needs of the class. The younger students enjoyed reading aloud and having the opportunity to share their work. The older kids enjoyed having a forum for discussing their feelings about everything, not merely the piece we were reading. The small class size lent itself to each child's receiving individualized attention. I also encouraged the class to work as one large group, several cooperative peer groups and individually.

Some of my classes were offered in communities known as *empowerment zones*. These children (many of them eight years old or younger) walked themselves to class through streets I'd be nervous about journeying through. There was an inner strength, a toughness, a wisdom in the eyes of some of these students that told me they had stories to tell that I could not even imagine. With these students I had to first get their respect. I had to create a classroom in which they felt safe, respected, understood and *intelligent*. I changed my usual way of speaking. I became more hip. I used street slang in my explanations of family or nature or feelings. Again I observed amazement on each child's face as I not only spoke the language of a teacher, but also spoke their language.

As inclusion and cooperative learning become realities in our typical classrooms, teachers will be called upon even more to incorporate intuition into teaching techniques. Responding to the diversity of all students is similar to "dropping" into a situation and looking at it from all angles. (Blanchard, 1993)

Many of the children in my classes were African American. I made it a point to use a broad ethnicity base when choosing writers to discuss in the class; however, an emphasis was placed on African American artists—with particular emphasis placed on artists who were raised in and/ or wrote about urban settings. I took in biographies of the writers and explained the particular awards they had received for their work.

When we used music as a vehicle for stimulating imagination, music from all genres (including rap and R&B) were utilized. I watched the wonderment in each child's eyes as I asked them to get up and dance to Arrested Development and then explained that their dance had been a creative expression of how the "art" of Arrested Development had made them feel. I watched many small jaws drop to the floor when I played Queen Latifah's "Just Another Day" and got them to realize that a "hood" was a _neighborhood_ which was part of one's _environment_, which was part of _nature_, which was our lesson for the day. (When I asked one 7-year-old why he looked so shocked by the music I was playing, he quickly responded, "I thought you was gonna play some old-timey somethin'." "Ah, I fooled ya, didn't I?" was my response.)

In _Developing Cross-Cultural Competence_ (1992), Lynch and Hanson ask interventionists to "consider a garden of lovely plants—all varied in form, blossom, and size. All share a basic need for soil, water and sun, yet each plant may have different needs. Each type of plant is of interest to the observer and offers its own beauty and special characteristics. But as a whole the plants make a wondrous garden to behold." The authors go further to explain that "communities and cultures are like gardens— made up of individuals who contribute their own unique characters to the place in which they live." (pp. 3-4) My classes were some of the most beautiful gardens that I have ever seen. I stressed the fact, the reality that each person in my class could use their writing to elicit emotion from their audiences. I taught them they could draw pictures for me and for themselves with their words. That they could tell the world what it was like to be them . . . and no one else could do it for them.

So with this introduction I invite you to peruse a few of the pictures that my classes drew for me—and themselves—with their words.

The Gathering

The sea is a comforter.
My place to relax.
The water is calm and clear.
We are gathered at a table having festival and fish.

The day has ended and it's time to depart.
As we gather our things, I turn to bid goodbye.
I turn to see moments of happiness and time well spent.
Moments that I shall treasure forever.
I am saddened by the fact that I am leaving, but even happier
that one day I shall return.

Monique Ferguson

What I Hear Outside

What I hear outside is boomboxes blasting in the max,
while children dance the night away on the corner.
They don't know that the next step they take
may be their last.
Low class idiots drive by in their urban assault vehicles, yelling pro-
fanities.
I watch the news and see that another youth is killed over a Starter
Jacket
or a pair of Nikes.
I say to myself, "is violence the key to solving the problem"
The only thing it's going to get you is 10 to 20 years.

So I'll leave you with this thought,
"It's better to buy something instead of facing 10 to 20"

Laurence Bass III

Untitled

When the sun shines,
When the birds sing,
People are happy, happier than anything.

When it is rainy,
When it is cold,
People are sad, very, very sad.

When it is thundering,
When it is lightening,
People are mad, so very mad.
Ronnie Reives

After reading a poem about what it was like to feel old and doing movement exercises that dealt with growing old, this student wrote an empathetic piece about the elderly:

Raining Cats and Dogs

Once there was a forgotten house with a forgotten old lady inside. She was very cold. Her family never came around anymore and she could not get around like she used to. Her house was very cold and she had five quilts. Her house was falling apart and had a big hole in the roof. All of a sudden it started raining. The old lady was awaken by the water dripping on her face. She said, "Just my luck, it's raining cats and dogs."
Edwin Russell

After a discussion about nature, animals, and humans (initiated and led by the class), one student wrote this story:

Wolle the Whale

Once there was a whale named Wolle. Wolle had a wife named Harriette and two children, Anansi and Sarafina. When Harriette swam, Sarafina swam right behind her. And every time Wolle would go swimming, Anansi would follow him.

So one day, Sarafina and Anansi went swimming by themselves. A human started to mess with them, so the whales fought back and won. Wolle swam over and said, "Wow, he's good for his skin and teeth." Then the whales walked on land and sold the humans so they would be humiliated.
Shannah Harris

Something's Under My Bed

Something's drooling
Something's crawling
Something's pushing
Something's gnawing
Something's pushing
Something's gnawing
Something's under my bed!

I have to go to the bathroom,
But that thing won't let me go,
I have to go to the bathroom,
But that thing makes me say no!
Something's under my bed.

It ate my doll
It ate my bear
My Mom won't come across the hall
Something's under my bed.

Mom and Dad have gone out to play.
The babysitter's here to stay,
I'll turn on the light next to my bed,
And Pray I won't turn out to be dead.
Something's under my bed.

IT'S A DOG!
I thought it was something from a bog.
Nothing's under my bed.

Sarah Estes

I Wish It Was Night

I wish it was night
There out in the jungle
I wish it was night
for kids to go to bed.
Oh yes it is night
I am so happy.

Robert Silver, Jr.

A seven-year-old used the diamante form to create the following poem:

Cody

Cody
Caring Lovable
Barking Crying Growling
Beagle Friend Playmate Beggar
Whining Smiling Meowing
Unlovable Mean
Wallaby

Ashley Hall

Untitled

D is for a dream that Dr. King had.
R is for respectful.

K is for kind.
I is for intelligent.
N is for nice.
G is for great.

It spell Dr. King.

Keith Figgs

Summertime

Summertime is a fun place we love.
I like to play in the pool.
Friends tell me it's time to go in the pool and dive.
It's hot outside.
A $1.25 it costs to go to the pool.
Sometime Mom says,
"Here the money."
Sometime she says,
"Too bad."
Then I lock myself in my room.
I get mad.
Mom says, "You better stop that crying."

POOSH!
I hear the sp sp splash
like somebody step in the snow.
After the pool I go home
drink some milk and take a nap.
It makes me feel cold.
Sometimes it's fun to dive in the pool
and the lifeguard can be any color,
black or white.

Chuckie Stith

Lastly, I'd like to share a poem I've written, using the techniques that I used with my class to inspire me:

Brown Eyes and Butter

When I think of you
(the one who somehow slipped away,
like the skin of a marlin—
proud and determined—
between two wet, tired palms)

I see the diner on the corner of Charles and Center
Number 1 Center Street, I believe.

"The Buttery"

The windows, caulked on all four sides,
do not open out or in.
They sit
(dusty, grease-stained)
as the hours and years go by,
unchanged. . .unmoving.

We walk through the door,
through the memories of burnt coffee and old scrambled eggs,
tumbling into our favorite table.

You comb your fingers through your yellow hair.
(It will not leave that easily, my dear.)

To the right sits a group of men:
50's, balding,
bulging bellies,
Marlboros in their sleeves—on their breath.
Faded tattoos of eagles and hearts and women's breasts:

*"I don't blame 'im 'cause sometimes them women deserve it.
They bring it on themselves, they ask fer it.
And up until then he was a model citizen . . .
'cept fer that little wife-beatin' incident."*

To the left sits a group of gay men
dressed in pink and lavender and shirts that say, "Just DO
    Me!":

*"Well, some people do think lesbians are part of the gay culture,
but I definitely don't agree. They should not be included.
They're all so bitchy!"*

At the counter sits a homeless man huddled in an old army
     jacket,
in the dead of this heat, with a bottomless cup of coffee.
His head is held low, with his chin on his chest and his mouth
     hanging limply open.
At the other end, on a deep red stool,
sits a women in stiletto heels and leather
with a fatigue in her eyes that pleads, "How did I ever get
     here?"

The waitress, Mae, usually slides from her low-back chair
and shuffles toward us with a quickness not bestowed upon
     the average customer.
We have somehow slipped into her favor.
Into her tired joints and wrinkled chocolate skin.

But tonight she is leaning listlessly against the lime green
     counter.
The AM radio behind the table
crackles out an aged melody that
takes Mae back to the days when she swooned to the tunes
from a jukebox in a tiny backroom speakeasy.

She rests her elbow on the counter
her chin in her hand
and is gone far away
to a time when she stood in the line labeled
"Colored Only"
to see Ella sing at the Palladium.
Swaying
back and forth,
humming
in and out
of this evening and that.

And in the midst of all this
all I can see is your eyes.

Brown.
    Brown.
        Brown.

In the middle of this "macabre cabaret"
I can only note the slope of your neck
as it disappears into your back,
around your silken shoulders.

The tilt of your chin and
softness of your cheeks
and temptation of your voice as it rises and lowers,
reminding me that some roads cannot be taken.

In the midst of all this there is
you and me,
and brown and butter,
and the fading trail of a bright-blue fin—
cutting deep and fast through darkened water—
never to be touched or thought of again.

References

Blanchard, M. *The Rest of the Deer: An Intuitive Study of Intuition*, Portland, ME: Astarte Shell Press, 1993.

Lynch, E., & Hanson, M. *Developing Cross-Cultural Competence: A Guide for Working with Young Children and Their Families.* Baltimore: Paul H. Brookes Publishing Co., 1992.

❀

INTUITION AND PROBLEM-SOLVING
Margaret Blanchard and S.B. Sowbel

Assuming intuition to be an indefinable process which visits us when we least expect it can prevent us from actively employing it in ordinary parts of our lives. Actually, the basic building blocks of intuition—image, symbol and story—have often been used for healing, personal growth and problem solving. If we stay cognizant of the fruits of the intuitive process—integration, synthesis and transformation—we see how they can be used to help ourselves and others move creatively through crisis or change in the cycle of life and how they can help us work together to resolve social issues.

The process of integration can easily be seen in psychological work which uses the Jungian concept of the shadow. Whenever we reclaim the parts of ourselves which have been despised, rejected or denied, we not only increase the resources from which we can draw, we reduce our vulnerability to hidden terrors. This kind of integration involves knowing the story we start with (who we believe ourselves to be in relation to family and history) and introducing new characters, settings and plots to the process. This, in turn, increases our potential to perceive ourselves in a different relationship to our old story and/or to embrace a new story.

The process of synthesis occurs whenever we bring together two or more conflicting or polarized positions out of which something new can emerge. Those positions may be within one person or between several people or groups. Whenever you feel internally divided, intuition can be used to place those separated parts into a context of wholeness. When several parties are involved, we can use the same process in the form of mediation. In mediation, the conflict may move to a place of harmony, may actually lead to reframing, which produces a solution not previously envisioned or at the very least may produce a larger understanding of the facets of discord.

The process of transformation enables us to imagine how we might move from where we are to where we want to be. While imagining how such a change might occur does not actually make it happen, this process allows us to clarify the elements necessary to prepare the soil for that transformation. It also gives us a sense of power and possibility which can inspire us to make or welcome change. For example, the social images for women of menopause are so negative that a woman facing this period of life can look forward to a pathologizing of this natural phase, pity for her lack of ability to procreate and visions of herself as a dried up prune. In the last few years considerable effort has been put into researching and transforming these images so that this stage is seen as a welcome initiation into a time of wisdom and freedom.

These aspects of intuition link creativity with healing from trauma, personal problem-solving and explorations of larger social issues.

ACTIVITIES

Integration, an aspect of the intuitive process, can serve to join previously adversarial elements, provide a synthesis of complementary elements or connect seemingly unrelated elements. This activity, THE INTEGRATION EXERCISE, provides the individual with an opportunity to experience integration in symbolic terms.

Through this activity, you will detect an unintegrated aspect of self, explore aspects of that unintegrated aspect via guided meditation, identify other arenas where integration activities would be of use and experience integration in symbolic terms.

You will need pencil and paper.

Steps:
1. Remember, we are often taught or may choose as a matter of developmental survival to neglect or reject aspects of ourselves. These aspects can be dimensions of self we need. Even though we might tend to disown, deny or denounce such parts of ourselves as the child self, the angry self, the powerful self, the opposite gender, integrating those aspects can yield options and resources previously unavailable.

2. Prepare for a guided meditation by getting comfortable and closing your eyes. Take three deep breaths and with each exhale, release any tension that may be in your body.

3. Ask a friend to read the following instructions or record them onto a tape recorder and play back when you are ready:

You are walking down a long hallway and notice doors of different colors. Behind each door is an aspect of yourself which may be positive and unaffirmed or negative and unacknowledged. It may be a child self or a monster self or an animal self or a fantasy self or any other possibility. Pick a door. Open the door and see what part of your self is there. Dialogue with that part.

When you are ready, meet that part at the threshold of the door and approach it until you merge with it. Realize how it feels. Speak with its voice. Understand what it wants and why.

When you are ready, return to where you started, feel yourself sitting in your chair and open your eyes.

4. Describe in writing the following:
* what the door looked like
* who or what the part of self behind the door was
* the dialogue you had with the part of yourself behind the door
* how you felt when you became it; what it had to say; what it wants and why.

5. If you are in a group, share your experiences and what they meant to you.

6. List examples of other issues or areas of your life where such integration might prove useful. Who or what would you like to integrate and how would the presence of that aspect of self help change various situations?

Synthesis can be defined as reconciling opposites or putting together distinct parts to make a whole. As an intuitive process synthesis can allow a discerning of possibilities where none previously seemed to exist. This activity, SYNTHESIS AND WHOLENESS, provides the individual with an opportunity to reframe an issue by joining polarized opposites through visual symbols. This can be useful as a form of problem solving.

You will identify a personal dilemma and its polarized parts, choose visual symbols for poles of that dilemma, conceive a synthesis of those poles. You will need crayons, colored pencils or pens and paper.

Steps:
1. Remember, problem solving can sometimes be approached from an intuitive, symbolic manner which then translates into a genuine solution.

2. Consider a no-win dilemma in your life. For example, time vs. money—in order to do the things we want, we need money; if we work to earn the money, we have no time. Other dilemmas might be personal needs vs. others' needs, a loved child vs. battering spouse, and so on.

3. Think of an image for each side of the conflict and draw each image separately.

4. Imagine an offspring of these two images, something with aspects from both of them, and draw it. If after some consideration this seems impossible for your particular dilemma, you might see if there isn't some way to transform one of the images so a new insight appears or some relationship/partnership between the images becomes possible.

5. If you are in a group, share your results and discuss whether any new solutions emerged from this symbolic reframing of the issue. If not a solution, did any new insights about your interaction with this issue arise?

GROUP ACTIVITY

If you're working in a group, you may want to try THE ROLE PLAY.

Many social issues which trigger strong emotional responses are viewed from simplified either/or positions. A debate mode merely amplifies the limitations of a rational, oppositional approach to such issues. This activity will allow the individual to examine the complexity of an issue from a situational perspective.

In this activity you will examine the various facets of a social situation, role play specific positions related to a social issue, understand the complexity of that social issue, consider solutions more appropriate to that complexity. You will need role play cards, pencil and paper.

Steps:

1. Remember, many people address social issues from an either/or perspective born of the rational model rather than the intuitive model. You're either for war or against it, a hawk or a dove. You're a liberal or a conservative, left or right. This results in very "charged" interactions and less than open exchanges around certain topics. We're going to look at a "charged" social issue from the vantage point of the intuitive. As we've seen, the intuitive approach often means accommodating the full complexity of a situation.

2. We'll approach this with a role play. Eight participants will present experiential aspects of the issue and the remaining participants will listen and ask questions. We'll be looking here at the issue of abortion, but any controversial issue—health care reform, domestic violence, equity in education—can be explored with this method.

3. Before anyone volunteers for the role play, everyone should write a brief description of their personal opinion, belief or position on this issue. Once it is down on paper, set it aside for the next half an hour and try to keep an open mind.

4. Eight people are asked to join the role-play, as long they are willing, for the moment, to play a part which may not cohere with their own personal experience or values.

5. Ask each of the eight volunteers to choose one of the ten role cards. The roles described on the cards include ten situations in which the issue of abortion would have been considered:

Five women who have had abortions—

* a woman who was date raped at age eighteen;

* a woman who has four children under the age of seven and has a very strained marriage on the brink of collapse;

* a woman who was in medical school on scholarship which she would lose if she dropped out;

* a woman who discovered that her family had a history of genetically-based degenerative disease.

* a sexually active teenager who has become pregnant three times and has had three abortions.

And five women who have not had abortions—

* a woman who had a child at seventeen, out of wedlock, which she gave up for adoption; she has since been married, had other children and grandchildren, is now a widow; she has always had to work;

* a woman with strong religious beliefs who was sexually abused by a relative;

* a woman who is the mother of six, who had been told there was a substantially increased risk to her health if she became pregnant again a few weeks before she became pregnant with her sixth child. She is supported by her husband, who is from a wealthy family.

* a woman who was the ninth child in a family of eleven children, who has never been pregnant and wants to be, though six of the boys in her family have hemophilia and she carries the trait.

* a lesbian who has never had a child herself although she is helping to raise her partner's three children.

6. Role play volunteers are encouraged to defend their character's position and may embellish their roles if they choose. This role play is an improvisation and new information may come out as the drama is acted.

7. The role play volunteers sit the center of an inner circle with the

witnesses surrounding them. A "talking stick" is passed around so each person, when it's her turn to hold it, can tell "her" story without interruption. She passes it on when she's finished and when someone else wishes to speak.

8. After each volunteer has told her story based on her role play character, the participants may ask questions of one another (staying in character). These questions should elicit more information or feelings about the experience but should not attempt to judge or debate it. The point is to explore the full experiential dimensions of the issue before making any generalizations about it.

9. Now open the floor to questions and comments from the outside circle. Again, stop the discussion as soon as it gets polarized or turns into a debate. Ask people to speak from actual experiences.

10. After comments and questions, imagine how, as a group, you can use intuition to help resolve or bring insights to the dilemma of abortion. Would any of the tools or techniques of intuition (as described more fully in *The Rest of the Deer* or *Restoring the Orchard*) be useful for reframing this issue, putting it in a broader perspective or finding alternative solutions?

Whoever is acting as facilitator must maintain a neutral position in this role play and may find it necessary to remind participants not to fall prey to arguing and/or debating the issue. A facilitator may observe that role play volunteers defend their positions well the first time around but during questioning, after having heard other positions, may move to questioning their original position. This process can help everyone recognize the complexity of any issue.

Other charged issues may be war, welfare, affirmative action, gun control, mandatory HIV testing or socialized medicine.

EMPATHY EXERCISE

There are many social splits in any society. These splits are based on facets of our lives which may differ. We may be of a different class, gender, sexual orientation or race from someone else. One way we may attempt to heal social splits around these differences, without trying to erase the differences or pretend a false unity, is to imagine ourselves as the other. This can help us see aspects of difference as well as assumptions we may have about differences. An issue that often causes discomfort is the area of sexual orientation, maybe because it touches on a topic that isn't easily discussed in our culture, sex, and an area that is crucial to any society, relationships.

Imagine that you wake up one morning with a different sexual orientation from the one you had when you went to bed (or a different race, gender, class, nationality, age or ability). How do you feel when you look into the mirror and see this new you? How would this change affect your relationships, social status, job, interests, self-esteem, political concerns, recreational activities? Describe one day in your life as "the other." What do you enjoy most about this life? What do you enjoy least? What insights does this new perspective provide?

*This essay was adapted from *Restoring the Orchard: A Guide to Learning Intuition* (Ft. Ann, N.Y.: Tara Press, 1994).

❀

EMPTY BOWLS
Lisa Blackburn

The *Empty Bowls* project (which I co-created with my partner John Hartom) began in earnest in August of 1991 although the original seed for it was planted in November of 1990. Each year the Bloomfield Hills, Michigan, school district has a Thanksgiving Day food drive in which each school participates. Traditionally the individual schools pledge to purchase a certain number of turkeys, all of which are gathered by the district and donated the week before Thanksgiving to needy families in the area. In 1990 one school had fallen short on their fundraising efforts to pay for the turkeys they had pledged. This left everyone with about two weeks to raise additional funds.

John teaches ceramics at one of the high schools in the district and felt that there must be a way for his students to contribute. After some brainstorming, we came up with the idea that his students could make enough ceramic bowls to serve a soup luncheon to the faculty and staff and ask them to donate what they would have otherwise paid for lunch that day. Interest among the students and staff was high, and someone suggested the home economics students participate by making soup and bread for the meal.

During the days of bowl making the students who were participating started to really learn to make bowls. They began to understand and recognize subtleties about design and form that they had not previously concerned themselves with. The same was true when it came time to glaze the bowls. Having 120 bowls to glaze in a short period of time presents the need for mixing(and learning how to mix) large quantities of glazes. John's students also chose to mix a variety of glazes so when it came time to apply them, the studio setting was ripe for experimentation. It is rare that all of these conditions would otherwise exist simultaneously in a classroom setting and further that they would exist along with the high level of enthusiasm and energy that was present in anticipation of the staff luncheon. A critique of the bowls with regard to form, function, glaze combinations and application which preceded the meal was extremely educational and in retrospect provided a quantum leap in the quality of work being created by many of the students in the program.

At some point during the preparatory process, and to a greater extent since, we have become aware of the power of the bowl as a symbol: a vessel for food, a symbol of all the empty bowls that exist in the world, a symbolic vessel for the spiritual emptiness and disconnection we face as a society. There is also another symbol contained within the bowl that is somewhat less obvious yet perhaps as powerful. Contained within the form of a bowl is a circle. A circle is symbolic (perhaps archetypal) of many things: completion, unity, wholeness and, depending upon its size, a feeling of opening (offering) or closing.

On the day of the meal this symbolism was felt deeply by those who participated. Everyone was asked to keep the bowl they chose to use for the meal as a reminder that someone's bowl is always empty. Many of the staff members had tears in their eyes as they left hugging their bowls. We discovered that there was great power in joining together, in community, for a simple meal and a common goal. We also discovered that there was great power in leaving with a concrete reminder of hunger, an empty bowl. The students displayed a sense of pride as they watched their teachers embrace their bowls. Everyone who participated that day was touched and connected in a very deep way, and the students raised six hundred dollars.

John and I knew at that time there was potential for expansion and agreed to explore the possibilities. For six months following, we bounced the idea around with colleagues in art education and ceramics and started to contact hunger relief agencies to solicit their input. We learned a great deal about hunger and received many suggestions regarding expansion. By August of 1991 we had compiled most of this information and put it into a format ready for distribution and decided to name the project *Empty Bowls*.

In August of 1991 the first "official" *Empty Bowls* meal was held in a private home locally for one hundred invited guests. Detroit Bishop Thomas Gumbleton from St. Leo's Church (and soup kitchen) and Leonna Patterson from the Robert Matchan Nutrition Center spoke to the guests about the organizations they represented and about the causes of hunger. The meal received publicity in the *Detroit Free Press Newspaper* and raised $8,000, which was divided between the two groups. Although this was a very different setting from the meal held at Lahser High School, many of the same feelings were expressed in the faces of the guests.

As a result of the publicity this meal received, requests for information packets started to pour in. We also gave presentations at local and national conferences, including the Michigan Art Education Association, Michigan Potter's Association, the National Council for Education in the Ceramic Arts and the Global Alliance for Transforming Education. We encouraged groups to focus at least in part on hunger awareness in all of their *Empty Bowls* projects and to include our contact information in all publicity so that word would continue to spread. It has.

From August of 1991 to present (April 1993), *Empty Bowls* has grown to include projects in all fifty states and several other countries. We hear from many groups who have decided to make Empty Bowls an annual event, in part because of its power as a fund-raiser but also because of its power to build community and to provide interactive hands-on learning.

Empty Bowls provides a vehicle for understanding and embracing our interdependence. We have purposefully provided enough information for people to be involved but with enough room for each individual or group to tailor the project to their needs and uniqueness. *Empty Bowls* challenges everyone involved to be creative not only in making bowls and soup but also in developing their own unique event.

Because of the need to bring together a variety of elements, this project also challenges individuals and groups who otherwise might never meet to work together for a common goal outside of themselves. We have found that when this occurs, many differences fall away.

We receive letters and telephone calls on a daily basis from individuals and groups who are involved in *Empty Bowls* events. Each time we hear from another group or individual we learn something new about *Empty Bowls* and the way it is affecting people's lives.

When Empty Bowls began, we intended for it to be an education project as well as a fund-raiser. The educational aspect, in particular, has evolved and deepened in many ways.

For instance, in 1991 we decided that in order to maximize the impact of the project and provide support for real change, we should address all of the members of Congress by giving them a bowl made by a child and ask them to pass the legislation necessary to bring an end to hunger. We brought this idea and a request for student-made bowls to members of the Michigan Art Education Association, and for several months prior to the event, we enclosed similar requests in each information packet that went out.

One of the first bowls that we received in response to this request was from Tyler Benjamin from Charlotte, Tennessee. It came with the following letter:

8-30-91

Dear Friends,
My name is Tyler Benjamin. I'm 9 years old in the fourth grade. I live on a farm in Charlotte, TN. My mother is a potter and my dad teaches special education. My big brother went off to college this year. Every year we plant a big vegetable garden so we have plenty of food in the summer. I know everyone can't do this and a lot of people go hungry. That is why I made this bowl to help people be aware of this problem.

Yours Truly,
Tyler

Tyler's bowl was carefully made and was decorated with a picture she had drawn in the inside with glaze. The drawing depicted two stick figures, one handing a bowl of food to the other.

We presented this bowl and letter to Representative Tony Hall from Ohio during a meeting in his office in Washington. At the time Tony Hall headed the Senate Select Committee on Hunger.

Another bowl that arrived around the same time was from Spencie. Spencie was four years old and attended the Friends School in Detroit.

His letter began, "Dear Washington,". . .and went on to request that there be something done for the children in the world who were hungry.

We were invited to attend the Friends School *Empty Bowls* meal, during which time we were presented with Spencie's bowl to take to the Congress. After his letter was read aloud, an adult from the crowd asked him in a somewhat condescending way, "But Spencie, do you know what the President's *name* is?" Spencie quickly responded by telling him that it didn't matter, children were hungry.

A few days following the meal we received a letter from Spencie's teacher.

> Dear Lisa and John,
> Many thanks for joining us for dinner on the seventh. It was a pleasure to meet the originators of this wonderful project that enable children to take responsibility for solving a community and world problem. The children and parents not only enjoyed making the bowls, they also found great satisfaction in helping with a growing need in our community. Eleven children and their families contributed $373. $85 went to tent city for food. The rest went to Manna Kitchens. I'm sure the children will remind their parents of hunger and their helping each time they use their bowls.
>
> Betty and the Friends School Pre-K

For both Spencie and Tyler, this experience offered an introduction to the problem of hunger, a time for reflection and an opportunity to feel empowered (I can make a difference) as they were helping to raise awareness through their bowls and letters.

Many other children sent bowls for us to distribute to the members of Congress, 800 in all. Many were accompanied by thoughtful letters (some even included photographs of the children holding their bowls in an outward gesture of offering) asking that hunger in the world be alleviated.

Prior to making this trip, we contacted several of the larger hunger organizations to see if there was some way to connect this with the work they were doing. OXFAM America responded by inviting us to participate in their annual Hunger Banquet in the Congressional Office Building. Each year OXFAM holds a hunger banquet in seven cities around

the country on the Thursday before Thanksgiving in order to demonstrate and draw attention to the inequity of food distribution in the world.
At a hunger banquet, the guests randomly draw a "lot in life" as they
enter the door. Sixty percent of the guests represent the third world and
sit on the floor with only rice to eat. Twenty-five percent sit on chairs
with rice and beans, and fifteen percent represent the first world and sit
at the tables with linen and are served a gourmet meal.

As a part of our cooperative effort with OXFAM America, we provided children's bowls to be used for the second and third world meals.
We were given an opportunity to speak at the meal about the *Empty
Bowls* project. The day before the banquet, volunteers from OXFAM
helped us distribute children's bowls, letters and requests for policy change
to every member of Congress.

While a variety of levels of understanding was demonstrated in the
children's letters which accompanied their bowls, it was clear that all of
the students had some grasp of the issues surrounding hunger in our
world. For many, this represented a first experience with clay and for
using their creativity to address a problem. It provided a sense of confidence and empowerment, and for some, a lesson in accessing the system.
Many of the children received a letter from the senator or representative
to whom their bowl had been given.

Another example of the learning process occurred at Upland Hills
School (a small private K-8 school) where I was teaching. We planned
an evening meal and community soup-making effort. The students created bowls for which we requested a minimum five-dollar donation.
During class one day I was fortunate enough to witness one of those
magic moments of teaching. The students were quietly busy making and
decorating their bowls when one of the eleven-year-old boys suddenly
looked up, as if a light bulb had gone off in his head, and said: "You
mean if I make one bowl, it will raise $5 to help feed someone?" I said
yes. "If I make three, they will raise $15?" Yes. "This is great! I'm only a
kid. I can't write a check, but this is something I can do to help!" At that
moment, and with a great sense of pride, he set a goal of making five
bowls, which he fulfilled before the meal. I later learned that this little
boy had recently experienced his father's leaving home abruptly, forcing
the family on welfare and food stamps until his mother found work. He
had experienced first hand what it was like to have some days each month
with very little food to eat.

The soups for the meal were created from community and school gardens, which the children planted. If someone needed something for their soup, they called around within the community until they found it. The children lovingly prepared "stone soup" and performed their own version of the play "Stone Soup" the day of the meal. Some of the children also baked bread during school and left a wonderful aroma lingering in the air as guests arrived for their evening meal. We held our first meal on October 16, World Food Day, and many adults within the community chose to fast for the day. Everything about the day and the efforts leading up to it carried the feeling of a holiday in which the entire community was participating. Others felt it too, and the school has decided to make this an annual event; in a sense the school community has turned this very simple process into an annual holiday, a creative ritual, a time for reflection, a time for giving back. Some of the students also went to a local soup kitchen to serve lunch every fall.

During that first meal, the Upland Hills School community raised $849, which was donated to the Food Bank of Oakland County. The director of the Food Bank joined us for our meal. He told us that for the Food Bank, a box of cereal costs six cents, how many boxes of cereal $849 would buy and how many families that might help. For several days following, I would hear the children comparing and translating everything to do with numbers into the equivalent number of boxes of cereal.

The second year we participated in Empty Bowls at Upland Hills, one of the staff members wrote a song about hunger and taught it to the children to share as a "grace" before our meal. They in turn taught it to a group of students at another area private school, Cranbrook Kingswood Academy. As a result, the Cranbrook students invited the Upland Hills students to their campus for a day of sharing when they were working on Empty Bowls. Now an exchange has begun between the two schools.

Through the two years' experience at Upland Hills, students—some as young as four—and the extended community have learned much. They have learned about hunger in their local and global community; the older students have explored some of the causes of hunger, including what hunger and malnutrition do to the body; they have learned about gardening and preparing nutritious foods. The concept of sharing and working together has been reinforced in a powerful way; they have learned that there are many creative ways to address the problems we face and that each of us can make a difference.

This was true also for students at the Arcadia Neighborhood Learning Center in Scottsdale, Arizona (a public school in the Scottsdale School District pioneering new approaches to education). This project was organized by a volunteer mom/potter and involved six classes of children grades K-4. The children, staff and parents worked together to make 162 bowls, soups, corn muffins and baked goods that were served. Over 300 people attended the meal and the school raised $1,010 Sherrie Zeitlin, the mom/potter who organized the event, sent the following letter to us shortly after their meal:

> Our event far exceeded our expectations and has left a glow around our school. The day of the event each classroom set up a soup station so that there were six stations to choose from. We spoke with the children about giving and sharing and caring so that there were no hurt feelings about trying to buy one's own bowl. . . .The kids did everything but dish up hot soup. They took the money, they helped parents with young kids and they generally had a great time. They sang two songs to all gathered about the homeless and about caring. News Channel 5 filmed the event and we were on the 9pm news with another group in Mesa who were doing the same project. We had newspaper coverage two days before and found that some people came to our campus after reading about the event.
>
> One of the things that is difficult at this age level is the comprehension on just what $1,010.00 means. So, we decided that to make this very meaningful we could take the children shopping and let them buy the food that they would then deliver to the food bank. We have contacted the food bank and they let us know what is especially needed and on November, 5 we will go shopping at ABCO Desert Market near the school. The children will calculate everything, it will be a total project for them that they will understand, instead of just a paper check to hand over to another adult. When we contacted ABCO they were thrilled of course to have us come and they have donated an additional $500 in food for our project. I guess our real total is now $1,510.00!

The students involved in all of the Empty Bowls projects I've just discussed experienced multi-disciplinary hands-on learning, tied to service. Each of these projects stepped outside of a direct "community service" approach and started to incorporate service-learning.

Inspired by Empty Bowls, Bloomfield Hills Schools seventh grade team teachers Anne Baldwin and Dave Barrett focused half of their school year on the theme of hunger, taking the evolution into service-learning one step further. As a part of the seventh grade social studies curriculum, the students studied the geography and sociology of each country in Africa. They learned about the famine in Somalia, the adequate amount of food in the world and some of the agricultural and political reasons for the persistence of hunger. Studies in language and literature were incorporated by writing to hunger relief organizations for information and to find out where and what kind of help was needed. Through the information they received, they began to learn the difference between famine, (and the way we respond to famine) and chronic persistent hunger (which is the larger problem). Science classes focused on what happens to the body and brain in the absence of adequate nutrition.

The study of chronic persistent hunger brought their attention back to this country and their local community. As they focused on hunger in the United States and specifically local hunger, they "adopted" one of the shelters/soup kitchens in our area. Each month they found out what was needed (diapers, clothing, food, for instance) and chose one thing to help with. They went to the soup kitchen once a month and served lunch, and their school year culminated with an Empty Bowls meal (the students made bowls, the meal was held for their families and teachers), which financially benefited the soup kitchen. By approaching the issue of hunger globally and then focusing locally with specific projects, the students were able to understand and make direct links to the ways they can help with what seem to be monumental problems. The assessment process included a verbal presentation from each student both for their classmates as well as for the students from a neighboring school district. The students from the neighboring school had been studying renewable resources and environmentally responsible agricultural, building and community planning practices. The exchange of information between the two groups dramatically extended the learning for all of the students.

Cranbrook Educational Community approached the Empty Bowls project from a service-learning perspective on a much larger scale. The entire community—which includes an elementary school, two preparatory schools and a graduate art academy—were involved.

The campus-wide focus for September, October and November of 1992 was hunger. Speakers from a variety of hunger organizations gave presentations to the students in an effort to address the root causes of hunger politically and economically and helped the students to learn about the systems we have which actually support hunger. Speakers also addressed hunger within the local community.

There were many opportunities for making bowls both within the classroom and outside, and the bowls they created took many forms. Some were drawn on paper, some were made of papier mache, some were photographed, some made of glass, wood and metal. There were clay bowls, bowls woven of reed and fabric and bowls made of mixed media. The students explored the bowls as metaphor, as symbol and as vessel. Pewabic Pottery in Detroit extended the help of artists from their community to work with parents and children as they created collaborative bowls during a Sunday "Bowls-a-thon." Altogether, they created 1,000 bowls, many of which were displayed in the Cranbrook Gallery the week preceding their meal.

A local photographer gave a slide presentation of his work entitled "Forgotten Lives" (a compilation of photographs taken of the homeless in Detroit) to the students earlier the same week. Another presentation focused around video footage taken by one of the staff members in the Cass Corridor in Detroit, one of the economically hardest hit areas in the city.

On the Thursday before Thanksgiving, the Cranbrook Educational Community held their Empty Bowls meal. Several well-known jazz musicians who live in the Detroit area volunteered their talents. The students also performed a jazz concert during the meal. The bowls were selected randomly by the guests, a process symbolic of the random selection of our "lot in life." The Cranbrook Educational Community's event served to educate many throughout the entire process.

Empty Bowls has evolved from a community service based project into a vital vehicle for interdisciplinary service-learning. From the early experiences of Tyler and Spencie, Empty Bowls has been providing a vehicle for children and adults to access their creativity and through the process created change.

In the spring of 1993 another evolution occurred. Lahser High School students themselves initiated two meals. One student band member solicited three school friends and her parents to help create bowls and put on an evening meal as part of their awards banquet. The student who organized this event shared what she had learned. Another student chose to hold his meal outside of school for a friend's birthday party. He, too, solicited the help of friends in school to create bowls and share information about local hunger.

The educational aspects of Empty Bowls have expanded the walls of the traditional educational environment and are extending into the community. There have been many examples of the Empty Bowls project functioning as a bridge between cultures and as a vehicle for learning and sharing. Perhaps one of the best examples of this occurred when Empty Bowls was integrated into a Passover celebration.

This Empty Bowls meal took place in April 1992 and was sponsored by the Detroit Women's Forum (a project of the American Jewish Committee) and combined beautifully the essence of the Seder ritual with a revised feminist Haggadah/Passover story and Empty Bowls. Many of us were not Jewish and had never attended a Seder before, so we had the experience of learning about another culture's religious ceremony and its historical significance. "Traditionally, the Passover story is retold each year to remind all—and to teach the children—that freedom from oppression must be defended."[1] The Cass Community Central United Methodist Church received the money raised through this meal for their soup kitchen, and their pastor, Ed Rowe, spoke to us about hunger in the Detroit area. By presenting us with an experience in which the service opportunity cut across cultural, religious and socio-economic lines, the need for cooperation and solidarity when we are dealing with social justice was underscored.

Leonna Patterson of the Matchan Nutrition Center is developing projects, including Empty Bowls, for teenagers which will allow them to become part of solutions and instill a sense of pride within the community. By working with this project, the teenagers will learn that there are constructive and creative ways to address their problems and that they can contribute to making changes within their own community.

Whether through Empty Bowls or another art for social action, creative expression provides us with methods of coming together over difficult if not controversial issues. The art allows us to speak from our hearts and allows us to make deep meaningful connections with our creativity, with ritual with one another and to move toward a more just world.

[1] Ruth Dricker Kroll and Wendy Watson, 1992 Detroit Women's Forum Feminist Haggadah.

❀

HOLISTIC METHODS OF THEORIZING
Sandra Wade Churchill

Ethical Theory as Collage

In this short essay,[1] I use the collage image/metaphor as an imaginative and creative framework through which ethical theory might be reconfigured. In particular, I will discuss principles, story and rhetoric as three compatible methodologies for theorizing. I offer collage as a means of pushing ethical thinking toward more intuitive, as well as more inclusive, analytical directions. I do not see intuition in opposition to analysis; indeed, such polarization is part of the very problem in theory-making that I want to correct through the use of collage. My objective is to tease out more holistic dimensions of ethical theorizing so that the makers and users of theory might become more responsive and responsible to multiple occasions for and practices of ethical reflection.

The collage image functions in this essay, as well as in ethical thinking, as an intuitive and creative metaphor to guide insight toward taking new and often critical risks— ones which displace our thinking from the comfort of established norms for what counts as "good" ethical theory. This dimension of ethical reflection is often hard to honor as we speak to our particular professional colleagues. Hence, a new image of the process of ethical thinking is needed.

Human ethical imagination and activity—the thinking and doing complex—are comprehensive, multifaceted and more open-ended than the language of professional ethics enacts (or acknowledges). Ethical imagination incudes reflection and contemplation, deciding and acting, sustaining and changing habits of thought and action, nurturing character and many other kinds of complex activities. Ethical thinking is a kind of poetic logic—part acts of imagination and insight, part acts of will, part turnings of sensibility, part trying and failing. Ethical theory, consequently, needs to be rich, diverse and as much dedicated to discovery of forms of imagination and intuition as it is dedicated to parsing of arguments, principles or other abstract (and often exclusively) cognitive modes of reasoning. Yet, this is frequently not the case.

The approach to theorizing I offer by way of the image of the collage is not a linear and progressive rational argument which makes additive and cumulative points for the purpose of unifying or totalizing a theory. "Collage" comes from the French *verb* "coller," meaning "to glue"— implying the playful activity of piecing together, of trying on parts, of intuitive and emergent meanings rather than predesigned or prescribed contexts for meaning. However, "collage" is typically used as a noun, to refer to an artistic production composed of various materials glued to a picture surface. To create a collage is to glue, bind, or hold together diverse fragments or ideas.

When I say that ethical theorizing is collage-like, I offer a way to configure ethical thinking in "transition," as Jane Flax says, . . . "without resort to linear, teleological, hierarchical, or binary ways of thinking and being."[2] By putting ethical theories together in collage-like conversation, their collaborative and interactive power is emphasized. The collage image allows us to eschew the battle for dominance among theories and to encourage a more complex and less exclusionary approach to moral interpretation. This method is required by the complexity and multifaceted character of human moral activity and its depth of meaning.

Collages have rough edges: cumulative and distinct meaning is not what they depict and not what an analysis of them can yield. Pictures in a collage collect, represent and frame meaning in a simultaneous and holistic manner, much like a bodily gesture holds meaning for those who give and receive it. Theory that is rooted in collage places emphasis on multiple interpretations, on showing how images are interdependent and gain their meaning from the whole, rather than being serially or chronologically anchored.

When we look at a collage, it is at first often disconcerting because we are required to set aside the desire to bring one dominant and unifying vision or perspective to bear. This desire is buried so deep in the norms for what counts as viable modes of reasoning that we often act from it without reflection on the hold it has over us. Appreciating a collage means letting go of the ordering norms and keeping the various media and meanings in flux, in transition. The more we try to systematize the meaning of a collage from a dominant, single angle of vision, the more the meaning of it is distorted and elusive.

Collage is intended to give ethical theory more interpretive power and less explanatory power. It brings to light in the activity of ethical reflection a shape which is temporally situated, but in which a unifying and totalizing perspective is not the goal. The collage image relieves ethical theorizing of the need to push for final resolutions, conclusions about which theory is preeminent or dominant and focuses on interpreting what is before us—the contexts of power which shape how ethics is applied as much as the "dilemma" or "decision-matrix" which needs elucidation by the application of ethical theory. Collage as a guiding metaphor for ethical reflection insists that the experience of ethics-in-use (both application and critical examination of methodological predispositions) demands multiple theoretical perspectives, multiple tools, which, when used, become part of the activity of excavating ethical encounters.

Hazards of Two Competing Theories: Principled Reasons and Normative Narrative

To continue with our discussion of how to reconfigure theory-making, I want to discuss two different, and often oppositional, dominant theories—principled reasoning and what I will call normative narrative. My use of *normative* will become clear below. My interests here are to characterize moral theory making itself so that we can see that a collage-like methodology might help us step back from and criticize ideologically-ingrained methodological commitments to polemical argument, competition between theories, dominance of one system or theory over another and totalizing the particular usefulness of one theory in a faulty manner. These methodological commitments typically characterize how theory is produced in most professional disciplines, not only ethics.

Principled reasoning—the analysis of principles at work in the decision-making process—has many proponents. It is not my intent here to rehearse the proponents or to survey representative literature. A few citations will have to suffice. Beauchamp and Childress, in their widely used medical ethics text, *Principles of Biomedical Ethics*, describe principles in a way which is general enough to apply to areas other than medical ethics. They commend principles as a way to bring "order and coherence" to the frequently "disjointed approach" that relies on cases or descriptions of particular instances. If time and space permitted, I would welcome an opportunity to analyze these rationalist principles of order, coherence and control, for they are suspect norms when viewed from a feminist analysis. However, in keeping with the theoretical balancing act we are entertaining here, in light of the use of collage, it is the faulty generalization and universalization of principled reasoning that makes it suspect, not so much the use of this theory, *per se*. When taken as the only model for ethical reasoning, rather than one piece of the collage, the model loses interpretive relevance, even as it attempts to enact ideological hegemony.

Three principles often excavated from ethical sites are autonomy, beneficence and justice. Autonomy, or more precisely respect for autonomy, is viewed by ethicists, as well as most persons in American culture, as a paramount value and respect for autonomy of others as a *sine qua non* of contemporary life. Although difficult to characterize without reference to specific ethical scenes, autonomy usually entails absence of coercion (even though covert coercion may often be a contested power aspect of autonomy). Autonomy usually encompasses a set of positive values and conditions for action as well, including clarity of thought in choosing, knowledge about alternatives and access to unbiased interpretations. Other conditions for autonomous action include consideration of whether actions are authentic, that is, whether actions are consonant with previous life choices, and, finally, honesty, that is, actions that are open to personal and political scrutiny.

Beneficence, as a principle by which ethical analysis proceeds, is one which positively promotes the good of others—to seek the good of others even when, *especially* when, self-interest or the interest of third (often politically expedient) parties is involved.

Justice often functions as an extension of beneficence as well as an extension of respect for autonomy. It entails the extension of the positive set of autonomy values beyond consideration of individuals into the socially connected nature of human relations. It involves recognizing that none of us is an isolated individual or moral atom—that all our actions affect others, sometimes profoundly. Justice recognizes multiple persons and interests at work. What this often means in ethical deliberations is treating the social context of particular ethical conflicts with equal weight as the individual aspects of the ethical scene.

To argue that principles are the primary mode of moral understanding is, therefore, to assume that the moral story or account opens itself to a principled analysis in some fundamental fashion, in some structurally normative way, as if the moral decision-maker should follow the account or the story told and simply insert the principles at the right spot.

Narratives and story telling make up one of the most pervasive organizing principles for experience. Human existence is "tensed" and would be incoherent with the "tensed unity of these three modalities, [past, present, future] in every moment of experience."[3] The thesis is as old as Augustine, who laid it out definitively in *The Confessions*. At another level this is a grandiose claim. The assertion that narrative form is logically and existentially primitive, that there is no way to get distance from it or get critical reflexivity on it as a category of experience, is immense. Features of this claim unfold when we study narrative or story telling as a moral interpretation which is supposedly superior to principled reasoning. Narratives, on this model, are designed to provide norms of moral interpretation. Narrative theory, despite its many different practitioners, operates in a Kantian fashion. That is, it is *not* the persistence or ubiquitous nature of stories in experience that provide theoretical interest and foundations. Rather, it is the *necessary*, and I argue normative, narrative structure of any and all human experience. Quite simply, experience *requires* a narrative quality as a condition of being what it is—a condition of there being experience at all. Narrative is, in short, an *a priori* inner form rather than an *interpretive category*. The competition between theories so that one theory might win out and claim dominance over another pushes theoretical commitments along the Kantian road toward categorical considerations and away from the kind of experientially contingent ranges of meanings the collage image allows us to appropriate.

Working from normative narrative instead of principled reasons, for example, the ethicist will ask different questions. She might ask, "Is the story or account a truthful or self-descriptive account?" "What virtues are displayed?" The sort of moral coherence narrative seeks is not that of the reason, but the coherence of characters and histories with whom it is possible to identify and lend our concurrence and admiration, our suspicion and disdain.

One hazard of a narrative approach, and one might speculate that this hazard could apply to an ethics of care as well, is the tendency to acritically adopt the point of view of the narrator as solely normative for the story presented. Too much empathy or sympathy can blunt our critical faculties and encourage premature closure on ethical conflicts.

Another hazard is the discouragement of multiple perspectives implied in a single narrator—a protagonist identification. A powerful narrative may serve only to reinforce our prejudices, especially if we strongly identify, either positively or negatively, with the narrator. It may be true that, in some sense, moral notions of the self are figured in a narrative. Yet care is required so that being figured in *a* narrative does not result in being grounded in a normative narrative—an absolute or privileged model.

We must learn to resist the move from "a" to "the"—from appreciating a particular story to "Story" as the model for all facets of the ethical encounter.

Indeed, this move is one we make frequently from faulty generalizations. Faulty generalizations often tacitly uphold faulty normative stances. Such stances are frequently buried deep within standard academic modes of doing business, in this case, modes of theorizing.

A third and less pedestrian problem has to do with the relentless, diachronic temporality which can accompany narrativity. Beginnings, middles and endings—neatly tied into temporal sequencing—can be as tyrannical over the moral imagination as the often abstracted logic of principled reasoning. Deductive systems of principles tend to trap moral agents with the exercise of logical maneuvering, as if agents were in an administrative posture over themselves and their actions. Principled reasoning, as a piece of the theoretical collage rather than a competing theory, however, can save moral analysis from an *ad hoc* approach and preserves consistency across a variety of actions and judgments. Recourse to principles also provides a way to account for choices, to say *why* one act or choice is morally preferable to another.

Narrative accounts of ethics correct for the deductive bias in principled reasoning but tend to confine the agent within a sequential, linear course. A tyranny of principles is avoided only to be replaced by a tyranny of teleology. Narrative forms threaten to turn the vertical logic of principles into the horizontal logic of the story. One form can be just as exclusionary and absolute as the other. By introducing rhetoric as a methodological choice for theorizing we are able to view narrative and principles as pieces in an inclusive collage.

Rhetoric as a Piece of the Collage—A Way to Reconfigure Agency

The meaning of "rhetoric" in today's highly sensationalized and often extremely polarized institutional languages is anything but normally associated with ethical thinking. So, why would I introduce rhetorical interpretation as a missing piece in the ethical collage, a missing interpretation of the moral encounter? Rhetorical interpretation allows us to put different texture into the theoretical collage. It asks different questions of how and why stories mean what they mean. It acknowledges, as Terry Eagleton says, that "meanings are products of language, which always has something slippery about it. It is difficult to know what it would be to have a 'pure' intention or express a 'pure' meaning."[4]

To put this in another, less linguistically oriented, way, the transfor mative and inventive character of theoretical innovation always already take place in circumstances and structures culturally situated; i.e., specific ethical dilemmas are always *already* a part of a larger cultural (and I will claim rhetorical) circumstance when any particular ethical encounter is discussed.

Richard McKeon, a twentieth century philosopher and historian of rhetoric, locates the definition of rhetoric in its *power*, a location I also endorse:

> The new art of rhetoric is the art of discovery. It is not a heuris-
> tic method or a radical interpretation but an art of topics or a
> selection of elements which opens the way to the recognition of
> new facts, new historical and political contexts, and to the per-
> ception of unnoticed structures and sequences.[5]

It is the discovery of new and broader historical and political contexts that rhetoric helps us accomplish when analyzing ethical dilemmas, as will become obvious later in this essay.

Rhetoric, then, following McKeon (who follows Aristotle on this point), is an architectonic productive art which combines technical and artisan qualities to produce new structures for thinking about any sub-ject. The goal of rhetorical analysis is not to end in knowledge, but rather to promote new action on the part of the subject as well as on the part of the theory. "Innovation and change in any discipline, therefore, arise by means of rhetoric, when old terms and ideas are transformed by new problems, uses and circumstances" (p. xxiii).

Following McKeon, I use rhetoric to displace the subject-agent posi-tions normative for theory in both principled reasons and normative narrative. I use rhetoric to invent new points of view and to help us discover new structures and contexts of meaning, so that the gaze of ethical theory considers broader and more politically contested circum-stances which surround particular ethical dilemmas.

As we have seen, rhetoric enlarges the ethical canvas so that founding ethical theory on being able to suspend historical reality must be aban-doned. Such founding in the past has required epistemological clarity and ontological purity when such is not possible.

It is difficult to know what it would be to have "full" possession of oneself and have "full" intentional control of my expression. In both principled reason and normative narrative, agency—the subject's production of ordered actions—relies on an understanding of how decisions mean or stories mean where meaning is capable of being fully separated from the rhetorical field of action. Both theories assume, in one fashion or another, that we *can* know the ethical encounter *as it is*, and that we can do this because the agent is the sole producer of meaning (principled reasons) or that its meaning can be made transparent in a canonical story (normative narrative).

In principled reason we have a picture of reason as the universal and apolitical arbiter of an agent in society: a self in full possession of itself and in full intentional control of its expression. The language of the agent looks much like the old "rhetoric of pure will." In normative narrative we have a picture of the subject completely knowable, or transparent, to the terms of a story. Here the agent's identity is not produced through reason, but supposedly fully discoverable through interpreting the story. Yet both these dominant theories present a picture of subject and meaning, a picture of actor and action of the story which is essentialist. Hence, questions of the rhetorical field —the already situated nature of the field of action—remain unattended. Questions of agency take the form of agent-as-subject: WHO is the SUBJECT of the story?

The rhetorical question of agency goes this way: WHO is the OBJECT of the story? We are trying, in this reconfiguration of agency, to introduce into the theoretical collage questions which actively scrutinize the agent's production of meaning, whether by reasons or narrative. This site of rhetorical activity is created when we ask about wider relations between an ethical story and the agent's purposes, audiences and constituencies which lie outside the particular scene of ethical deliberation. In this manner, an intentional agency does not have to bear all the weight of the ethical gaze. It is the rhetorical appeal which takes a center stage. How the story represents its motives and *whom* it appeals to—audiences, constituencies, a larger professional destination—become a vital part of its ethical dimensions.

Conclusions

Principled reasoning and normative narratives are powerful and important tools, or methods, in ethics. I do not argue that the introduction of rhetoric should "win" or "falsify" their theoretical efficacy. I argue that it

282 • FROM THE LISTENING PLACE

is mistaken to see them, or any other particular theory, as all-embracing alternatives which must subsequently compete for dominance. Competition leads to assumptions about dominance and subservience, winners and losers.

These theories are not still shots competing for representational control. The collage metaphor is intended to undercut the cultural hegemony of this mode, of this way of doing academic business. Theories in ethics are not like photographic images, to be judged by monodimensional or isomorphic "fit" to the world. Collage-like theory-making encourages the incomplete or intuitive capacity of moral reasoning along with the stepping back or analytic scrutiny which is part of well-rounded narrative theory. What is there to be grasped in ethical theory, and always grasped incompletely, is no simple, stable moral reality. But as rhetorical analysis in particular reveals, there are agents in complex webs of social and political/power relationships, as well as agents interpreted for strictly moral meaning. Theory which is even partially adequate must be layered, textured and open-ended like a collage and capable of multiple interpretations and perspectives. With this broadly intuitive goal, the value of the addition of rhetorical analysis to the collage of ethical theories is in the style of reflexivity it introduces: its power to turn ethical discourse back upon itself, frequently at cross-purposes with principled reasoning or normative narrative.

The collage as an intuitive metaphor for theory making allows us to find meaning without locating it solely in the subject or agent's productive capacities. Rhetorical analysis embodies within the collage a view of moral interpretation which crisscrosses the vertical lines of reason and the horizontal planes of a story. On the collage model, the efficacy of ethical theory resides not in how well it founds or justifies the claims of the system—principles' reasons or narratives' stories. Rather, the truth-making capacity of ethical theory, figured in the intuitive metaphor of the collage, resides in its framing capacity: in the ability of theory to frame the ethical encounter in as many different perspectives as necessary to keep footing and friction—for thinking and judging wisely.

Footnotes

[1] I have discussed these methodological issues and applied the collage theoretical framework, uniting principles, narrative and rhetoric, to a particular medical case, in the following paper, on which Larry R. Churchill collaborated with me, Reason, Narrative and Rhetoric: A Theoretical Collage for the Clinical Encounter. In G. P. McKenny and J.R. Sande (Eds), *Theological Analyses of the Clinical Encounter*, 171-184. Kluwer Academic Publishers, 1994. I pursued using the collage metaphor as a tool for critically assessing how our disciplines teach us *not* to be able to collaborate in the following, unpublished paper: "Methodological Reflections on Theory Building and Collaboration." This paper was delivered at a conference in May 1993, "Writing and Responsibility," which concluded the work of the year-long Carolina Seminar on "Gender and History, 1992-1993."

[2] *Thinking Fragments: Psychoanalysis, Feminism, and Postmodernism in the Contemporary West*. Berkeley: University of California Press, 1990, p. 15.

[3] Stephen Crites. "The Narrative Quality of Human Experience," *Journal of the American Academy of Religion* XXXIX, 3 (September 1971), 291-311.

[4] *Literary Theory. An Introduction*. Minneapolis: The University of Minnesota Press, 1983, p. 69.

[5] "Philosophy of Communications and Arts," in *Rhetoric: Essays in Invention and Discovery*, Woodbridge, CT: Ox Bow Press, 1987, p. 110.

❂

POEMS
Norma Bradley

Passage

Life will be better
so we came
with a dream of America

Thousands running walking
passing through towns villages

The walk toward boats

Mom, Dad, Sister and Brother
lost to the dust
Here take what is left of me.

Here, take me
I'll be good
I'll make you proud
I'll hide under veils of sorrow
I'll fit in your way
I'll lie, I'll deceive
I'll never let you know
Know how it was back there
Know what it is like inside.

I'll give you
some small pieces
Stories
that I'll allow myself to remember
Stories so hard, I will forget
All but a few
the most sacred memories

The dream of America.
Freedom
Freedom to love, to live, to feel connected.

I'll live out my fears
pass them on to you
Daughters, Sons
in unknown ways.
You'll pass them on
in unknown ways.

We will laugh cry love hate
Until one day
all will be told

The dream of America will be real.
A return to love, to hope, to life, to feeling connected.

STAR OF FREEDOM
1' x 25' x25'
Anderson Elementary School, Bayboro, NC   1991

Earth Quilt Reflections

I woke one morning
with an image, an idea.

In the morning light
with pencils ruler paper
The image grew into a garden
of smooth raked white pebbles
Like those I read about.

Peaceful simple lines
to rebut the revolution
going on from within.
Simple playful lines in the sand.

Placed at the center
A white picket fence appeared
Paths of soft mulch
leading from four directions.

Please come
see for yourself
This is the American Dream
House   Garden   Mother Earth

You can't take it away.
I will not let you take it away.

STAR BURST
1' x 22' x 22
Union Elementary, North Wilkesboro, NC   1990

TRIANGLES
2' x 22' x 22'
Estes Elementary, Chapel Hill, NC   1989

ON THE ROAD AGAIN
6' x 15' x 15'
Strathmore Hall Arts Center, Bethesda MD   1990

SEA TALES AND SAND-DO-INS
5' x 21' x 27'
Ocracoke School, Ocracoke Island, NC   1992

Summer 1995

My garden grew like the quilt
thirty-two patches
squares triangles circles octagons

Kinder/Garden   Earth Tie   Rising Star   Starlight
Star of Freedom   Turning Point   Crossroads   Gentle Spirits
Free Flight   Towering Spirits   Vessel of Hope....

Hundreds now help
We celebrate people
and our Mother Earth

Now in this year of 1995
I remember the People
Faces   Hands   Hearts
filled with love and sometimes fear.

Moving On, I return to my own garden
New Directions   Mother Earth   Gentle Spirit

Raked pebbles
Simple playful lines in the sand.

❁

THE SYBIL POEMS
Margaret Blanchard

Sybil is one voice of many ancient female oracles (Delphi, Eritrea, Libya, Cumae) who lived in caves and underground caverns.

Sybil Murmurs to Mist

You tease and tug at my cave's frontiers, nudge against
my rocky home, harsh to a stranger's touch, sharp
to his sight, impenetrable except to the most knowing
feet—I blur and shine, blessings enter, contours glow
and shift—you soften the lines of my confinement here.

With you reflections swim in my waters, shimmer
off my damp walls, calling into me the green
outside, giving me soft shapes of my own truth.

Sybil Hums at the Moon

You startle me.

Were I brighter, I'd know when you were
coming, where your beams might slip
onto my cool dirt floor.

But steady as granite myself,
just as immobile,
I enjoy the surprise of you,
sometimes coming, sometimes going,
sometimes not here at all.
And I like to guess each time
what shape you'll be in—
a slice, a slant, filling up,
pouring out; what color—
silver, pumpkin or flame—
how you'll appear—unveiled,
behind clouds flirting.

You're always changing,
I'm as predictable as this rock
I live within.
I'm here, I'm always here.
That's why I must hide.
You can count on me
to notice your mood;
my movement
shifts with you.

Sybil Chats with Rain

Here you come, my other visitors, uninvited
guests too modest for announcements or appointments,
persistently tap, tap, tapping
at my openings, dancing at my doorway
as you journey from anonymity
to anonymity, from clouds to streams,
multitudinous as stars but oh so different,
transient where stars abide, chattering
where stars are solemn, impressionable
while stars impress, willing
to fall while stars remain aloof.

Such comforting companions,
echoing my fluency, filling
my cracks, soothing my faults,
playing in my pools, you soft,
humble drops, asking nothing,
giving so much relief.

Sybil Speaks to the Sun

When I invite you in, welcome you
through my mossy gates, allow you
to stroke my tender edges, feel
the moist seed buried, luminous
keystone arched above the keynote,
music pours across my silence,
harmony bounds back
as margins merge
in the dark, sounds
the song whose source is mystery,
I hear my hidden voice
chant our secrets.

Sybil Talks to a Star

I'm not divine. I never descended
with an explosion of light
into this place. I was simply
born here, grew into it and stayed
because whenever I left,
I lost my voice.

You never guided anyone to me
and those who come to visit
are not necessarily wise men.

But sometimes I wonder—
watching you streak across my blue hole—
what it's like up there, floating above us,
sharing your light with eons of watchers,
sending out signals through vacant space.
Are you eclipsed daily by sunlight?
Are you able to curl into dark to rest?
In your perpetual dance with other stars,
can you touch across the vast
distances between you?

I'm alone here too. The people
who come to listen to me signify
what they're afraid to see
never really talk to me. But I have my animals,
friends who press their warmth into mine
on cold nights, hungry days.

Though I'm not divine, a divine fire
resides in me, rises when the wind
sounds through my hollows and eventually

implodes. Its sparks spill
crystal runes through midnight crevices.

You know you don't just pulse
through my nightly rhythms?
Stars in the stream remind me of you.
Stars in the oven, steady as dough,
stars in dew, frosty stars on spider webs,
sparks, sparks, sparks all mirror you.

No, you needn't lose your light to be here with me,
but please don't ask me to shine up there with you.

❁

Sybil Communes with Darkness

Hug me, dear friend, you who know
the whole of me, how I melt
into you when the wind blows shrill
out there, when I doubt myself far more
than those who come with rapt attention
to listen with such deaf ears.

You do not need me to show off
your radiance, as background for your
brilliance, you embrace the sharp and
the flat of me, the dumb and the loud
of me, the sour and the bitter too.
All are one to you, all worth holding
every day in your depths and every
night in your blossoming.

You do not flicker and go, tease and fade
like rainbows or snow, you are here
always, steadier than this ground,
firmer than these walls, with me
before I was born and after
I am buried.

Out of you my wisdom flows.

Margaret Blanchard's poetry is included in
Unlacing: Ten Irish-American Poets. For twenty-five years
she lived in Baltimore where she was an editor for
Women: A Journal of Liberation, served on the staff of
The Women's Growth Center and taught women's studies
and writing at Towson State University.
Her Ph.D in Literature is from The Union Institute.
She is the author of *The Rest of the Deer*, and with S.B.Sowbel,
Restoring the Orchard: A Guide to Learning Intuition.
Her poetry has been published in *The Atlantic Monthly*
and many other periodicals.